Emptiness Appraised

Emptiness Appraised

A Critical Study of Nāgārjuna's Philosophy

David Burton

MOTILAL BANARSIDASS PUBLISHERS
PRIVATE LIMITED • DELHI

First Indian Edition: Delhi, 2001
First Published in 1999 by Curzon Press

ISBN: 81-208-1814-8

Also available at:
MOTILAL BANARSIDASS
41 U.A. Bungalow Road, Jawahar Nagar, Delhi 110 007
236, 9th Main III Block, Jayanagar, Bangalore 560 011
8 Mahalaxmi Chamber, Warden Road, Mumbai 400 026
120 Royapettah High Road, Mylapore, Chennai 600 004
Sanas Plaza, 1302 Baji Rao Road, Pune 411 002
8 Camac Street, Kolkata 700 017
Ashok Rajpath, Patna 800 004
Chowk, Varanasi 221 001

Printed in India
BY JAINENDRA PRAKASH JAIN AT SHRI JAINENDRA PRESS,
A-45 NARAINA, PHASE-I, NEW DELHI 110 028
AND PUBLISHED BY NARENDRA PRAKASH JAIN FOR
MOTILAL BANARSIDASS PUBLISHERS PRIVATE LIMITED,
BUNGALOW ROAD, DELHI 110 007

CONTENTS

Preface ix
Abbreviations xiii

1 Introduction 1
The Purpose of this Study 1
Three Readings of Nāgārjuna's Philosophy 2
Some General Reflections on the Interpretation of Nāgārjuna 5
The Philosophical Study of Madhyamaka 11
The Problem of Authorship 13

Part I 17

2 Nāgārjuna and Scepticism 19
Introduction 19
The Nature of Scepticism 20
Scepticism, Negative Dogmatism, and Positive Dogmatism 21
The Scope of Scepticism 21
Undogmatic and Dogmatic Global Scepticism 22
Present Global Scepticism and the Future 23
Classical Scepticism 23
Isosthenia and *epoche* in Classical Scepticism 24
Academic and Pyrrhonian Scepticism 27
Nāgārjuna Interpreted as a Sceptic 30
A Refutation of the Sceptical Interpretation 34
Nāgārjuna's Knowledge-Claim 34
A Non-Sceptical Reading of *MMK* XIII, 8 37
A Non-Sceptical Reading of *YṢ* 50–51 38
The Non-Sceptical Purpose of Nāgārjuna's Method of Argumentation 39
A Final Objection Considered 40

3 Non-Conceptuality and Knowledge of Reality 45
Introduction 45
Conceptualizability and Expressibility 48
Interpretation (1): Non-Conceptual Knowledge of an Unconceptualizable Reality 49
The Unconceptualizable Reality – Immanent or Transcendent? 52
Is Interpretation (1) Supported By Textual Evidence? 53
A Philosophical Critique of Interpretation (1) 55
The Paradox of Unconceptualizability and Ineffability 55
The Problem of the Two Truths 57
The Night In Which All Cows are Black 62
S. Katz, etc on Non-Conceptual Religious Knowledge 64
Concluding Philosophical Reflections on Interpretation (1) 65
Interpretation (2): The Non-Conceptual Meditative Knowledge Experience of Emptiness 66
Knowledge of Reality Versus the Reality Which is Known 68
Knowledge of Reality is an Experience 69
A Short Digression. The Private Nature of Experience 70
(1) Knowledge by Acquaintance 73
(2) Lack of Explicit Conceptualization 77
(3) Focussed Conceptualization 79
Concluding Remarks on and Criticisms of Interpretation (2) 81
The Problem of Emptiness as a Mere Absence 82
Interpretation (2) and the Question of Nihilism 83

4 The Problem of Nihilism 87
Introduction: The Charge of Nihilism and Nāgārjuna's Response 87
The Abhidharma Notion of *svabhāva* 90
Nāgārjuna's Notion of *niḥsvabhāva* Understood in the Abhidharma Context 92
A Terminological Difference? 92
Universal Absence of *svabhāva* as Equivalent to *prajñaptimātra* 93
Evidence for *prajñaptimātra* in Nāgārjuna's Writings 95
Dependence on Parts 95
'*Saṃvṛti*' and '*sāṃvṛta*' in the *AS* 96
'*Saṃvṛti and 'vyavahāra*' in *MMK* XXIV 96
Synonyms for *prajñaptimātra* 97
The Non-Origination of Dependently Originating Entities 98
Comparisons with Dreams, Illusions, etc 99
MMK XXIV, 18: An Analysis 101
Prajñaptimātra and *karma* 104
Prajñaptimātra and the Possibility of a Public World 107
The Nihilistic Consequences of *prajñaptimātra* 109
An Alternative Reading 111
Textual Difficulties 113

A Philosophical Problem 114
Conclusion 116

Part II 123

5 The Purpose of Part II 125

6 The Nyāya *Pramāṇa* Theory 127
Introduction 127
Cognition (*Jñāna*) 130
Cognition in the *NS* 130
The Developed Nyāya Theory of Cognition 131
Pramāṇa-s 133
Prameya-s 135
Nyāya Realism 136

7 Nāgārjuna's Non-Apprehension of Entities 141
The Opponent's Objection at *VV/VVC* 5–6 141
Nāgārjuna's Response at *VV/VVC* 30 142

8 Mutually Dependent Existence 145
Nāgārjuna's Position 145
Mutual Dependence and *niḥsvabhāva* 146
A Critical Analysis of Nāgārjuna's Position 147

9 The Attack on Validation: Introduction 151
Nāgārjuna's Challenge to the Realist 151
The Purpose of Nāgārjuna's Attack 152
The Theories of Validation Refuted by Nāgārjuna 154
The Validation of Knowledge-episodes Versus the Reflexivity of Consciousness 155

10 The Attack on Intrinsic Validation 157
Intrinsic Validation (1): The *pramāṇa*-s are Validated by Other *pramāṇa*-s 157
Nāgārjuna's Refutation of Intrinsic Validation (1) 158
A Solution to the Infinite Regress Problem 158
Intrinsic Validation (2): The *pramāṇa*-s are Self-Evident 160
The Fire/Lamp Analogy 161
Nāgārjuna's Refutation of Intrinsic Validation (2) 162
Critical Analysis of Nāgārjuna's Five Arguments 166
Some Further Reflections on Self-Evident Knowledge-episodes 172
An Argument Against Both Intrinsic Validation (1) and (2) 175

11 The Attack on Extrinsic Validation 181
Extrinsic Validation (1): The *pramāṇa*-s areValidated by the *prameya*-s 181
Nāgārjuna's Refutation of Extrinsic Validation (1) 183

Extrinsic Validation (2): *Pramāṇa*-s and *prameya*-s are Mutually Validating 186
Nāgārjuna's Refutation of Extrinsic Validation (2) 186
A Reply to Nāgārjuna's Refutation 186

12 The Attack on Validation: Conclusion 189

13 The Argument from the Three Times 191
Analysis of the Argument 191
The Naiyāyika Objection 194
Nāgārjuna's Response to the Naiyāyika Objection 195
Another Mādhyamika Response Considered 196

14 Further Arguments in the *Vaidalyaprakaraṇa* 201
The Analysis of the Perception of a Pot 201
Refutation of the *pramāṇa* as a Cognition which Corresponds to the Object as *prameya* 204
The Object Cognized is Just a Condition of the Knowledge-episode 204
The Cognition is a *prameya*, According to the Naiyāyikas Themselves 206

15 Conclusion 209

Appendix: Some Further Reflections on *Svabhāva* in Indian Madhyamaka 213
Candrakīrti's Claim that the Actual *svabhāva* of Entities is Their Lack of *svabhāva* 213
Adumbrations of Candrakīrti's View in Nāgārjuna's Writings 214
A *gzhan stong* Interpretation of *AS* 44–45b 218

Bibliography 221
Index 228

PREFACE

'Emptiness' (*śūnyatā*) is a religious/philosophical concept which is central to much Buddhist thought. It is employed in numerous contexts, by different thinkers and schools, with a variety of meanings. A thorough comparative study of the uses and meanings of the notion of emptiness throughout the history of Buddhism is certainly a desideratum.

The present study has a more modest ambition, however. This book is an investigation into the philosophy of emptiness as expressed by the second century Indian Buddhist thinker Nāgārjuna. Nāgārjuna came to be known as the founder of the Madhyamaka school, a school which was particularly influential in Tibetan and Chinese Mahāyāna Buddhism. Nāgārjuna's philosophy of emptiness has also been the subject of considerable interest and controversy amongst modern scholars of Buddhism.

My study of Nāgārjuna's philosophy of emptiness has two principal concerns. These might be summarily described under the headings of *ascertainment* and *appraisal*. Nāgārjuna's philosophy of emptiness has famously (perhaps infamously) yielded many diverse, divergent (often contradictory) interpretations. My first principal concern in the present book is, through close study of texts reliably attributed to Nāgārjuna, to ascertain the possible meaning or meanings of Nāgārjuna's philosophy of emptiness. My second principal concern is with critical analysis. There is a need for an assessment of Nāgārjuna's philosophy. Too few books about Nāgārjuna, it seems to me, take the crucial step from exposition to evaluation. I intend to take this (admittedly danger-fraught) step.

Having ascertained the character of Nāgārjuna's philosophy of emptiness, I shall subject this philosophy of emptiness to an appraisal. I shall investigate to what extent Nāgārjuna's notion of emptiness, and his arguments in support of this notion, withstand rational scrutiny.

This book is, then, a *philosophical* study of Nāgārjuna's writings. I hope that this book may, therefore, be of use and interest to both students/scholars of Buddhism and philosophers. There is, I think, a great need to engage with historically significant Buddhist writers, such as Nāgārjuna, as serious thinkers who address fundamental philosophical questions. I am confident that, whether or not one finds Nāgārjuna's arguments and ideas convincing, the critical consideration of Nāgārjuna's philosophy of emptiness can be a valuable stimulus for one's own reflections about the nature of existence.

There is a common interpretation that Nāgārjuna's philosophy of emptiness is simply a re-assertion of the Buddha's original teaching (in the early *āgama*-s) of dependent origination (*pratītyasamutpāda*). This re-assertion was required, this interpretation continues, because some Ābhidharmikas had departed from the Buddha's original teaching of universal dependent origination by asserting the autonomous, permanent existence of the atomic *dharma*-s out of which the dependently originating world is formed.[1] Thus, Nāgārjuna's philosophy of emptiness re-affirms, in the face of this Abhidharma heterodoxy, the orthodox teaching that *everything* in the world arises and ceases in dependence upon conditions. All the manifold entities of the world, including the atomic *dharma*-s themselves, have a dependently originating sort of existence, and thus are *empty of* independent, permanent existence.

The present book rejects this interpretation. I accept neither that Nāgārjuna's Abhidharma opponents *departed from* (though they certainly did develop) the original teaching of dependent origination nor that Nāgārjuna's philosophy of emptiness is simply a *re-assertion* of this original teaching. Nāgārjuna's Abhidharma opponents did not think that the *dharma*-s out of which the dependently originating world is formed are themselves not dependently originating. But they did claim that these *dharma*-s, unlike the entities formed out of them, have an existence

1 See, for example, Kalupahana (1986), pp. 5–7.

independent of the constructing activity of the mind. Nāgārjuna's philosophy of emptiness is, I shall argue throughout this book, fundamentally a rejection of this Ābhidharmika claim that *dharma*-s have a more-than-conceptually constructed existence. For Nāgārjuna, *all* entities, including the *dharma*-s, originate entirely in dependence upon mental construction. All entities whatsoever are thus *empty of* unconstructed existence. So, Nāgārjuna's philosophy of emptiness is not simply a re-statement of the basic teaching of dependent origination; emptiness means, furthermore, that *all* dependently originating entities – including the dependently originating *dharma*-s which the Abhidharma says exist independent of mental fabrication – have a conceptually constructed existence (*prajñaptisat*).

No doubt Nāgārjuna felt that his philosophy of emptiness, i.e. his position that all dependently originating entities (including the *dharma*-s) are conceptual constructs, was justified by *buddhavacana*. (Nāgārjuna often declares, especially in his 'verses of praise' (*stava*), that emptiness is the Buddha's teaching). However, I suspect that the *buddhavacana* which Nāgārjuna would rely on here would be not so much that of the early *āgama*-s as that of early Mahāyāna *sūtra*-s, especially of the *Prajñāpāramitā* tradition, the main theme of which is that all entities (including even the *dharma*-s) are empty, i.e. *lack* more-than-conceptually constructed existence. Or, at least, his reading of the *āgama*-s would have been heavily influenced by the theme of emptiness as found in the early *Prajñāpāramitā sūtra*-s.

* * *

This book is a substantially revised version of my doctoral thesis, which was written between 1994 and 1997 while I was a research student at the Centre for Buddhist Studies of the University of Bristol. Many people and institutions have played an important part in its development. Particular thanks are due to the University of Bristol, Curzon Press, Mark Izard at LaserScript, Dr Rupert Gethin, Dr John Peacocke and Dr Damien Keown.

I would like to express my heartfelt gratitude to Professor Paul Williams for so much kind encouragement, and for so many invaluable criticisms of this book at various stages in its development. Thank you also for all of the stimulating and enlightening conversations. I have been greatly inspired by your enthusiasm for and knowledge of Buddhist philosophy.

Franky Henley has been a genuine and very generous friend over the years that I have been writing this work, especially at times of great need. Thank you. I rejoice in your tremendous energy and positivity!

I have undertaken this study as a Buddhist who wishes to understand more deeply the spiritual tradition (with all its philosophical strengths and weaknesses) to which he is committed. I would like to thank my benevolent preceptor, Dharmacari Suvajra, for first suggesting that I undertake this project, and for his unfailing support.

This book is dedicated to Sangharakshita, as a token of gratitude.

David Burton
(Dharmaçari Asanga)
Oxford, 1998

ABBREVIATIONS

I have placed a question-mark (?) after the name of the author if the attribution has been seriously questioned.

AKBh *Abhidharmakośabhāṣya*. Vasubandhu. French translation of the Sanskrit text in De la Vallée Poussin (1971/1980). English translation by Pruden of the French translation of the Sanskrit text in De la Vallée Poussin (1988).

AS *Acintyastava*. Nāgārjuna. Sanskrit text and Tibetan text in Lindtner (1982) and Tola and Dragonetti (1995b).

BC *Bodhicaryāvatāra*. Śāntideva. Sanskrit text in Sharma (1990).

BK *Bhāvanākrama*. Kamalaśīla.

BV *Bodhicittavivaraṇa*. Nāgārjuna (?). Tibetan text in Lindtner (1982).

CS *Catuḥstava*. Nāgārjuna. Sanskrit text and Tibetan text in Lindtner (1982).

CŚ *Catuḥśatakaśāstrakārikā*. Āryadeva. Tibetan text and Sanskrit fragments in Lang (1983).

DN *Dīghanikāya*. English translation in Walshe (1987).

DS *Dharmadhātustava*. Nāgārjuna (?).

HV *Hastavālanāmaprakaraṇa*. Āryadeva (?). Tibetan text in Tola and Dragonetti (1995b).

JIP *Journal of Indian Philosophy*.

LS *Lokātītastava*. Nāgārjuna. Sanskrit text and Tibetan text in Lindtner (1982) and Tola and Dragonetti (1995b).

MA *Madhyamakāvatāra*. Candrakīrti. Tibetan text in Fenner (1990).

MABh *Madhyamakāvatārabhāṣya.* Candrakīrti. Partial German translation of the Tibetan text in Tauscher (1981).
MMK *Mūlamadhyamakakārikā.* Nāgārjuna. Sanskrit text in Inada (1970).
MS *Madhyamārthasaṅgraha.* Bhāvaviveka. Tibetan text in Sastri (date unknown).
NS *Nyāyasūtra.* Gotama. Sanskrit text in Vidyābhuṣana (1913, 2nd ed. 1975).
NSBh *Nyāyasūtrabhāṣya.* Vātsyāyana. English translation of the Sanskrit text in Jhā (1984).
NSV *Nyāyasūtravārṭika.* Uddyotakara. English translation of the Sanskrit text in Jhā (1984).
OP *Outlines of Pyrrhonism.* Sextus Empiricus. English Translation in Annas and Barnes (1994).
PhS *Philosophical Studies.*
PP *Mūlamadhyamakavṛttiprasannapadā.* Candrakīrti. Sanskrit text in Vaidya (1960). Tibetan text of chapters 18–22 in de Jong (1949). Tibetan text of chapters 2–4, 6–9, 11, 23–24, 26–27 in May (1959).
Prj *Prajñāpradīpa.* Bhāvaviveka. Partial English translation in Eckel (1980), Ames (1993).
RS *Religious Studies.*
RV *Ratnāvalī.* Nāgārjuna. Sanskrit text and Tibetan text in Hahn, vol 1 (1982).
SC *Studies in Central and East Asian Religions.*
ŚS *Śūnyatāsaptati.* Nāgārjuna. Tibetan text in Lindtner (1982) and Tola and Dragonetti (1995b).
sTong *sTong thun chen mo.* mKhas grub dGe legs dpal bzang. Tibetan text in lHa mKhar yongs dzin bsTan pa rGyal mTshan (1972).
TJ Tibet Journal.
TJv *Tarkājvālā.* Bhāvaviveka. Tibetan text of chapter 3, 1–136 in Iida (1980).
TS *Tattvasaṃgraha.* Śāntarakṣita. English translation in Jha (1986).
Vaid *Vaidalyaprakaraṇa.* Nāgārjuna (?). Tibetan text in Tola and Dragonetti (1995a).
VaidC *Vaidalyaprakaraṇa, commentary.* Nāgārjuna (?). Tibetan text in Tola and Dragonetti (1995a).
VS *Vaiśeṣikasūtra.* Summary in Potter (1977).
VV *Vigrahavyāvartanī.* Nāgārjuna. Sanskrit text edited by E.H. Johnston and A Kunst in Bhattacharya (1978).

VVC *Vigrahavyāvartanī, commentary.* Nāgārjuna. Sanskrit text edited by E.H. Johnston and A Kunst in Bhattacharya (1978).

YṢ *Yuktiṣaṣṭikā.* Nāgārjuna. Tibetan text and Sanskrit fragments in in Lindtner (1982), Scherrer-Schaub (1991), and Tola and Dragonetti (1995b).

YṢV *Yuktiṣaṣṭikāvṛtti.* Candrakīrti. Tibetan text in Scherrer-Schaub (1991).

CHAPTER ONE

Introduction

The Purpose of this Study

Is Nāgārjuna a sceptic? In what sense is knowledge of the ultimate truth (*paramārthasatya*) or reality (*tattva*) non-conceptual for Nāgārjuna? Does Nāgārjuna's understanding of the ultimate truth/reality as emptiness (*śūnyatā*) condemn him to nihilism? These are the principal questions which the first part of this study will address. In the second part of this study, I shall consider Nāgārjuna's critiques, in the *Vigrahavyāvartanī* and the *Vaidalya-prakaraṇa*, of the Nyāya theory of knowledge (*pramāṇa*). What is the Nyāya *pramāṇa* theory which Nāgārjuna attacks? What is the precise purpose of Nāgārjuna's critiques? Are Nāgārjuna's criticisms successful, from a philosophical perspective? These will be my main questions in the second part of this study.

The dominant concern of this book might be, broadly speaking, described as the epistemological and ontological implications of Nāgārjuna's philosophy of emptiness. Which is to say that, in the various chapters of this book, I will try to ascertain both: (i) what, for Nāgārjuna, might be the nature of knowledge and (ii) what, for Nāgārjuna, is the real nature of things. I will, furthermore, undertake an appraisal of Nāgārjuna's epistemology and ontology. I will subject to critical scrutiny Nāgārjuna's understanding of (i) the nature of knowledge, and (ii) the real nature of things.

(i) and (ii) are clearly intimately linked. If, for example, the real nature of things is a possible object of knowledge for Nāgārjuna, then the nature of this ultimate truth will determine the character of the knowledge the Mādhyamika might have of it. If the ultimate truth were ineffable and unconceptualizable, for instance, then knowledge of it must be of a non-conceptual and non-linguistic variety (whatever precisely that might mean). And if for Nāgārjuna all entities are without *svabhāva* ('inherent existence' or 'own being'), and, hence, have a merely conceptually constructed existence (*prajñaptisat*), this has implications for the character of the knowledge-claims which one makes about these entities. If all entities have conceptually constructed existence this would preclude, for example, a theory of knowledge which describes knowledge as a matter of correspondence with entities which exist in a mind-independent manner. Finally, were Nāgārjuna's ontology found to entail nihilism, i.e. that no entities exist, then this would necessarily have the epistemological implication that there could be no knowledge of entities. In important ways, then, the character of Nāgārjuna's epistemology follows from the nature and implications of his ontology.

Three Readings of Nāgārjuna's Philosophy

There are, broadly speaking, three divergent interpretations of Nāgārjuna's philosophy. One interpretation sees Nāgārjuna's philosophy as primarily an attack on knowledge. This attack is interpreted as a refutation of *all* knowledge-claims about how things actually are, in which case Nāgārjuna might be described as a sceptic. Nāgārjuna has no views (*dṛṣṭi*), no philosophical position (*pratijñā*), because he claims that he knows nothing about things in their actual nature. A second interpretation sees Nāgārjuna's philosophy as primarily an attack on all *conceptual and expressible* knowledge-claims about how things actually are, in which case Nāgārjuna might be described as a 'mystic', who advocates a 'trans-rational', 'non-linguistic' gnosis. Nāgārjuna has no views, no philosophical position, because his knowledge of things as they actually are is not of the type which can be formulated in propositional terms. A third interpretation understands Nāgārjuna's philosophy as, not an attack on knowledge, but rather a refutation of a particular (wrong) ontological assumption, viz. that entities have *svabhāva*. There can be knowledge of things in their actual nature and – although this knowledge can have a 'non-conceptual' form (involving a direct perception, i.e. knowledge by acquaintance, of the emptiness of entities, and not simply the factual knowledge of this emptiness) – this knowledge can be correctly formulated in the proposition that 'all entities lack *svabhāva*'. According to this third interpretation, Nāgārjuna's ontological critique has epistemological implications, however. It entails that knowledge-claims (such as those of the Ābhidharmikas and Naiyāyikas) that assert the *svabhāva* of (some) entities are wrong, and knowledge-claims that assert the absence of *svabhāva* of all entities are right. Nāgārjuna has no views, no philosophical position in the restricted sense that he does not assent to any proposition which asserts that entities have *svabhāva*.

These three types of interpretation have had their adherents within the modern, (predominantly) western scholarly community. Hayes and Matilal, for example, have described Nāgārjuna's epistemology as 'scepticism'.[1] There have been numerous interpretations of Nāgārjuna's philosophy as asserting a trans-rational reality, known only by a non-conceptual, inexpressible gnosis. See, for example, Inada and Bhattacharya.[2] Other scholars – for example, Ruegg and Williams[3] – have argued that, for Nāgārjuna, the attack is on the notion of *svabhāva*, not on the possibility of knowledge, or conceptual/expressible knowledge, of how things actually are.

And there have clearly been proponents of the second and third interpretations, at least, in the Tibetan Madhyamaka tradition (traditions?) as well. Sa skya Paṇḍita (1182–1251) writes, in the *mKhas pa 'jug pa'i bzhag pa*, that the actual nature of things is beyond conceptual diffusion (*spros pa=prapañca*), and hence is not an object of language or the conceptual mind.[4] Dreyfus notes that the Sa skya pas, most especially Go rams pa bSod nams seng ge (1429–1489), claim that the central teaching of Madhyamaka philosophy is that the actual nature of things or the ultimate truth is beyond conceptual diffusion.[5] How things actually are is, one might say, transcendent, in the sense that it is inaccessible to the rational mind (but open to a non-conceptual gnosis).

This also appears to be the position of Mi bskyod rdo rje (1507–1554), the eighth Karma pa, who sees the actual nature of things as quite 'other' than the conceptualizable world and for whom, according to Williams, 'all language becomes skill in means; it has a purely pedagogic purpose, it doesn't in any way reflect a position claiming doctrinal correctness.'[6] There is knowledge of how things actually are, to be sure, but it is not a knowledge which is conceptual or expressible.

By contrast, mKhas grub dGe legs dpal bzang (1385–1438) and, indeed, most dGe lugs pas, say that Nāgārjuna (and other Indian Mādhyamikas) accept the absence of *svabhāva* of entities as the correct position, i.e. it accurately expresses how things actually are. What is refuted by Nāgārjuna, rather than conceptual knowledge of how things actually are, is the view that (any) entities exist with *svabhāva*. There is no incompatibility between the conceptual knowledge of the emptiness of entities, and the non-conceptual (i.e. directly perceptual) knowledge of this *very same* emptiness in the context of meditation.[7]

These three interpretations admittedly require much more elucidation (not to mention assessment). It shall be the business of the present book to accomplish (or, at least, to contribute to) this task.

In this study, I shall be in sympathy with the third interpretation. Nāgārjuna's philosophy is probably intended, I shall argue, as an attack on a particular ontological assumption, viz. that entities have *svabhāva*, rather than as an attack on all knowledge-claims, or all conceptual knowledge-claims, about the actual nature of things. Which is to say that Nāgārjuna thinks that there can be correct conceptual knowledge of reality, viz. that all entities lack *svabhāva*. Nāgārjuna is not a sceptic, and he is not a proponent of a trans-rational gnosis.

However, the word 'sympathy' needs some explanation and qualification. While I am sympathetic to the third interpretation in the sense that I consider that the third interpretation is probably closest to the philosophical position Nāgārjuna himself intends to communicate, it does not follow that I am sympathetic to Nāgārjuna's philosophical position.

On the contrary, as my argument in this study will make clear, I believe that the knowledge-claim that all entities lack *svabhāva* entails nihilism (despite Nāgārjuna's advocacy of the Middle Path between nihilism and eternalism). Expressed very briefly, this is because, understood in the Abhidharma context in which Nāgārjuna functions, the universal absence of *svabhāva* means, not simply that all entities dependently originate, but furthermore that all entities have an entirely conceptually constructed existence (*prajñaptisat*). And, I shall argue, if there is nothing unconstructed *out of which* and *by whom/which* conceptually constructed entities can be constructed, then it is impossible that these conceptually constructed entities themselves can exist.

In which case, Nāgārjuna's epistemology would appear to fall into contradiction, for he claims to have knowledge of the ultimate truth, yet the ultimate truth of which he (supposedly) has knowledge entails that nothing exists, including Nāgārjuna's knowledge of this ultimate truth. So, it would seem that the implication of Nāgārjuna's critique of the ontology of *svabhāva* is, after all, the impossibility of any knowledge whatsoever. (Though I do not think that this is an implication which Nāgārjuna himself intended. On the contrary, I think that he probably did mean to tread the Middle Path).

Even if somehow Nāgārjuna were to avoid the nihilistic implications of his position, I would find his philosophy quite implausible. It seems highly unlikely (and is certainly counter-intuitive) that all entities have an entirely conceptually constructed existence (*prajñaptisat*). Although I certainly believe that trees, mountains, and elephants, for example, are dependently originating, I do not believe that in all respects such entities (and, indeed, even their atomic constituents (*dharma*-s)) are, as Nāgārjuna contends, *conceptually constructed.*

Some General Reflections on the Interpretation of Nāgārjuna

In his influential book about the thought of Nāgārjuna, *The Central Philosophy of Buddhism*, T.R.V. Murti writes that,

> The Mādhyamika system seems to have been perfected at one stroke by the genius of its founder – Nāgārjuna. There have not been many important changes in its philosophy since that time.[8]

With the greatest respect to Murti, this statement strikes me as very naive. I shall dwell on this naivity not out of malice but because I think that such an analysis reveals some dangers (to which it is easy to fall prey) to be avoided by the interpreter of Nāgārjuna. Such an analysis will serve to highlight, then, some of the interpretative principles which underpin this present study. Let me suggest three senses in which Murti's statement is naive.

(1) Murti's claim seems extraordinary that 'there have not been many important changes in its [i.e. the Madhyamaka] philosophy' since Nāgārjuna wrote. Are we to believe that later Mādhyamika thinkers, such as Candrakīrti, Bhāvaviveka, Śāntarakṣita, Kamala-

śīla, and so on – not to mention the great Chinese and Tibetan Mādhyamikas – simply repeated Nāgārjuna's thinking with, perhaps, some minor variations? Such an idea is ahistorical; it fails to recognize that the Madhyamaka tradition is very long and complex, with numerous, often conflicting interpretations having been made.

Madhyamaka philosophy, of course, changed in response to numerous influences which were not present yet in Nāgārjuna's time. One thinks, for example, of the developments in the Nyāya tradition, to which the Indian Mādhyamikas responded (see especially Bhāvaviveka[9]), and also of the emergence of Yogācāra thought, which plays a very important part in later Indian Madhyamaka thought, both as an object of critiques (for example, in the case of Candrakīrti[10] and Bhāvaviveka[11]) and in attempts at synthesis (for example, in the case of Śāntarakṣita[12]). And one cannot imagine the thought of Tsong kha pa (1357–1419) without the influence of Dharmakīrti,[13] nor would the *gzhan stong* Madhyamaka have occurred without the advent of the various *tathāgatagarbha* texts.[14] Numerous other examples of historical development and transformation could be cited. The Madhyamaka tradition has produced a long series of creative thinkers who responded to the new philosophical demands of their historical circumstances. To suggest, then, that there were not many important changes in Madhyamaka philosophy after the time of Nāgārjuna is simply false.

This point is very important in the context of the present study. I will be dealing with Madhyamaka at its very earliest stage of development. I intend to be careful not to import what are actually later Mādhyamika concepts, terminology, and arguments, attributing them naively to Nāgārjuna. (In fact, the term 'Mādhyamika' itself appears to be an importation. It is not used by Nāgārjuna. Nāgārjuna does however refer to 'the proponents of emptiness' (*śūnyatāvādin*) at *VVC* 69, and seems to include himself among their number. In the *VaidC* also, Nāgārjuna seems to refer to himself as a **śūnyatāvādin* (*stong pa nyid du smra ba*)).[15] There is a great danger of simply reading Nāgārjuna from the perspective of later Mādhyamikas.

This is not to say, however, that I shall not refer to later Mādhyamikas in my attempts to understand Nāgārjuna's thought. Such references are, I think, illuminating and actually often indispensable (especially given the laconic nature of Nāgārjuna's statements). Nevertheless, it is necessary to distinguish clearly what Nāgārjuna says, in the texts available to us, from what later (often much later) Mādhyamika commentators and thinkers have said about these texts.

Some of the most important commentators to which I refer (for example, Tsong Kha Pa and mKhas grub rje) lived over one thousand years after Nāgārjuna (and in a different country, using a different language, etc). Even Candrakīrti and Bhāvaviveka lived centuries after Nāgārjuna. One should not, and I certainly do not, expect that their thoughts are identical to those of Nāgārjuna. In fact, one should expect that their thoughts are often somewhat different from those of Nāgārjuna, because these thinkers are responding to different issues or have explicated points in a manner of which Nāgārjuna never conceived. (For a case in point, see the appendix of the present study. Candrakīrti, I argue, clearly writes of emptiness, i.e. the lack of *svabhāva* of entities, as the actual *svabhāva* of entities. However, although there are adumbrations of this usage in Nāgārjuna's texts, Nāgārjuna himself never explicitly says that the actual *svabhāva* of entities is their lack of *svabhāva*).

(2) Murti's statement that Nāgārjuna 'perfected' Madhyamaka philosophy 'at one stroke' is highly dubious. It is my contention – to which surely anyone who tries to read Nāgārjuna's texts will assent – that, far from being 'perfect', Nāgārjuna's thought, as expressed in his texts, is inchoate and obscure. So much is left unsaid that it is not uncommonly difficult to ascertain what Nāgārjuna might mean.

Understanding Nāgārjuna's thought is thus partly a matter of appreciating that a range of interpretations is possible with regard to some of his puzzling proclamations. In not a small number of cases understanding Nāgārjuna's thought means, perhaps not so much arriving at the correct interpretation, but rather noticing and being sensitive to the fact that a text supports more than one reading. One task of the present study will be to explicate some of the interpretations which Nāgārjuna's texts might support.

But – and this is important – this is not to say that Nāgārjuna's texts support any reading whatsoever. On the contrary, the interpreter must, I contend, pay careful attention to the actual words, concepts and arguments which Nāgārjuna employs, and also the interpreter must see these words, concepts, and arguments in their wider philosophical and historical context. It is this method which will ensure a considered and plausible interpretation of Nāgārjuna, though not an indubitably correct interpretation.

For example, that Nāgārjuna's philosophy is the same as that of Wittgenstein or Derrida (or whoever happens to be the popular philosopher of the moment) is a highly unlikely interpretation (by which I do not mean that people are unlikely to make such an interpretation – there are, after all, plenty of people who see in Nāgārjuna a proto-Wittgenstein[16] or proto-Derrida, etc – but that they are unlikely to be representing Nāgārjuna's thought in an accurate fashion), given that Nāgārjuna lived in (probably) the second century in India as a Buddhist monk with Abhidharma and Hindu realist opponents to contend with (conspicuously absent from the writings of Wittgenstein, Derrida, etc!).

This is not to say that one should eschew all comparisons between Nāgārjuna's thought and that of thinkers who function in very different intellectual, spiritual, and historical circumstances. There are, I believe, universal philosophical and spiritual issues which recur in otherwise disparate contexts. It is just that such comparison needs to be done with great sensitivity to both the authentic (as opposed to superficial) similarities and the inevitable differences.

That an understanding of Nāgārjuna's thought will be facilitated by an appreciation of the Abhidharma and Nyāya philosophies is certainly true, given that these are the thinkers and traditions to which Nāgārjuna is responding. Abhidharma and Nyāya concepts and arguments are the language in which Nāgārjuna would have been versed. (This is clearly evident from even a cursory examination of his texts). If one is to understand Nāgārjuna's philosophy, one must grasp this language. Thus, by paying sufficient attention to the philosophical context in which Nāgārjuna's thought is embedded, one's interpretation is far more likely to represent something like what Nāgārjuna had in mind.

I am here in disagreement with Tuck, who sees the history of scholarship concerning Nāgārjuna's thought as 'a collection of intelligent misreadings', which he says, 'may be enough'. [17] I agree that there have been numerous misinterpretations of Nāgārjuna (some of them intelligent, some of them not intelligent), but I think also that there is such a thing as careful scholarship which – though it might not arrive at a definitive interpretation of Nāgārjuna's philosophy – does not misinterpret, paying as it does considerable attention to context, and always advancing its conclusions in a tentative way. My approach here is certainly in discord with that of Huntington, for whom the ideal interpreter of Nāgārjuna, etc 'asks neither the author nor the text their intentions but simply beats the text into a shape which will serve his own purpose.'[18] (Huntington's hermeneutic theory, I might add, is strangely at odds with his own scholarship, which is often quite meticulous).

In this book, then, I will endeavour to follow closely arguments which Nāgārjuna employs and, in a context-sensitive way, draw-out the possible philosophical content and implications of these arguments. I will not simply repeat what Nāgārjuna says, but I will give textual (and other contextual) support for the interpretations which I make.

(3) Even when Nāgārjuna's points seem textually relatively clear, or when one has come to what seems like a textually plausible interpretation of obscure points, these points often seem philosophically doubtful, to say the least. If this is 'perfection' for Murti, then there has been a radical re-definition of the term, of which I am unaware!

Murti's remark, it seems to me, in this respect betrays an unhealthy tendency in the study of Madhyamaka, which the present study will resist. Scholars of Madhyamaka, and of Nāgārjuna especially, are often overly deferential to the object of their studies. There is a tendency to view Nāgārjuna as a great thinker, whose thoughts are quite probably right. Any philosophical obscurity or apparent flaws which one might find in his thinking are thus usually considered to be attributable to one's inability to understand what Nāgārjuna means, rather than to Nāgārjuna's own failure as a thinker.

While I certainly think that it is important to be receptive to what Nāgārjuna says, and to evaluate carefully the various ways in which what he says might be taken (rather than arrogantly and prematurally refuting his claims), it is my considered opinion that such receptivity leads, not to a resolution of the various philosophical problems which appear, but to an intensification of them. It one really pays attention to Nāgārjuna's writings, one becomes aware of just how bizarre are some of his claims and arguments. This will become apparent, I trust, in the course of the present study.

So, modern interpreters, for a variety of reasons, tend to view Nāgārjuna as an authority whose thoughts or words are very likely to be true. Recent scholarship suggests, it may be noted, that in thinking this way one perhaps rates Nāgārjuna's thought more highly than did Nāgārjuna's contemporaries and the later Indian (non-Buddhist and Buddhist) tradition. It is arguable that many Indian thinkers, non-Buddhist and Buddhist alike, did not take Nāgārjuna's ideas very seriously, because of their obvious nihilistic consequences or because of Nāgārjuna's blatantly fallacious reasoning.[19] The modern interpreter (and I include here the modern practitioner) must be open to the possibility that Nāgārjuna's philosophizing was not as meticulous as is often assumed!

Hayes writes[20] that '... the interest that modern scholars of Buddhism have in Nāgārjuna may be out of proportion to the influence that Nāgārjuna had on Buddhists themselves.' Hayes points to the fact that there was no attempt on the part of the Ābhidharmikas to reply to Nāgārjuna's criticisms, and – despite Nāgārjuna's critique of the *pramāṇa*-s – the epistemological school of Dignāga and Dharmakīrti, which was very influential in later Indian Mahāyāna philosophy, made no explicit reply to his works. Hayes suggests that perhaps these Buddhist philosophers considered Nāgārjuna's criticisms to be so outlandish that they did not require a response.

Furthermore, there is, in fact, strong evidence (textual and archeological) that Mahāyāna Buddhism as a whole, and not simply Madhyamaka, was a marginal and minority movement in India, especially before the fifth century.[21] It is quite likely, then, that many Indian Buddhists had simply never *heard* of Nāgārjuna. Perhaps those who had heard of him considered him to be a member of a fringe-group (prone to sophisms and nihilism), and thus not worthy of serious refutation.

However, Nāgārjuna must have been known to and respected by at least certain segments of the Indian Buddhist population. There is, after all, an Indian commentarial tradition on his works, and a succession of thinkers in India who derive inspiration from his thinking, stretching for about one thousand years after his time. Further, it seems difficult to explain the fact that Nāgārjuna's writings came to be so widely influential in China and Tibet unless he already had *some* importance (at least in certain sections of the Indian Buddhist community) in India itself. Nevertheless, perhaps the very *lack* of general popularity of Mahāyāna (including Madhyamaka) thought in India may have contributed to its success in China and Tibet. A religious movement which is not very popular in its home-country would be naturally disposed to seek converts elsewhere. (However, the issue of why Mahāyāna Buddhism (including Madhyamaka) became so popular outside India, given that it probably was not popular within India, admittedly is a large and difficult puzzle, many of the pieces of which are (perhaps irretrievably) missing).[22]

Thus, perhaps the picture which emerges is of a generally unpopular movement, which failed to gain mainstream acceptance in India, and which inclined to foreign missionary activity because of its marginalization in its home-country. But even within this fringe-group, Nāgārjuna was only one of a number of significant figures, and many Mahāyāna thinkers would not have accepted his position. As Williams[23] says, 'the tendency to see the history of Mahāyāna thought as a series of complementary footnotes to Nāgārjuna should be firmly resisted.' (For example, there is arguably a real and basic philosophical disagreement between Madhyamaka and Yogācāra about whether or not *everything* is conceptually constructed. Also, the *tathāgathagarbha* texts, unlike (in all probablity) Nāgārjuna's writings can in some cases be read as positing an Absolute Reality).

The Philosophical Study of Madhyamaka

It could of course be objected that my comments betray a rather rationalistic approach to the study of Madhyamaka. The thoughts of an ancient Buddhist master should not, the objection might run, be assessed in terms of the standards of philosophy (understood here as the evaluation of the validity and soundness of arguments). After all, the Mādhyamikas were first and foremost religious thinkers practising within a particular spiritual tradition.

I entirely accept that Madhyamaka needs to be understood in the context of Buddhist practice, and that such practice has very important dimensions other than the philosophical (for example, meditation, ethics, ritual and worship, spiritual community). However, the Mādhyamikas (including Nāgārjuna), at least, clearly and often employ *arguments* as part of their Buddhist practice. The precise significance of these arguments on the path to liberation is debatable, but that they had some importance is beyond doubt. According to some forms of Madhyamaka (for example the dGelugs tradition) ultimate truth (*paramārthasatya*, *don dam bden pa*) itself is accessible to rational analysis.[24] Other interpreters claim that such analysis has an essential but preparatory role in the apprehension of ultimate truth.[25] In either case, it seems necessary, if one is to take Madhyamaka thought seriously, to assess the arguments which the Mādhyamikas present.

Clearly, we do not know precisely what importance Nāgārjuna gave to his arguments and his philosophical positions. But, unless he considered them to be simply rhetoric, they need to be properly evaluated as arguments and as statements which convey something about how things really are.

I propose, then, to take Nāgārjuna's truth-claims seriously. To take his truth-claims seriously, I believe, means to examine critically the arguments which Nāgārjuna employs in support of these truth-claims. Perhaps unfortunately, much of what Nāgārjuna says does not withstand the rigorous philosophical scrutiny which I am advocating (and which, in this study, I make some efforts to begin to carry-out), but I trust that one may be a little wiser for having made the effort.

But it might be thought that any assessment of what constitutes a valid/sound argument is conditioned by one's own historical and cultural perspective. My methodology thus wrongly assumes a trans-historical, trans-cultural rationality in terms of which Madhyamaka thought may be judged. It is incorrect, in fact arrogant, the objection might continue, to assess Nāgārjuna's thought in terms of a rationality which is actually of western provenance.

My answer to this objection, in brief, is that I *do* assume such a trans-historical and trans-cultural rationality, but that I believe that I am justified in doing so. (Presumably those who claim that rationality is itself culturally specific wish to *argue* for this claim, and to assert that it is a (non-culturally specific) truth. Which is to say that it is *rational* (in a non-culturally-specific way) to uphold that rationality is culturally specific. The proponents of this sort of relativism are thus caught in a paradox, for they must presuppose the very (non-culturally-specific) rationality which they aim to refute[26]). Rationality – and here I mean basic logical laws such as the principle of non-contradiction, the law of the excluded middle, the avoidance of fallacies such as circular reasoning, infinite regress, etc. – was understood and accepted by ancient Indian philosophers. The *Nyāyasūtra*, for example, is largely devoted to the topic of valid inference, and to the various fallacies which can make inference invalid. Nāgārjuna, as we shall see, is quite aware of fallacies such as circularity and infinite regress. And, as Ruegg has shown,[27] Nāgārjuna's arguments assume the principles of non-contradiction and the excluded middle. Ancient Indian philosophers did not reason in an essentially different way than the modern westerner. Appraisal of their thinking by a modern westerner is therefore possible. This study attempts just such an appraisal of Nāgārjuna's philosophy of emptiness.

The Problem of Authorship

Any book which concentrates on the study of Nāgārjuna's philosophy must confront the vexatious issue of authorship. Numerous texts have been attributed to Nāgārjuna. Which texts are to be accepted as genuinely by Nāgārjuna?

All attributions of texts to Nāgārjuna, it is fair to say, are more-or-less doubtful/probable. This is with the exception of the *Mūlamadhyamakakārikā* which is, by definition one might say, by Nāgārjuna. Or, perhaps it would be more accurate to say that who Nāgārjuna was is defined by his authorship of the *MMK*. That is to say, the person (assuming, of course, that it was one person) whom we call Nāgārjuna was whoever wrote the *MMK*.

It is not my intention to become involved here in the complexities of the arguments for and against the attribution of individual texts to Nāgārjuna. The most valuable work in this area has been done by Lindtner.[28] Perhaps, however, Lindtner is rather liberal in some cases; he attributes to Nāgārjuna some texts which are probably not by Nāgārjuna. For example, Williams[29] has argued convincingly that the *Bodhicittavivaraṇa*, attributed by Lindtner to Nāgārjuna, is in fact a later work. At any rate, the texts which my present study will primarily draw on are precisely those texts which are least controversially attributed to Nāgārjuna. That is, in addition to the *MMK*, I shall rely on the *Vigrahavyāvartanī* (and its commentary), the *Śūnyatāsaptati*, the *Yuktiṣaṣṭikā*, the *Catuḥstava* (including, most importantly, the *Acintyastava* and the *Lokātītastava*) and the *Ratnāvalī*.

I also refer often to the *Vaidalyaprakaraṇa* and its commentary. The attribution of this text to Nāgārjuna is perhaps more dubious.[30] But I have taken the liberty of using it as a principal source, mainly because it contains a detailed early Madhyamaka critique of the Nyāya theory of knowledge (*pramāṇa*). I have relaxed somewhat in this case my generally conservative views on the issue of authorship because there is so much useful information in the *Vaid/VaidC* on early Indian Madhyamaka epistemology, and also because the critique of the Nyāya *pramāṇa* theory in the *Vaid/VaidC* begs to be compared with the similar critique which occurs in the *VV/VVC*.

One cannot honestly claim to know that any texts other than the *MMK* are definitely by Nāgārjuna, even if they are traditionally attributed to him (although one can know that some – in fact, many – of the texts traditionally attributed to Nāgārjuna are certainly not by him). What one can say, however, is that there is a group of early Indian texts which is coherent insofar as it teaches a set of ideas which came to be identified as Madhyamaka. Whether these texts have one or several authors it is impossible to say, given the paucity of extant historical records. That the texts teach a basically common philosophical perspective is, however, attested by their content. Insofar as this is a philosophical study of a particular philosophical perspective, which came to be called 'Madhyamaka', the issue of the precise dating and authorship of these texts is of secondary importance, the basically shared philosophical outlook (regardless of authorship or precise dating) being the primary concern. For the purposes of the present study, then, I shall be content to refer to the author(s) of the *MMK*, *VV/VVC*, *ŚS*, *YṢ*, *CS*, *RV*, and *Vaid/VaidC* as 'Nāgārjuna'.

Notes

1 See Matilal (1986), pp. 47–50, Hayes (1988), pp. 53–62.
2 See Inada (1970), Bhattacharya (1990).
3 See Ruegg (1977) and (1991), Williams (manuscript 2).
4 See Jackson (1987), p. 342, 398.
5 Dreyfus (1997), p. 459.
6 Williams (1983), p. 132.
7 See *sTong* 294–315. Cabezón (trans.) (1992), pp. 257–272. See also Hopkins (1996).
8 Murti (1960), p. 87.
9 See Eckel (1980).
10 See *MA* VI, 45–97.
11 See *Prj* 25, translated in Eckel (1980).
12 See Ruegg (1989).
13 See Ruegg (1981), pp. 87–100.
14 See Hookham (1991).
15 See *VaidC* 1.

16 Huntington (1989) has produced one of the more interesting studies of this variety.
17 Tuck (1990), p. 100.
18 Huntington (1989), p. 8.
19 See here Williams (manuscript 2) and Hayes (1994).
20 Hayes (1994), p. 299.
21 See Schopen (1987).
22 The reflections in this paragraph have been inspired by a lecture given by Prof. G. Schopen (University of Bristol, Centre for Buddhist Studies, June 5, 1997).
23 Williams (1994), p. 976.
24 See, for example, Hopkins (1996), pp. 91–94, Williams (1991), p. 514.
25 This version of Madhyamaka also had its proponents in Tibet, such as Mi bskyod rdo rje. See Williams (1983).
26 For more discussion of this issue, see Nagel (1997).
27 See Ruegg (1977).
28 Lindtner (1982). See also Ruegg (1981).
29 See Williams (1984).
30 See Tola and Dragonetti (1995a), pp. 7–15.

PART I

CHAPTER TWO

Nāgārjuna and Scepticism

Introduction

It is my intention to ascertain the nature of knowledge-claims about reality (*tattva*, *dharmatā*) or the ultimate truth (*paramārtha-satya*), according to Nāgārjuna. However, it might be objected at the outset that such a project is ill-founded. After all, there are various texts attributed to Nāgārjuna which appear to state that the objective of Madhyamaka is to purge oneself of all pretensions to knowledge about the nature of reality. Thus, at *VVC* 29 Nāgārjuna declares that he does not have any thesis (*na mama kācidasti pratijñā*). *YṢ* 50a–b states that the great individuals (*che ba'i bdag nyid can=mahātman*), i.e. the enlightened persons, do not have a position (*phyogs=pakṣa*). And, in the *MMK*, Nāgārjuna says that,

> *śunyatā sarvadṛṣṭīnāṃ proktā niḥsaraṇaṃ jinaiḥ/*
> *yeṣāṃ tu śūnyatādṛṣṭistānasādhyānbabhāṣire//*
>
> The Victorious Ones proclaimed emptiness to be the remedy for all views. But those for whom emptiness is a view were declared to be incurable. (*MMK* XIII, 8).

On the basis of these statements, it might be thought that Nāgārjuna is a sceptic. A number of scholars have in fact advocated a sceptical interpretation of Nāgārjuna's thought.[1] But in order to evaluate this interpretation, it is necessary first to ascertain the precise nature of 'scepticism'.

The Nature of Scepticism

Scepticism is characterized by not-knowing.[2] Scepticism may be succinctly described as 'lack of knowledge whether x or $\sim x$'. The sceptic does not know whether x or $\sim x$. This is a formulation which I will repeat throughout this chapter as the common core of the various types of scepticism which I shall discuss. There are two components of this formulation which need clarification, however. What is meant here by: (i) 'x or $\sim x$', and (ii) 'knowledge/know'?

(i) x here, and throughout this chapter, can mean 'it is the case that x exists' or 'it is the case that x is y'. $\sim x$ here, and throughout this chapter, can mean 'it is not the case that x exists' or 'it is not the case that x is y'. Thus, one might be a sceptic because one does not know whether x exists or x does not exist. Or else one might be a sceptic because one does not know whether x is y or x is not y. For example, one is sceptical concerning the existence and non-existence of God if one does not know whether God exists or God does not exist. One is sceptical concerning the benevolent quality of God if one does not know whether God is benevolent or God is not benevolent. In fact, then, the sceptic who does not know whether x is y or x is $\sim y$ is not sceptical about the existence or non-existence of x. Rather, he is sceptical about the existence or non-existence of y as a quality of x.

(ii) 'Knowledge' here means, to borrow an expression from modern epistemology, justified true belief.[3] Which is to say that to know x must include proof that x. If I say that I have knowledge that God exists, for example, I mean that I have a correct belief that God exists, and also that the correctness of this cognition has been substantiated. To know $\sim x$ must include proof that $\sim x$. If I say that I have knowledge that God does not exist, I mean that I have a correct belief that God does not exist, and the correctness of this cognition has been substantiated.

Of course, the moot point here is precisely what is to count as proof. It might be argued, for example, that proof means evidence which is indubitable. But it can be countered that such a criterion for proof is too strict. Perhaps, then, simply good evidence will be a sufficient criterion for proof. (But in this case, it is debatable at what point evidence becomes 'good'). I do not want to enter into the details of this controversy, but it is as well to be aware that what level of justification is required for a true belief to qualify as knowledge is debatable.

So, the sceptic's claim that he does not know whether *x* or ~*x* means that he does not have proof (whatever precisely he means by 'proof') that *x*, and he does not have proof that ~*x*. Consequently, he does not have the means to determine whether a belief that *x*/~*x* is correct or incorrect.

Scepticism, Negative Dogmatism, and Positive Dogmatism

Scepticism must be distinguished from dogmatism, both positive and negative. Note that the term 'dogmatism' does not have here the pejorative sense of an arrogantly held, unsupported belief. Positive dogmatism occurs when 'it is known that *x*.' For example, it is known that the Queen of England is rich. Negative dogmatism occurs when 'it is known that ~*x*.' For example, it is known that the moon is not made of cheese. Thus:

Positive dogmatism: It is known that *x*.
Negative dogmatism: It is known that ~*x*.
Scepticism: It is not known whether *x* or ~*x*.

I contend, then, that any position which accepts, for some matter *x*, that 'it is not known whether *x* or ~*x*' is sceptical. However, not all such sceptical positions are the same. In fact, the rubric of genuine scepticism encompasses a number of different positions, all of which, however, accept the basic formulation that 'it is not known whether *x* or ~*x*'. Let me explain.

The Scope of Scepticism

Scepticism can be of varying scope or range. One might be sceptical in some matters, but not in others. In this case one's scepticism is 'local'. Local scepticism is, then, compatible with (in fact, necessitates) negative and/or positive dogmatism concerning the matters about which one is not sceptical. For example, one might consistently uphold:

Local scepticism: It is not known whether or not Henry is ill.
Local positive dogmatism: It is known that the book is red.
Local negative dogmatism: It is known that the dog is not old.

(Of course, whether in any particular matter one is a dogmatist or a sceptic will partly depend on the criteria which one accepts for proof. If, for example, one accepts that only matters about which there is absolute certainty count as knowledge, then one is likely to be sceptical about far more than if one accepts a less stringent criterion for proof, such as good (though not indubitable) evidence. If I demand absolute certainty, then I am a sceptic about the existence of Martians; I do not know (i.e. I am not absolutely certain) whether Martians exist or do not exist. If I am content with good evidence, then I am a negative dogmatist about Martians; I know (i.e. have good evidence) that Martians do not exist).

However, scepticism also can have an unrestricted (often called 'global'[4]) form:

> {It is not known whether *x* or ~*x*} [where *x* stands for any matter whatsoever].

Global scepticism states, then, that there is no knowledge concerning the existence or non-existence of any matters (be they the qualities of entities, or the entities themselves). Global scepticism is, obviously, incompatible with negative and positive dogmatism. If {it is not known whether *x* or ~*x*} [where *x* stands for any matter whatsoever] it would be contradictory also to assert that, in any specific case of *x*, there is knowledge of *x* or knowledge of ~*x*. It is global scepticism which is of primary interest to me in this study. As we shall see, the interpretation of Nāgārjuna as a sceptic understands his philosophy as a form of global scepticism.

Undogmatic and Dogmatic Global Scepticism

Global scepticism might be dogmatic or undogmatic. Whereas all global sceptics agree that:

> {It is not known whether *x* or ~*x*} [where *x* stands for any matter whatsoever].

the dogmatic global sceptic asserts that:

> It is known that {it is not known whether *x* or ~*x*} [where *x* stands for any matter whatsoever],

whereas the undogmatic global sceptic asserts that:

> {It is not known whether *x* or ~*x*} [where *x* stands for any matter whatsoever] and this is not a knowledge-claim.

Undogmatic global scepticism is consistently sceptical. The undogmatic, global sceptic does not even have knowledge of his total lack of knowledge. By contrast, dogmatic, global scepticism is inconsistently sceptical. The dogmatic global sceptic, like Socrates, has knowledge of his otherwise total lack of knowledge.

Present Global Scepticism and the Future

The global sceptical statement 'it is not known whether *x* or ~*x* [where *x* stands for any matter whatsoever]' is, of course, in the present tense. As such, present global scepticism can be conjoined with a variety of different positions about the future possibility of knowledge whether *x* or ~*x* [where *x* stands for any matter whatsoever]. Consider, for instance, the following possibilities (which, I will show shortly, correspond to Academic and Pyrrhonian scepticism respectively):

(1) (a) It is known that {it is not known whether *x* or ~*x*} and (b) it is known that {it cannot be known whether *x* or ~*x*} [where *x* stands for any matter whatsoever].

(2) (a) {It is not known whether *x* or ~*x*} and (b) {it is not known whether or not it can be known whether *x* or ~*x*} [where *x* stands for any matter whatsoever].
Neither (a) nor (b) is a knowledge-claim.

(1) is dogmatic, global scepticism about both present and future matters. (2) is undogmatic, global scepticism about both present and future matters. (2) is a stronger form of scepticism than (1), because (1) – unlike (2) – mitigates its scepticism by making the knowledge-claims that nothing is and nothing can be known. (2), by contrast, does not even make these knowledge-claims. It is scepticism through and through. (2) is scepticism *par excellence*. One could not be more sceptical than a proponent of (2). I shall, therefore, call (2) 'radical scepticism'. It is undogmatic, global scepticism extended into the future.

Classical Scepticism

I have written so far in abstract, ahistorical terms about scepticism. But scepticism is an historical phenomenon as well. It has taken diverse forms in the course of western philosophy. Broadly speaking, there is classical scepticism and modern scepticism. Modern scepticism originated in the sixteenth century, with the revival of knowledge of and interest in classical scepticism.[5] I shall comment here primarily on classical western scepticism (with some parenthetical remarks about modern scepticism) because, I believe, it is here that the apparent parallels with Nāgārjuna's philosophy are most striking.

Classical scepticism is global. Which is to say that the classical sceptic claims not to know anything about any phenomena as they exist in their real nature (*phusei*).[6] He does not even know whether or not any phenomena have a real nature. In any matter *x*, the classical sceptic does not know whether or not *x* exists, nor whether or not *x* is *y*. The classical sceptic does not know, for example, whether or not the oak-tree he sees really exists, nor does he know whether or not the green oak-tree which he sees is really green. So, the classical sceptic maintains that one does not have any knowledge (justified true beliefs, in modern epistemological terms) about things as they actually are.

The classical sceptic does not deny that he has subjective impressions/experiences (*phantasia*) of phenomena. He continues to acquiesce in these impressions. (It is this acquiesence which makes practical life possible for the sceptic). As Sextus Empiricus writes,

> Those who say that the Sceptics reject what is apparent have not, I think, listened to what we say. As we said before, we do not overturn anything which leads us, without out willing it, to assent in accordance with a passive appearance – and these things are precisely what is apparent.[7]

But the classical sceptic does not claim either that these impressions correspond to reality, or that they do not correspond to reality. He simply does not know, i.e. cannot adequately demonstrate, one way or the other. The classical sceptic claims not to have proof that any of his impressions are true or false. The classical sceptic sees the oak-tree and he accepts that this is his subjective experience. He acquiesces in the oak-tree experience. But he does not claim that his experience does or does not correspond to a real oak-tree. And the same principle applies to his entire experience of phenomena.

Isosthenia and *epoche* in Classical Scepticism

How does the classical sceptic reach his conclusion that he has no knowledge whether or not any of his impressions correspond to phenomena in their real nature? The classical sceptic's answer, in brief, is that, in every case, there will be conflicting knowledge-claims, and there will be no good reason for choosing between them. Even if one knowledge-claim did appear to be compelling, new evidence or circumstances might suggest otherwise in the future. Conflicting knowledge-claims are thus in equipollence (*isosthenia*), and there is no way to resolve the dispute. In which case, there is no justification for choosing one of the conflicting knowledge-claims as correct, i.e. as a true apprehension of phenomena in their real nature. 'The chief constitutive principle of scepticism', Sextus Empiricus writes, 'is the claim that to every account an equal account is opposed; for it is from this, we think, that we come to hold no beliefs.'[8] The impossibility of choosing (with good reason) between the various conflicting knowledge-claims induces the sceptic to suspend judgement (*epoche*).[9]

(Classical scepticism may be contrasted here with Cartesian scepticism. The classical sceptic claims that he does not have knowledge because there is unresolved dispute in all matters. In other words, for any knowledge-claim, there will be equal evidence for opposing knowledge-claims. Thus there is no way to decide which of the knowledge-claims is in fact a case of knowledge. By contrast, the Cartesian sceptic states that he does not have knowledge in matters about which he cannot be certain. For the Cartesian sceptic, then, scepticism is a result – not of equal evidence for a knowledge-claim and its contrary but rather – of lack of certainty. That is, for the Cartesian sceptic, there might be much greater evidence for one knowledge-claim than for the opposing knowledge-claims, but – insofar as this evidence is not sufficient to make the knowledge-claim indubitable – one does not have knowledge, and hence scepticism results.)[10]

The classical sceptics present a number of arguments to demonstrate the equipollence of opposing knowledge-claims about phenomena in their real nature. These arguments are summarized as the 'ten modes of Aenesidemus.' All ten modes share a common logical structure. It is argued that {x appears y to a}, and {x appears z to b or to a at a different time or in different circumstances}, where {z is incompatible with y}. However, {x cannot in its real nature be both y and z}. But there is no way to know whether {x is in its real nature y or z} (if, indeed, it is either). Therefore, one should suspend judgement about the real nature of x. For example, the first mode is that the same phenomenon will appear differently to different animals, depending upon their biological composition. Thus, a bird's eyes are constructed differently than a lion's; therefore the bird will perceive phenomena differently than the lion. How is one to know which, if either, of these varying, incompatible perceptions corresponds to the perceived phenomenon in its real nature? That is, how is one to prove which of these perceptions (if either) is correct? The sceptic says that there is no such proof, and thus one should suspend judgement. The tenth mode states that phenomena appear differently and incompatibly to different people depending on their culture and values. Thus, actions which are considered good in one culture, or according to one system of beliefs, are deemed bad by another culture or system of beliefs. There is no way to ascertain which (if either) culture is right. Thus, it is, the sceptic argues, impossible to know whether the actions in question are good or bad in their real nature. Therefore, one should suspend judgement. And so on.[11]

The suspension of judgement is said by the classical sceptic to have a dual psychological effect: (i) the cognitive repercussion of non-assertion (*aphasia*). One does not make assertions, i.e. does not make knowledge-claims, about phenomena in their real nature,[12] and (ii) the emotional and volitional repercussion that one possesses tranquillity (*ataraxia*). Sextus Empiricus says that *ataraxia* follows *epoche* like a shadow follows a body.[13] It is attachment to knowledge-claims about phenomena in their real nature, and the inevitably disappointing search for knowledge about these phenomena in their real nature, which – according to the classical sceptic – create mental turmoil. With the cessation of such knowledge-claims there will be, according to the classical sceptic, a corresponding equanimity. (I note, however, that the classical sceptics' claim here is debatable. It does not appear to me to be logically necessary that tranquillity follow from suspension of judgement. It would seem to be just as plausible that someone who knew/had the impression that he knew nothing about phenomena in their real nature would feel very insecure and anxious. If it is to work, the sceptics' argument that *ataraxia* follows from *epoche* must be inductive rather than deductive. It might be that people who suspend judgement do experience tranquillity, but one cannot argue *a priori* that this is the case; one would have to examine the evidence.) The mechanics of the classical sceptical method are summarized in Table 1.

Here, then, is an important difference between modern scepticism and classical scepticism. The classical sceptic considers

$$\text{isosthenia} \Rightarrow \text{epoche} \Rightarrow \begin{matrix} \text{aphasia} \\ \updownarrow \\ \text{ataraxia} \end{matrix}$$

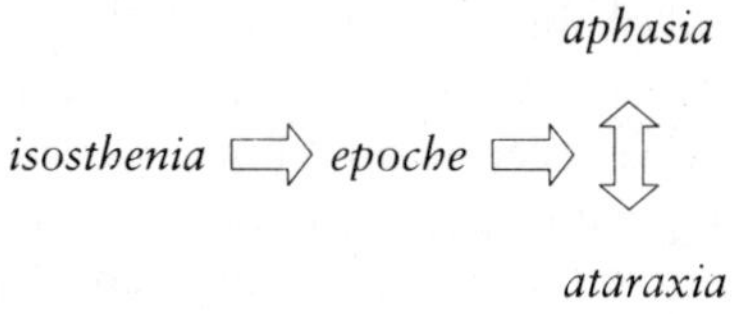

Table 1 The classical sceptical method

his philosophy to have implications for his entire life. By contrast, the tendency in modern scepticism is to insulate one's scepticism from life as a whole. Modern scepticism tends to be, one might say, a merely theoretical exercise. Hume, for example, contends that it would in fact be impossible to live a sceptical life. Descartes' scepticism is methodological, intended as a means to establish a secure foundation for science. (The insulation of theory from life as a whole is, it may be added, a (pernicious?) tendency, not only in modern scepticism, but in modern philosophy in general).[14] In this respect, Nāgārjuna is certainly in agreement with the classical sceptic rather than the modern sceptic. That is, Nāgārjuna, as a practitioner of Buddhism, is not engaging in an insulated, merely theoretical pursuit (although, I will argue shortly, the way of life which he is advocating is not in fact — despite superficial similarities — a *sceptical* way of life).

Academic and Pyrrhonian Scepticism

Roughly speaking, there are two forms of classical scepticism: (1) Academic scepticism, and (2) Pyrrhonian scepticism.[15] I say 'roughly speaking' because, evidently, other classical thinkers display sceptical tendencies (one need look no further than Socrates). But it is the Academics and the Pyrrhonians who were called sceptics and who had the most explicit and extreme sceptical doctrines.[16]

Pyrrhonian scepticism is named after its supposed founder, Pyrrho of Elis (c. 360–c. 270 B.C.E.). Academic scepticism is so-called because of its association for many centuries with the Academy founded by Plato. Arcesilaus (c. 318–c. 243 B.C.E.) introduced the sceptical influence into the Academy. Our chief source for both forms of scepticism, but especially Pyrrhonism, is the *Outlines of Pyrrhonism* by Sextus Empiricus (who lived no earlier than the end of the 2nd century CE).

Academic scepticism is dogmatic, global scepticism conjoined with dogmatic global scepticism about the future. Pyrrhonian scepticism is undogmatic, global sceptic conjoined with undogmatic, global scepticism about the future. That is, the Pyrrhonian sceptic is a radical sceptic. The Academic sceptic contends that he knows that phenomena in their real nature (if there is such a thing) are not and cannot be known whereas the Pyrrhonian sceptic states that: (i) phenomena in their real nature (if there is such a thing) are not known, and (ii) he does not know whether or not phenomena in their real nature can be known. He is open to the possibility that the phenomena in their real nature might become known in the future, but he does not know that this will happen.[17] The word '*skeptikos*' means 'an inquirer', or 'someone who looks, or examines' (*skopein*, *skeptesthai*). Thus, the pure sceptic, i.e. the Pyrrhonian sceptic, has not stopped looking for the truth. He does not know whether or not he might find it in the future. But he has the impression that he has not found truth as of yet. By contrast, Academic scepticism is mitigated because the Academic sceptic no longer looks for the truth, as he claims to know both that the truth is and always will be inaccessible. (One wonders, however, how seriously one can take the Pyrrhonian's claim that he is still searching for the truth. It is hard to conceive of any future situation in which a Pyrrhonian would be willing to accept that the truth had been found).[18] Furthermore, the Pyrrhonian sceptic says that his statement of (i) and (ii) is not itself a knowledge-claim.

The Academic sceptic, then, makes at least one knowledge-claim. He claims to know that phenomena are not and cannot be known in their real nature, and that it is not and cannot even be known whether or not they have a real nature.

One might, however, object that this exception is arbitrary. Why should the Academic sceptic accept one knowledge-claim, i.e. the knowledge-claim about knowledge-claims, but not others? And if the Academic sceptic admits one type of knowledge, what is there to prevent there being other cases of knowledge?

I think that the Academic sceptic might reply that the knowledge-claim which he accepts is qualitatively different from the knowledge-claims which he rejects. The Academic sceptic, in effect, might make a distinction between first-order knowledge of phenomena in their real nature, and second-order knowledge about knowledge of phenomena in their real nature. There is and can be, the Academic sceptic claims, no first-order knowledge, but there is the second-order knowledge that there is no first-order knowledge.[19]

Hankinson thinks that there is such a qualitative distinction. There is a clear difference, he argues, between knowledge-claims concerning factual matters (phenomena in their real nature), which transcend one's subjective experience, and a report of what is occurring in one's experience (the knowledge that one does not know anything about phenomena in their real nature). The knowledge of one's lack of knowledge is a matter simply of introspection, and requires only access to one's immediately available mental contents.[20]

I am not sure, however, that this explanation of the qualitative difference works for the Academic sceptic. If one *knows* (and does not simply have the subjective impression) that one does not know anything about phenomena in their real nature, surely this is not simply a matter of introspective awareness of mental contents? It includes, in addition, a truth-claim. One must think not simply that 'it feels like or is my impression that I don't know anything about phenomena in their real nature'; rather, one must think that 'it is in fact the case that I don't and cannot know anything about phenomena in their real nature.' That is, one must think that 'it is true – objectively, demonstrably the case – that I don't and cannot know anything about phenomena in their real nature.' One's knowledge that one does not know is not simply a matter of subjective belief, but of justified (and hence objective) belief.

I think that the real qualitative difference between first-order knowledge and second-order knowledge is a difference in *what counts as proof*. For the Academic sceptic, first-order knowledge-claims would be proved only if it could be adequately shown that they, as opposed to conflicting first-order knowledge-claims, correspond to phenomena in their real nature. But, as I have explained, the classical sceptic thinks that no such proof in any case is forthcoming. By contrast, the second-order knowledge-claim is proved simply by the *lack of proof* for all first-order knowledge-claims. That is, *because* there is no proof that first-order knowledge-claims apprehend phenomena in their real nature, *therefore* the second-order knowledge-claim that one does not have first-order knowledge is established. The second-order knowledge-claim is, in modern epistemological terminology, a justified true belief that one does not have any justified true beliefs about phenomena in their real nature. Far from being arbitrary, the Academic sceptic will claim that this second-order knowledge is an entailment of one's lack of first-order knowledge. So, perhaps the Academic sceptic can, in this way, reply successfully to the charge that he has made an arbitrary exception to his otherwise total scepticism.

The Pyrrhonian sceptic, by contrast, does not make any knowledge-claims. The Pyrrhonian sceptic is not prepared to admit that he knows that he does not know phenomena in their real nature. Nor is he prepared to admit that he knows that he does not know whether or not phenomena can (in the future) be known in their real nature. If it is objected that this is incoherent and self-refuting, the Pyrrhonian sceptic will reply that it is (or, rather, appears to him to be!) not so; he is simply being consistently sceptical. His belief that he does not know phenomena in their real nature, and his belief that he does not know whether or not phenomena can be known in their real nature, are simply impressions (*phantasia*) which he is left with on the basis of his investigations. He does not claim that he has proof that these impressions are true, although he does acquiesce in them.[21] Which is to say that, the Pyrrhonian sceptic's radical scepticism:

> (a) {It is not known whether *x* or ~*x*} and (b) {it is not known whether or not it can be known whether *x* or ~*x*} [where *x* stands for any matter whatsoever]. Neither (a) nor (b) is a knowledge-claim.

means:

> It is one's impression that: (a) {it is not known whether *x* of ~*x*} and (b) {it is not known whether or not it can be known whether *x* or ~*x*} [where x stands for any matter whatsoever].

The Pyrrhonian sceptic, then, need not make the distinction between first-order and second-order knowledge-claims, for he does not think that his impression that he has no knowledge of phenomena in their real nature, and his impression that he does not know whether or not he can have such knowledge, are knowledge-claims.

Nāgārjuna Interpreted as a Sceptic

Is Nāgārjuna a sceptic? The passages from his works which I have quoted at the beginning of this chapter might lead one to believe so.

The declarations that Nāgārjuna has no views, no thesis or position certainly sound like assertions that he knows nothing at all about the how things actually are. Understood in this way, emptiness would be a remedy (*niḥsaraṇam*) for views about how things actually are. Emptiness would mean, then, that Nāgārjuna states that he has no knowledge of entities in their real nature. Emptiness would be the emptiness of all knowledge-claims concerning how things really are.

At *MMK* XIII, 8 Nāgārjuna says, as we have seen already, that those who understand emptiness, which is the remedy for views, itself to be a view are incurable (*asādhya*). This would mean, according to a sceptical interpretation of emptiness, either that:

(i) emptiness involves a second-order knowledge-claim about views about how things actually are, i.e. it is the knowledge that one does not have and cannot have knowledge of how things actually are. It is when one (mis)understands emptiness to entail a knowledge-claim about how things actually are (e.g. emptiness means 'there is an Ultimate Reality', emptiness means 'nothing exists', even emptiness means 'entities dependently originate') that one becomes incurable, or

(ii) Nāgārjuna simply has the impression that he does not know and the impression that he does not know whether or not he can have knowledge of how things actually are. That is, Nāgārjuna acquiesces in this impression, but he does not claim that he knows that it is true. One becomes incurable when either one: (a) (mis)understands emptiness to entail a knowledge-claim about how things actually are (as in (i)) or (b) wrongly thinks that emptiness means that one knows that one does not and cannot know how things actually are.

(i) corresponds to Academic (dogmatic, global) scepticism, whereas (ii) corresponds to Pyrrhonian (undogmatic, global) scepticism.

Like the sceptic, this interpretation (in either of its varieties) would say, Nāgārjuna suspends judgement (*epoche*). Consequently, he: (i) does not assert any knowledge-claim about how things actually are (this non-assertion is equivalent to *aphasia*), and (ii) achieves tranquillity (*ataraxia*), free from the disputes and emotional turmoil which characterize the pursuit of such knowledge. One might perhaps construe the following passage in such a way:

che ba'i bdag nyid can de dag/
rnams la phyogs med rtsod pa med/
gang rnams la ni phyogs med pa/
de la gzhan phyogs ga la yod//
gang yang rung ba'i gnas rnyed nas/
nyon mongs sbrul gdug gyo can gyis/
zin par gyur.te gang gi sems/
gnas med de dag zin mi 'gyur//

The great individuals do not have a position [and] are without disputes.
How can there be an opposing position for those who do not have a position?
Through acquiring any resting-place one will be destroyed by the deceitful poisonous snakes of the afflictions.
Those whose minds are without a resting-place will not be destroyed. (*YṢ* 50–51).

'Resting-place' is my translation of the Tibetan word '*gnas*'. Lindtner[22] gives 'standpoint'. Lindtner says that the Sanskrit original is *sthāna* which, Monier-Williams says,[23] can mean 'place of standing or staying, any place, spot, locality, abode, dwelling, house, site.' Scherrer-Schaub[24] suggests that the Sanskrit original might be *āśraya*. She gives various possible translations: 'Un "point d'appui", un "support", ou une "base" ... un "endroit où résider", une "position".' According to Monier-Williams,[25] '*āśraya*' means 'that ... on which anything depends or rests ... the person or thing in which any quality or article is inherent ... seat, resting-place ... depending on, resting on ...'

It is clear that for Nāgārjuna a '*gnas*' is what causes the afflictions (*nyon mongs*). The sceptical interpretation of emptiness would maintain that it is by having any resting-place, i.e., any knowledge-claim, any position (*phyogs*) which is depended upon, that one will be destroyed by the afflictions. It is by not having any such knowledge-claim that one will not be so destroyed. Because the wise man does not have any position, i.e. because he does not make any knowledge-claim, he is in opposition to no one, and does not engage in disputes. Hence having no '*gnas*' is equivalent to suspending judgement.

In support of the sceptical interpretation of Nāgārjuna's thought, one might also cite the undeniable (indeed, striking) formal similarities between a number of Nāgārjuna's arguments and those employed by classical western sceptics. (The purpose of these comparisons, it should be noted, is to suggest a possible philosophical similarity between classical scepticism and Nāgārjuna's philosophy. I am not here interested in the issue of historical influence. At any rate, speculations about historical influence appear to me to be futile, given the paucity (in fact, complete absence!) of reliable evidence).

For example, the classical western sceptic argues that any attempt to establish a knowledge-claim, i.e. to prove that it – as opposed to conflicting knowledge-claims – apprehends phenomena in their real nature, will entail an unestablished assumption, an infinite regress or circular reasoning.[26] Nāgārjuna too,[27] in his critique of *pramāṇa*-s (knowledge-episodes) and *prameya*-s (objects of knowledge), claims that attempts to establish the *pramāṇa*-s will entail an unestablished assumption (if the *pramāṇa*-s are held to be self-evident), an infinite regress (if the *pramāṇa*-s are held to be established by other *pramāṇa*-s) or circularity (if the *pramāṇa*-s are held to be established by the *prameya*-s). Also, Aristocles' summary of Pyrrhonian doctrine mentions the sceptics' use of the 'quadrilemma', which has a formal resemblance to the *catuṣkoṭi*.[28] Further, the sceptics use various arguments to refute the knowledge of causes (aetiology),[29] while Nāgārjuna also criticizes a variety of theories of causation.[30] In fact, the following argument recorded by Sextus Empricus resembles closely Nāgārjuna's reasoning that a cause cannot precede, follow, or exist simultaneously with its effect:[31]

> A cause must either co-subsist with its effect or precede it, or exist after its effect has come about. Now to say that a cause is brought into existence after the coming about of its effect is ridiculous. Nor can it precede its effect; for it is said to be thought of relative to it, and they [i.e. the dogmatists] themselves say that relatives, insofar as they are relatives, co-exist and are thought together with one another. Nor can it co-exist with it; for if it is to effect it, and if what comes into being must come into being by the agency of something which already exists, then a cause must first become a cause and then in this way produce its effect.[32]

Note also the similarity of the following sceptical argument, recorded by Sextus Empiricus, which casts doubt on the existence of arguments:

> Thus arguments are composed of statements and compound objects cannot exist unless the things from which they are composed co-exist with one another (this is clear from beds and the like). But the parts of an argument do not co-exist with one another. For when we say the first assumption, neither the second assumption not the consequence yet exists; when we say the second assumption, the first assumption no longer exists and the consequence does not yet exist; and when we utter the consequence, its assumptions no longer subsist. Therefore the parts of an argument do not co-exist with one another. Hence arguments will seem to be unreal.[33]

with this passage, refuting the Naiyāyika parts (*avayava*) of the syllogism, from the *VaidC*:

> *gang gi tshe dam bca' ba brjod pa de'i tshe gtan tshigs la sogs pa med la gtan tshigs brjod pa na yang dam bca' la sogs pa med do/ de'i phyir gtan tshigs la sogs pa dag yod pa ma yin no/*
>
> When the thesis is uttered, the reason, etc [i.e. the other parts of the syllogism] do not exist, and when the reason is uttered, the thesis, etc do not exist. Therefore, the reason, etc do not exist. (*VaidC* 48).

This represents a selection of some of the formal parallels between Nāgārjuna's philosophy and classical scepticism. No doubt further examples could be cited.[34]

A Refutation of the Sceptical Interpretation

Nevertheless, Nāgārjuna is not a sceptic. Why not?

Nāgārjuna's Knowledge-Claim

Nāgārjuna's assertions that he has no view/position/thesis must be seen in the context of his philosophy as a whole. One finds repeatedly throughout Nāgārjuna's works[35] that his basic philosophical position is that entities (*bhāva*) lack *svabhāva*. Nor is Nāgārjuna averse to asserting overtly that this position entails a knowledge-claim:

skye ba shes pas 'jig pa shes/
'jig pa shes pas mi rtag shes/
mi rtag nyid la 'jug shes pas/
dam pa'i chos kyang rtogs par 'gyur//

By the knowledge of arising, destruction is known.
By the knowledge of destruction, impermanence is known,
and by the knowledge which penetrates into impermanence,
the supreme doctrine [that all entities lack *svabhāva*] is
understood. (*YṢ* 22).

dngos la mkhas pa rnams kyis ni/
dngos po mi rtag bslu ba'i chos/
gsog dang stong pa bdag med pa/
rnam par dben zhes bya bar mthong//

Those who know reality see that entities are impermanent,
deceptive phenomena, vain, empty, selfless, and isolated.
(*YṢ* 25).

('Isolated' translates *rnam par dben* which is itself a translation of *vivikta. Vivikta* has a range of meanings in Buddhist thought, but in the present context it is used, I think, as a synonym for *śūnya*. Candrakīrti's commentary on this passage (*YṢV* 25), says that 'isolated' (*dben*) here means 'empty' (*stong pa*)).

The ultimate truth (*paramārthasatya*) is, Nāgārjuna says, that all entites are empty, i.e. without *svabhāva*:

dngos po thams cad rang bzhin gyis/
stong pa yin pas dngos rnams kyi/
rten 'byung de ni de bzhin gshegs/
mtshungs pa med pas nye bar bstan//
dam pa'i don ni der zad do/

Since all entities are empty of *svabhāva*, the incomparable
tathāgata taught the dependent origination of entities. The
ultimate (*paramārtha*) is no more than that [literally, 'is
exhausted in that']. (*ŚS* 68–69a)

As I will show in greater detail in chapter 4, emptiness (the absence of *svabhāva* of entities) appears to mean both that entities are dependently arisen (*pratītyasamutpanna*), and that they do not have foundational existence (*dravyasat*). Which is to say that all dependently arisen entities have merely conceptually constructed existence (*prajñaptisat*). Thus entities which dependently arise are like a dream, a reflection, etc.

Emptiness is thus essentially an ontological doctrine, rather than an attack on all knowledge-claims. It states something about how things actually are. Namely, it states that all entities have a dependently arisen and conceptually constructed existence; an existence without *svabhāva*.

Although primarily an ontological teaching, emptiness does have epistemological implications, but these are implications which follow from the fact that entities are in reality without *svabhāva*. Thus, an epistemological implication of the ontological doctrine of emptiness is that views/positions/theses which assert the existence of entities with *svabhāva* are false, and the assertion that entities are universally dependent arisings (and are, furthermore, conceptual constructs) is true:

gang dag brten nas dngos po rnams/
chu yi zla ba lta bur ni/
yang dag ma yin log min par/
'dod pa de dag bltas mi 'phrog//

Those who assert dependent entities
to be neither real nor false,
like the moon in water,
are not carried away by views. (*YṢ* 45).

This passage implies, it would seem, that 'views' (*blta=dṛṣṭi*) are knowledge-claims which assert that entities have *svabhāva*. (See also *YṢV* 45, in which Candrakīrti makes it abundantly clear that entities exist like the moon in water, and are neither real nor false, in the sense that they lack *svabhāva*). These include both doctrines that assert that (any) entities exist in an independent, permanent manner, and also those Buddhist doctrines which assert that all entities dependently originate, but that (at least some of) these entities are *dravyasat*.[36] When Nāgārjuna says that he does not have a view/position/thesis, this means that he does not have a view/position/thesis which asserts the *svabhāva* of entities. But Nāgārjuna does uphold the position that entities lack *svabhāva*. Unlike the sceptic, for whom there is no knowledge of phenomena in their real nature, Nāgārjuna contends that there can be knowledge of entities in their real nature. Emptiness is not a doctrine which denies that there is knowledge. Entities as they really are exist without *svabhāva*, and this is knowable.

It strikes me, furthermore, that when Nāgārjuna claims that he *knows* that all entities lack *svabhāva*, he is using the term 'knowledge' in a very strong sense. Nāgārjuna thinks that it is indubitably correct that entities lack *svabhāva*. He does not mean merely that there is good evidence, or it is quite likely, that all entities lack *svabhāva*. His proclamations have the ring of certainty about them – there is no tentativeness or suggestion that the truth *might* be otherwise. Entities lack *svabhāva* – this is how things *actually* are (as seen, according to Nāgārjuna, by the Buddha), not how things *quite probably* are! See here especially *AS* 41, in which Nāgārjuna describes emptiness (*śūnyatā*) as the 'incontrovertible (*avisaṃvādin*) truth (*bhūtam*).'

A Non-Sceptical Reading of *MMK* XIII, 8

As I have already explained, Nāgārjuna states, at *MMK* XIII,8, that emptiness is the remedy for all views, but that those who take emptiness to be itself a view are incurable. This does *not* mean, as the sceptical interpretation in both its varieties ((i) and (ii) explained on p. 31) claims, that one becomes incurable if one misunderstands emptiness to entail a knowledge-claim about how things actually are. Nor does Nāgārjuna mean, as the radical (Pyrrhonian) sceptical interpretation ((ii) above) will further claim, that one becomes incurable if one considers emptiness to mean that one knows that one does not and cannot know how things actually are.

On the contrary, emptiness is a negative dogmatic assertion about how things actually are. Nāgārjuna claims to know that the real nature of entities is that they do not have *svabhāva*. This negative dogmatism implies, it seems, a corresponding positive dogmatic assertion, viz. that there are entities which exist without *svabhāva*, i.e. which have a merely conceptually constructed existence. Nāgārjuna claims to know that there are no entities with *svabhāva*, and he knows that there are entities without *svabhāva*.

Emptiness is an incurable view, according to my interpretation, if it is misunderstood by falling into either of the two extremes of nihilism or eternalism.[37] The nihilist would misunderstand emptiness to mean that entities do not exist (rather than that entities with *svabhāva* do not exist). As Nāgārjuna says,

vināśayati durjñāto dharmo 'yamavipaścitam/
nāstitādṛṣṭisamale yasmādasminnimajjati//

> This teaching [i.e. emptiness], poorly understood, ruins the unwise man. In this way he sinks down into the filth of the nihilist view. (*RV* II,19).

The eternalist misunderstanding, one might speculate, could have a gross and a subtle form. Emptiness might be misunderstood as an Absolute Reality. (See here Nāgārjuna's famous statement (at *MMK* XXV, 19) that there is no difference (*viśeṣa*) between *nirvāṇa* and *saṃsāra*. This might mean, then, that *nirvāṇa* is the true nature of cyclic existence, viz. its absence of *svabhāva*, rather than being a non-dependently originating Absolute Reality which is separate from the dependently originating world). Or, more subtly, although it might be understood that emptiness means that entities dependently originate, it might not be understood that emptiness also means that dependently originating entities are one and all conceptual constructs.

A Non-Sceptical Reading of *YṢ* 50–51

Earlier in this chapter (see pp. 31–32), I gave a sceptical reading of *YṢ* 50–51. However, I would strongly contest this sceptical interpretation of these verses. Nāgārjuna says that it is through having a resting-place (*gnas*) that one is destroyed by afflictions (*nyon mongs*). I would argue that a '*gnas*' is not, as the sceptical interpretation says, a knowledge-claim. On the contrary, a '*gnas*' is in fact any entity with *svabhāva* (in the Abhidharma sense of foundational, more-than-conceptually-constructed existence (*dravyasat*)) That is, a '*gnas*' is any *svabhāva*-endowed entity which is depended on by or is the basis for entities which do not have *svabhāva*. The (false) position (*phyogs*) that there are such entities with *svabhāva* is, according to Nāgārjuna, what causes the afflictions. (Believing entities to have *svabhāva*, one gets attached, etc to them). It is thus the knowledge that there are no such entities with *svabhāva* which destroys the afflictions. Disputes arise between people who believe in the *svabhāva* of entities and hold opposing positions about these *svabhāva*-endowed entities. The person who realizes that entities do not have *svabhāva* does not get caught up in such disputes. He sees that entities are in fact unreal (conceptual constructs), and are thus not worth arguing about.

My interpretation is supported by Candrakīrti's commentary on this verse, which makes it clear that it is the belief in the *svabhāva* of entities which causes the afflictions,

> *gang dag gzugs la sogs pa'i rang bzhin dmigs kyang nyon mongs pa rnams spang du rung bar 'dod pa de dag la ni nyon mongs pa rnams spang bar 'gyur ba med do/*
>
> Whoever claims that it is possible to abandon the afflictions although apprehending the *svabhāva* of form, etc, they cannot abandon the afflictions. (*YṢV* 51).

Candrakīrti does not say that it is knowledge-claims which cause the afflictions. On the contrary, his statement would seem to imply that it is the knowledge that entities lack *svabhāva* which brings an end to the afflictions.

There is further evidence for my non-sceptical interpretation of *YṢ* 50–51 at *YṢ* 46–49. Here Nāgārjuna states quite clearly that it is the ignorance of emptiness, i.e. the absence of *svabhāva* of entities, which produces the afflictions (*nyon mongs*) and, consequently, disputes (*rtsod pa*). It is the knowledge of emptiness which puts an end to afflictions and, consequently, disputes. This is certainly by contrast with the classical sceptic, who abstains from disputes (*aphasia*) and achieves tranquillity (*ataraxia*) (comparable here, perhaps, to the absence of afflictions) by means of his knowledge/impression of his lack of knowledge of reality.

The Non-Sceptical Purpose of Nāgārjuna's Method of Argumentation

There is another consideration. The classical sceptic, as I have explained, employs various arguments in order to demonstrate the equipollence (*isosthenia*) of all knowledge-claims. In every case, there will be conflicting knowledge-claims, and there will be no adequate justification for choosing between them. It is this technique which is intended to produce suspension of judgement (*epoche*), and, consequently, non-assertion (*aphasia*) and tranquillity (*ataraxia*). But there is no similar method present in Nāgārjuna's texts. The arguments which Nāgārjuna presents are not intended to demonstrate that there is equally good evidence for conflicting knowledge-claims. On the contrary, Nāgārjuna invariably *refutes* the views of his opponents which he examines. For example, in the first verse of the *MMK*, Nāgārjuna states his position that,

> *na svato nāpi parato na dvābhyāṃ nāpyahetutaḥ/*
> *utpannā jātu vidyante bhāvāḥ kvacana kecana.*
>
> No entities whatsoever exist – anywhere, at any time – arisen from themselves, from others, from both [self and others], or from no cause. (*MMK* I,1).

Nāgārjuna does not say that there are equally good reasons for asserting that entities originate in each of these four ways, and therefore he does not know in which way entities originate. He does not suspend his judgement. On the contrary, his point is that entities do not originate in any of these four ways. Here one must understand, I think, that Nāgārjuna means that entities with *svabhāva* do not originate in any of these four ways. And, as there is no other conceivable way in which their origination might occur, therefore there are no entities with *svabhāva*. There is no sceptical doubt in this statement. Nāgārjuna is not unsure about whether or not entities (with *svabhāva*) originate in any of these four ways. Nāgārjuna's statement is a negative dogmatic knowledge-claim. Nāgārjuna claims to *know* that entities (with *svabhāva*) do not originate in any of these four ways (and, therefore, entities (with *svabhāva*) do not exist), and his arguments are intended to provide the justification which makes his statement a case of knowledge.[38] Nāgārjuna is no sceptic. His arguments are not designed to show that knowledge is impossible. On the contrary, they are designed to *produce* the knowledge that entities lack *svabhāva*.

A Final Objection Considered

It might be objected that I have demonstrated only that Nāgārjuna is not a sceptic in the sense of classical scepticism. Perhaps, the objection might continue, Nāgārjuna's philosophy is similar to some form of modern philosophical scepticism. However, it would seem that modern philosophical scepticism in its diverse forms shares with classical scepticism the essential characteristic of 'not knowing'. For example, Descartes' methodological doubt is sceptical insofar as he doubts his ability to *know* the external world, etc. Hume's philosophy is sceptical in that he does not think that one has any *knowledge* of anything beyond one's impressions and ideas. And so on.[39] It is precisely this basic characterisitic of scepticism – modern as well as classical – which is absent in Nāgārjuna's philosophy. Nāgārjuna is confident that he knows how things actually are. He is, then, profoundly unsceptical.

Notes

1 See, for example, Matilal (1986), pp. 47–50, Hayes (1988), pp. 53–62. See also Garfield (1995), pp. 88–89.

2 See Hankinson (1995), pp. 13–30.

3 See Dancy and Sosa (1992), p. 509. In Part II of this book I will examine Nyāya epistemology, which has a quite different notion of knowledge. For the Naiyāyika, knowledge (*pramāṇa/pramā*) is simply the correct cognition of *x*/~*x*. The *justification* or *proof* of this knowledge is a separate issue. Knowledge, for the Naiyāyika, is knowledge regardless of whether or not it has been proved. But in the present chapter I am working with a conception of knowledge which includes proof/justification. According to this conception of knowledge, one does not know *x*/~*x* unless one's belief that *x*/~*x* has been proved to be correct.

4 See Hankinson (1995), p. 19.

5 See Popkin (1992), p. 462.

6 See Hankinson (1995), p. 156.

7 *OP* I, 19 (trans. Annas and Barnes (1994), p. 8). See also *OP* I, 21–24, and Burnyeat (1983b), pp. 117–148, Frede (1984), pp. 255–278.

8 See *OP* I, 12 (trans. Annas and Barnes (1994), p. 6).

9 See *OP* I, 10.

10 See Klein (1992), pp. 457–458.

11 See Hankinson (1995), pp. 155–178 for a critical analysis of the ten modes of Aenesidemus. See also *OP* I, 35–163, Striker (1983), pp. 95–115, and Barnes (1988).

12 On *aphasia*, see *OP* I, 192–193.

13 See *OP* I, 29.

14 See here Burnyeat (1983b), pp. 117–148, and Burnyeat (1984), pp. 225–254.

15 For the distinction between the Pyrrhonian and Academic sceptics, see *OP* I, 226. See also Burnyeat (1984), p. 227, and Hankinson (1995), p. 45.

16 For a history and philosophical study of the precursors to classical scepticism, see Hankinson (1995), pp. 55 *ff*.

17 See Hankinson (1995), pp. 13–30.

18 See Burnyeat (1984), p. 227, Frede (1984), p. 267, Hankinson (1995), p. 13.

19 The Academic sceptics' distinction between first-order and second-order knowledge is made explicit, for example, by Aenesidemus. See Hankinson (1995), p. 122, 'Aenesidemus appears to say that there is no ground for holding that anything is apprehended; but he is happy to allow . . . that that fact at least can be known.'

20 See Hankinson (1995), p. 17.

21 See Burnyeat (1983b), p. 127, Frede (1984), pp. 265–267.

22 Lindtner (1982), pp. 116–117.

23 Monier-Williams (1899), p. 1263.

24 Scherrer-Schaub (1991), p. 295.

25 Monier-Williams (1899), p. 158.

26 Infinite regress, reciprocity (circular argument), and hypothesis (unestablished assumption) are three of the five modes of Agrippa. See *OP* I, 164–177. See also Barnes (1990), pp. 204–224, Hankinson (1995), pp. 182–188.

27 See Part II of the present study.

28 See Hankinson (1995), pp. 58–65.

29 The sceptical critique of theories of causation is recorded by Sextus Empiricus as the eight modes of Aenesidemus. See *OP* I, 180–186. Sextus Empiricus also, at *OP* III 13–29, presents a general critique of notions of causation. The sceptical attack on causes was a response to the complex theories of causation developed by the dogmatists, especially the Stoics. See Barnes (1983), pp. 149–203.

30 See *MMK* I.

31 See *MMK* XX, *ŚS* 6, *RV* I, 47, and especially *Vaid/VaidC* 12 (examined in Chapter 13 of the present study).

32 *OP* III, 26–27. Translated by Annas and Barnes (1994) pp. 149–150, slightly amended from Hankinson (1995), pp. 218–224. The material in the square brackets has been added by me.

33 *OP* II, 144. Translated by Annas and Barnes (1994), p. 105.

34 See also Garfield (1995), p. 107, 118, 129, 246, 254, 356 for further comments on parallel arguments.

35 See, for example, *MMK* XXIV, *VV/VVC* 21–22, *ŚS* 3, 15–16, *LS* 24, *AS* 18, etc.

36 See here *YṢ* 40, 'If the proponents of existence abide in attachment to entities [and] continue in that same way, there is not any wonder in that!' (*gal te yod par smra ba rnams/ dngos la zhen par gnas pa ni/ lam de nyid la gnas pa ste/ de la mtshar cung zad med//*). In his commentary, Candrakīrti explains that Nāgārjuna here criticizes the theories of the non-Buddhists (*mu stegs can*), i.e. the followers of Sāṃkhya, who accept the three *guṇa*-s as eternal and the Vaiśeṣikas, who accept that atoms are permanent entities (*rtag pa'i dngos po*). *YṢ* 41 states, 'The proponents of universal impermanence, relying on the path of the Buddha, who remain attached to entities by [their] disputes, they are admirable!' (*sangs rgyas lam la brten nas ni/ thams cad mi rtag smra ba rnams/ rtsod pa yis ni dngos po la/ chags gnas gang yin de rmad do//*). Here, Candrakīrti continues, Nāgārjuna is criticizing his fellow Buddhists – the Vaibhāṣikas, the Sautrāntikas, and the Vijñānavādins (a very dubious interpretation on Candrakīrti's part, as the Vijñānavāda school almost certainly arose after Nāgārjuna's time) – who maintain that, though all entities dependently arise, (some of?) these dependently arising entities have *svabhāva*, i.e. are *dravyasat*. Candrakīrti also explains that Nāgārjuna's statement that such Buddhists are admirable (*rmad*) is an expression of sarcasm (*bsting ba=ullāpana*). See Scherrer-Schaub (1991), p. 274.

37 For Nāgārjuna's rejection of the views of eternalism (*śāśvatagrāha/śāśvatīdṛṣṭi*) and nihilism (*ucchedadarśana*) see, for example, *MMK* XV, 7, 10–11, and *AS* 22.

38 I must stress, however, that knowledge of emptiness, in its full sense at least, is not for Nāgārjuna *simply* a true belief, justified by his arguments. It is furthermore a direct experience, a knowledge by acquaintance, of the very emptiness about which one holds the justified true belief. Presumably, however,

having the true belief, justified by Nāgārjuna's arguments, that entities are empty is at least an aid to, and possibly a prerequisite for, a direct encounter with this emptiness (in meditation). For some more discussion of the meditative knowledge by acquaintance of emptiness, see chapter 3.

39 See here Popkin (1992), pp. 462–464.

CHAPTER THREE

Non-Conceptuality and Knowledge of Reality

Introduction

In the previous chapter I have argued against the interpretation that Nāgārjuna's epistemology is a form of scepticism concerning the ultimate truth (*paramārthasatya*), or reality (*tattva, dharmatā*). Instead, I have maintained, Nāgārjuna claims to know that the nature of reality is the absence of *svabhāva* of all entities. Nāgārjuna's declarations that he has no view/position/thesis are to be understood as statements that he has no view/position/thesis which asserts that entities have *svabhāva*. But, I have claimed, he does make the truth-bearing statement that entities are – in reality – without *svabhāva*.

There appears, however, to be a problem with this interpretation. There is a number of passages in texts attributed to Nāgārjuna in which it is stated that reality is (in some sense) non-conceptual and inexpressible (for now I leave the issue of the exact meaning of 'non-conceptual' and 'inexpressible' undetermined). Most famously, this point is made in the *MMK*,

> *nivṛttamabhidhātavyaṃ nivṛtte cittagocare/*
> *anutpannāniruddhā hi nirvāṇamiva dharmatā//*

> When the domain of thought has ceased, the named object has ceased. Indeed, like *nirvāṇa*, the true nature of things is without origination, without cessation. (*MMK* XVIII, 7).

> *aparapratyayaṃ śāntaṃ prapañcairaprapañcitaṃ/*
> *nirvikalpamanānārthametattattvasya lakṣaṇam//*

Not dependent on another, calm, not diffused by conceptual diffusion, free from conceptual discrimination, without diversity – this is the description of reality. (*MMK* XVIII, 9).

Similar declarations are made in the *LS*,

lakṣyalakṣaṇanirmuktaṃ vāgudāhāravarjitam/
śāntaṃ jagadidaṃ dṛṣṭaṃ bhavatā jñānacakṣuṣā//

You [the Buddha], having the eye of knowledge, saw this world – which is free from characterized objects and characteristics, without expression by words – as calm. (*LS* 12).

animittamanāgamya mokṣo nāsti tvamuktavān/
atastvayā mahāyāne tatsākalyena deśitam//
yadavāptaṃ mayā puṇyaṃ stutvā tvāṃ stutibhājanam/
nimittabandhanāpetaṃ bhūyāttenākhilaṃ jagat//

You have said that without entering into the signless there is not liberation. Therefore you comprehensively taught it in the Mahāyāna. May the whole world become free from the bond of signs, by means of the merit obtained by me, having praised you, the worthy recipient of praise! (*LS* 27–28).

While the *AS* states that,

astīti śāśvatī dṛṣṭirnāstītyucchedadarśanam/
tenāntadvayanirmukto dharmo 'yaṃ deśitastvayā/
catuṣkoṭivinirmuktāstena dharmāstvayoditāḥ/
vijñānasyāpyavijñeyā vācāṃ kimuta gocarāḥ//

'It exists' is the eternalist view. 'It does not exist' is the nihilist doctrine. Therefore, you [the Buddha] taught this *dharma*, which is free from [these] two extremes. Thus, you declared *dharma*-s to be free from the four positions. They are unknowable even to consciousness, how much less are they the domain of words? (*AS* 22–23).

bhāvābhāvadvayātītamanatītaṃ ca kutracit/
na ca jñānaṃ na ca jñeyaṃ na cāsti na ca nāsti yat//
yanna caikaṃ na cānekaṃ nobhayaṃ na ca nobhayam/
anālayamathāvyaktamacintyamanidarśanam//
yannodeti na ca vyeti nocchedi na ca śāśvatam/
tadākāśapratīkāśaṃ nākṣarajñānagocaram//

> That which has gone beyond the duality of existence and non-existence, but has not gone beyond to anywhere, is neither knowledge nor an object of knowledge, is neither existing nor not existing; that which is neither one nor many, not both [one and many] nor neither [one nor many], is without basis, is, moreover, unmanifest, inconceivable [and] incomparable; that which does not appear and is not concealed, is neither annihilated nor eternal – that, similar to space, is not the domain of words and knowledge. (*AS* 37–39).

I do not want to comment at this point on the precise meaning of these and other similar passages. However, they clearly communicate that for Nāgārjuna reality, and hence presumably knowledge of reality, is in some sense beyond concepts and inexpressible.

Why does this appear to be a problem for my interpretation of Nāgārjuna's philosophy? I have claimed that, according to Nāgārjuna, reality is the absence of *svabhāva* of entities. The true nature of entities is that they do not have, they are empty of, *svabhāva*. In which case my interpretation entails that knowledge of reality is both conceptual and expressible. That is, 'all entities are without *svabhāva*' is both a conception of and a statement about the true nature of things. It would appear, then, that my interpretation of Nāgārjuna's theory of knowledge of reality contradicts what Nāgārjuna's texts themselves say about this knowledge. Yet, as I have already shown, these texts also often assert that the nature of reality is the absence of *svabhāva* of entities. In which case the contradiction would appear to exist in Nāgārjuna's texts themselves. That is, Nāgārjuna's texts express both that the ultimate truth/reality is the absence of *svabhāva* of entities, and that the ultimate truth/reality is beyond conceptions and inexpressible. Is this contradiction real or merely apparent? If the contradiction is to be resolved, one must give an account of how it is that reality is correctly known by the conception and statement that 'all entities are without *svabhāva*', yet reality is also beyond conceptuality and language.

It is my intention in this chapter to explain and assess two distinct ways in which this apparent contradiction might be resolved. I shall call these two distinct resolutions of the apparent contradiction interpretation (1) and interpretation (2). These two interpretations are not only distinct but also they are incompatible.

Which is to say that it would be contradictory to hold both interpretation (1) and interpretation (2). I shall argue that, although interpretation (1) and interpretation (2) are plausible readings of texts attributed to Nāgārjuna, interpretation (2) is probably closer to Nāgārjuna's intentions. However, I shall also argue that both interpretation (1) and interpretation (2) entail serious philosophical difficulties. It is not clear to me, then, that either interpretation (1) or interpretation (2) is a *philosophically* successful resolution of the apparent contradiction in Nāgārjuna's statements that there is conceptual, expressible knowledge of reality, and that reality is beyond conceptualization and inexpressible.

Conceptualizability and Expressibility

Before I begin, however, there is a point which needs some clarification. I have been saying that, for Nāgārjuna, reality is in some sense beyond both concepts and words. But what exactly is the relationship between concepts and words here? The issues of the conceptualizability and the expressibility of reality are clearly intimately linked. It might be suggested, then, that in fact concepts and words are identical. However, there seems to be a strong case for a real distinction between concepts and words. For there is the case of 'not being able to find the right words to express one's ideas' (there may be, as Evans[1] says, 'a gap between what a speaker says and the thought he has in his mind'). Also, there is the fact that different words can express the same concept. Further, words can in certain situations (e.g. the young child or the parrot) be uttered without expressing any concept whatsoever. It might be countered that such utterances are not really words, but rather 'meaningless sounds'. However, if a sound only becomes a word by being attached to, or expressive of, a concept, then this demonstrates that a word is not the concept, but rather the vocal (or sub-vocal) expression of the concept. Finally there is the case of people who can certainly have concepts, but who cannot speak at all.

It seems true to say that words are founded on concepts, insofar as a word is an expression of a concept. And it may be that a concept is always potentially expressible as a word, even if it is not actually expressed, or if it is instead expressed in a non-linguistic way (e.g. by a gesture). Concepts are not identical with words but they do seem to be transparent to words. Words are not identical with concepts, but there is no word if a sound fails to express a concept.

Thus, in the context of the present study, a conceptualizable reality would be always (potentially) expressible linguistically. And, an unconceptualizable reality would necessarily be inexpressible. (I am not, however, claiming that Nāgārjuna himself was aware of this relationship between concepts and words).

Interpretation (1): Non-Conceptual Knowledge of an Unconceptualizable Reality

One way to overcome the apparent contradiction is by means of an equivocation in the term 'reality'. It is unavoidably contradictory to state that 'it is the case that there is conceptual knowledge of reality and it is not the case that there is conceptual knowledge of reality' if the affirmation and the negation is of 'conceptual knowledge of reality' in the same sense. However, it is not contradictory to state that 'it is the case that there is conceptual knowledge of reality in one sense of the term "reality"' and 'it is not the case that there is conceptual knowledge of reality in another sense of the term "reality"'.

The point might be expressed as follows:

There is {conceptual knowledge of reality} and there is not {conceptual knowledge of reality} = a contradiction.

There is conceptual knowledge of $\{\text{reality}\}_1$ and there is not conceptual knowledge of $\{\text{reality}\}_2 \neq$ a contradiction.

If this is the case, then what is required is a delineation of the different senses of the term 'reality'. Interpretation (1) says that on this basis one might hold together, without contradiction, Nāgārjuna's claims that there both is and is not conceptual knowledge of reality.

According to interpretation (1), reality_1 is the absence of *svabhāva* of entities. Thus, reality_1 is conceptualizable, and is the object of the conceptual knowledge that 'entities are without *svabhāva*.' Which is to say that the conception and statement that 'entities are without *svabhāva*' is a true conception and statement. This conception and statement accurately apprehends reality_1. This explains why it is that Nāgārjuna not infrequently declares the ultimate truth to be the absence of *svabhāva* of entities[2].

By contrast, as the passages quoted above suggest (see pp. 45–47), $reality_2$ is unconceptualizable. Something which is unconceptualizable cannot be conceptualized. $Reality_2$ is therefore not a possible object of conceptual knowledge. In fact, according to interpretation (1), $reality_2$ can only be apprehended by non-conceptual knowledge. According to interpretation (1), there is an extraordinary cognitive faculty (*tattvajñāna*), non-conceptual in nature, which apprehends an unconceptualizable $reality_2$. (I leave aside for the moment the troublesome issue of the intelligibility, of 'non-conceptual knowledge of unconceptualizable $reality_2$.') Thus,

> Interpretation (1) = There is conceptual knowledge of $\{reality\}_1$ and there is not conceptual knowledge of $\{reality\}_2$. There is non-conceptual knowledge of $\{reality\}_2$.

Note that interpretation (1) is not *sceptical* about $reality_2$. It does not say that there is not knowledge of $reality_2$. More precisely, it claims that $reality_2$ is not to be known conceptually but that $reality_2$ is to be known non-conceptually. Interpretation (1) rests, then, on a distinction between two means of knowledge, viz. knowledge by means which are conceptual (and expressible) versus knowledge by means which are non-conceptual (and inexpressible). Interpretation (1) states that in the matter of $reality_2$ there is no knowledge by means which are conceptual, but there is knowledge by means which are non-conceptual. (This of course raises the philosophical problem of what a non-conceptual means of knowledge might be. I shall discuss this issue shortly).

Interpretation (1) might derive textual support from Bhāvaviveka's teaching that the ultimate (*don dam pa*) has two aspects (*rnam pa gnyis*), viz. the ultimate which cannot be specified (*rnam grangs ma yin pa'i don dam*) and the ultimate which can be specified (*rnam grangs kyi don dam*). The first aspect is, he says, among other things, supramundane (*'jig rten las 'das pa*), without impurity (*zag pa med pa*) and without conceptual diffusion (*spros pa med pa*). The second aspect is described by Bhāvaviveka as, along with various other appellations, (the object of?) pure mundane knowledge (*dag pa 'jig rten pa'i ye shes*), and having conceptual diffusion (*spros pa dang bcas pa*). It is this second aspect of the ultimate, Bhāvaviveka says, which is expressed by his thesis (*dam bca'*) or position (*phyogs*) that all entities are without *svabhāva*. The first aspect of the ultimate, being beyond conceptual diffusion, is inexpressible by means of a thesis. It is, he claims, beyond the extremes (*mtha'*) of existence (*yod pa*) and non-existence (*med pa*).[3]

Perhaps the implication here is that all conceptualization takes place in accordance with the notions of existence and/or non-existence. That is – to employ the formulation often referred to as the *catuṣkoṭi* (see *AS* 23, quoted and translated on p. 46) – *x* exists, does not exist, both exists and does not exist, or neither exists nor does not exist. There are no other conceptual possibilities. To claim that the ultimate (in its unspecifiable aspect) is beyond the categories of existence and non-existence is, it would appear, to place it beyond the reach of conceptual knowledge. Existence and non-existence is the basic duality in terms of which the conceptual mind functions. To go beyond this duality is to attain a gnosis of a reality which transcends conceptualization.

This sort of understanding of Madhyamaka has certainly had numerous proponents. In Chinese Madhyamaka, Chih-tsang (458–522), for example, declares that the ultimate truth transcends all verbalization, because it transcends the *catuṣkoṭi*.[4] In Tibetan Madhyamaka, there is a rather similar interpretation of Madhyamaka referred to as the *yod min med min* (not existence, not non-existence) position.[5]

See also the modern rNying ma scholar Mi pham rgya mtsho (1846–1912). Williams writes that,

> For Mi pham any suggestion of going beyond entity and negation, *x* and not-*x*, is a chance to introduce a third value which in its very impossibility as that which is neither of two contradictories forces the mind to a new level beyond which there can be none higher, the level of the Great Madhyamaka, the level of that gnosis which is the calming of all verbal differentiations (*spros pa thams cad zhi ba'i ye shes*).[6]

What is more, Williams notes that Mi pham quotes from the *MMK* in support of his position. Mi pham cites the following passage,

> *astīti śāśvatagrāho nāsītyucchedadarśanaṃ/*
> *tasmādastitvanāstitve nāśīyeta vicakṣaṇaḥ//*

> 'It exists' is the grasping of permanence. 'It does not exist' is the view of annihilation. Therefore, the wise man should not depend on existence or non-existence. (*MMK* XV, 10).

There is also the following passage in the *RV* (though it is not cited by Mi pham):

> *dharmayautakamityasmānnāstyastitvavyatikramam/*
> *viddhi gambhīramityuktaṃ buddhānāṃ śāsanāmṛtaṃ//*

> Therefore, know the unique doctrine transcending non-existence and existence, the ambrosia which is the Buddhas' teaching called 'profound'. (*RV* I, 62).

The Unconceptualizable Reality – Immanent or Transcendent?

But what precisely is $reality_2$? It seems that there is a basic ambiguity in the sense of the term. Is the non-conceptual knowledge a knowledge of an unconceptualizable $reality_2$ which is the true nature of entities? Or is the non-conceptual knowledge a knowledge of an unconceptualizable $reality_2$ which is transcendent to, i.e. quite other than, entities? The two possibilities might be placed in opposition as follows: How entities really are is unconceptualizable, known only by non-conceptual knowledge, versus an unconceptualizable Absolute Reality – known only by non-conceptual knowledge – which is placed apart from the world of dependently originating entities. Thus, interpretation (1) might be understood in (at least) two divergent ways:

> (1a) There is conceptual knowledge of $\{reality\}_1$ [= the absence of *svabhāva* of entities] and there is not conceptual knowledge of $\{reality\}_2$ [= the unconceptualizable true nature of entities]. There is non-conceptual knowledge of $reality_2$.

> (1b) There is conceptual knowledge of $\{reality\}_1$ [= the absence of *svabhāva* of entities] and there is not conceptual knowledge of $\{reality\}_2$ [= the unconceptualizable Absolute Reality, placed apart from the world of dependently originating entities]. There is non-conceptual knowledge of $reality_2$.

The distinction here is between an unconceptualizable reality which is immanent, as the innermost nature of the world of dependently originating entities (1a), and an unconceptualizable reality which is transcendent to these dependently originating entities (1b). In both cases, however, $reality_1$, the absence of *svabhāva* of entities, is a surface-level sort of reality. It is reality in a provisional sense. Reality$_1$ is, according to these interpretations, the object of what Bhāvaviveka calls 'pure mundane knowledge' (*dag pa 'jig rten pa'i ye shes*). It is taught for those who are not able yet to know reality$_2$ (which, according to these interpretations, Bhāvaviveka calls the supramundane (*'jig rten las 'das pa*) ultimate) because of spiritual ineptitude. Perhaps also reality$_1$ is taught in order to facilitate the transactional, worldly or conventional (*vyavahāra*) conduct of those who have realized reality$_2$. That is, the true nature of entities or the transcendent Absolute is unconceptualizable, but in order for those who know reality$_2$ to continue to act in the world it is necessary for them to view entities as without *svabhāva*.

As I shall explain in more detail later, however, the notion of two realities – one final and unconceptualizable, the other provisional and conceptualizable – is surely problematic. For the relationship between these two realities appears to be obscure. (Not to mention the perplexing difficulty concerning what sense if any can be made of an unconceptualizable reality – be it the true nature of entities or a transcendent Absolute). But more about this shortly.

Is Interpretation (1) Supported By Textual Evidence?

It appears to me that, if Nāgārjuna is upholding interpretation (1), it is probably of type (1a) rather than type (1b). There is no textual evidence to support (1b). There is no indication given by Nāgārjuna that he is referring to an Absolute Reality, placed apart from the dependently originating world. On the contrary, several of the passages which I have quoted above (see pp. 45–47) state explicitly that the reality being described is precisely the true nature *of* entities. It is, Nāgārjuna declares, *this world* (*jagadidam*) which is free from characterized objects and characteristics (*lakṣyalakṣaṇanirmuktam*), without expression by words (*vāgudāhāravarjitam*). It is *dharma*-s – i.e. the basic constituents of existence – which are said to be free from the four positions (*catuṣkoṭi*), not some reality placed elsewhere. And Nāgārjuna states that the domain of thought (*cittagocara*) and, hence, the named object (*abhidhātavya*) have ceased with respect to the *dharmatā* – a term used in Mahāyāna Buddhism, as Griffiths notes,[7] to denote the true nature of the *dharma*-s themselves. The impression which these passages give, then, is of an unconceptualizable reality which is the true nature of the entities of the dependently originating world, not some transcendent Absolute.

It seems undeniable that the verses from Nāgārjuna's texts which I have already quoted and translated at the beginning of this chapter might be understood as an assertion of an unconceptualizable reality, i.e. the true nature of entities, accessible only to non-conceptual knowledge. Further, when Nāgārjuna says that he has no view, no position, no thesis, one might take this to mean that the true nature of entities is not amenable to conceptualization and expression. As Lang writes,

> The Mādhyamikas use logic and the techniques of argumentation to expose the limitations of their opponents' theories. Their critique of other philosophical positions is intended to demonstrate the inability of language to express ultimate truth, not to supplant one thesis by another.[8]

It is also the case that the quite common statements by Nāgārjuna which declare that the absence of *svabhāva* of entities is the ultimate truth might conceivably be interpreted as a provisional statement of the ultimate truth – to be finally replaced by a non-conceptual knowledge of the unconceptualizable true nature of entities. (Although, it must be admitted, this would be very much an interpretation. There is no explicit textual evidence in these passages that this is what Nāgārjuna in fact meant.) Nāgārjuna's verses are malleable, it must be acknowledged, and it does seem possible to mold them into a shape which fits interpretation (1). If one wants to find an unconceptualizable reality, known only by a non-conceptual knowledge, in Nāgārjuna's writings it is quite possible to understand some of his statements in such a manner. And, with some effort and ingenuity, there is usually some way to accommodate statements by Nāgārjuna which seem to contradict this interpretation.

This having been said, interpretation (1) does not appear to me to be the most plausible reading of Nāgārjuna's texts. It should be noted that explicit statements which might be construed to support the 'unconceptualizable reality' thesis are not very common in Nāgārjuna's writings (though they certainly do occur). Might the advocate of interpretation (1) therefore be guilty of what R. Robinson calls the fault of 'mosaic interpretation'? That is, might he be laying excessive weight on isolated verses which might be simply passing remarks, unintegrated with the mainstream of Nāgārjuna's thought? One might also suspect that advocates of interpretation (1) commit what R. Robinson calls the fault of 'insinuating the future.'[9] That is, proponents of interpretation (1) might be reading into Nāgārjuna's works a doctrine (that is, of an unconceptualizable reality) which is present in a developed form only later in the history of Madhyamaka

My own judgement is that Nāgārjuna probably meant to assert that there is no other ultimate truth/reality than the absence of *svabhāva* of entities. He does not mean to claim that there is an unconceptualizable reality, known only by a non-conceptual knowledge. The occasional verses in which Nāgārjuna writes of non-conceptuality can be explained as descriptions of a meditative knowledge-experience of the absence of *svabhāva* of entities, rather than as references to an unconceptualizable reality. This is the position, in brief, which I have called interpretation (2), and which I shall explain in detail later in this chapter (see pp. 66–83).

A Philosophical Critique of Interpretation (1)

As I have explained, interpretation (1), in both its varieties, relies on the notion of an unconceptualizable reality (reality$_2$), apprehended only by non-conceptual knowledge. It follows, then, that interpretation (1) will only make sense if one can make sense of this notion. And it is precisely here that the great philosophical problem with interpretation (1) lies. It appears to be difficult to make a philosophically respectable case for an unconceptualizable reality, apprehended by non-conceptual knowledge. I shall explain here some of the difficulties.

The Paradox of Unconceptualizability and Ineffability

The statement that there is an unconceptualizable (and inexpressible) reality seems open to the easy refutation that this statement is itself conceptual, (and expressible). It is a case of conceptual knowledge of a (supposedly) unconceptualizable reality. The statement that there is an unconceptualizable reality is therefore self-refuting. If the statement is true, then it is false. I shall suggest two possible solutions to this (apparent) paradox:

(i) The proponent of interpretation (1) might retort that reality is unconceptualizable, with the exception that it can be conceptualized as unconceptualizable. In other words, reality is *almost entirely* unconceptualizable. The only exception to the rule is the concept of reality's unconceptualizability. No other concept of the (almost entirely) unconceptualizable reality is possible.

The proponent of interpretation (1) might, in other words, introduce a two-tiered hierarchy of conceptuality with regard to the unconceptualizable reality. The tier of legitimate conceptualization of the unconceptualizable reality would contain only one member – the concept that reality is unconceptualizable. All other conceptualization would belong to the tier of illegitimate conceptualization concerning the unconceptualizable reality.

It might be objected that this introduction of two-tiers of concepts is an artificial and arbitrary strategy, a case of special pleading designed to evade (rather than solve) the insoluble problem of the paradox of unconceptualizability. If one concept is permitted with regard to the supposedly unconceptualizable reality, why are other concepts not equally legitimate? Simply to assert that one concept is permitted concerning an unconceptualizable reality, but not others, does not explain how it can be that this one concept has such privileged status.

I am not sure that this objection is convincing, however. Maybe reality *is that sort of matter* about which nothing can be conceived, *except that* it is unconceptualizable. Other concepts are not legitimate wih regard to reality *because reality is the way that it is* – unamenable to any concepts, *except* the concept that it is not amenable to concepts. Hence the 'privileged status' of the concept that reality is unconceptualizable. That is, the privileged status of the concept 'unconceptualizable' stems from reality's nature as unamenable to conceptualization, except the concept 'unconceptualizable'. (It might still be objected, however, that it has not been explained *how it is* that reality is by nature, unlike other entities, only accessible to the concept 'unconceptualizable'. Which is to say, why does reality have this privileged status?).

(ii) The second possible solution to the paradox can be explained by means of an argument by analogy. If I say, for example, that I have no concept of NewYork, then I have the concept that I have no concept of New York. But it would be wrong to suggest that I am here caught in a paradox. My concept that I have no concept of New York is not a quality possessed by New York itself. It is not that I have the concept of New York as having the quality 'not conceived of by David'. Rather, my concept that I have no concept of New York is a concept of my inability to form a concept of New York. By contrast, if I have the concept that

New York is large, exists on the east coast of America, and has a high crime rate, these are (if I am correct) qualities possessed by New York itself.

Similarly, perhaps, the concept that reality is unconceptualizable might plausibly be understood as a concept about the *inability* of concepts to apprehend this reality (the difference being, of course, that unlike the case of New York, it is (supposedly) not even *possible* for concepts to apprehend reality). It is not that reality has the quality 'unconceptualizable' anymore than the inability to conceive of New York is a quality of New York itself. Thus the statement that reality is unconceptualizable is not actually paradoxical, because what is conceptualized by this statement is the inability of concepts to apprehend reality, rather than a quality of reality itself.

Still, it might be objected that if it is not possible to have a concept of reality, then this is *not simply* a concept of the inability of concepts to apprehend reality. There must be – the objection might continue – something about, a quality of, *reality itself* which makes it impossible to form a concept of this reality. This quality of reality itself is reality's 'unconceptualizability.' In other words, if one asks *why* is it impossible to form a concept of reality, the answer must be that it is impossible to form a concept of reality because *reality* is unconceptualizable. In this case the paradox of non-conceptuality is not resolved, for one has the concept of the quality, 'unconceptualizability', possessed by the unconceptualizable reality!

In conclusion, it is not clear to me whether the paradox of unconceptualizability (and ineffability) can be resolved. (Which is to say that I am not sure whether or not it is a *real* paradox). There appear to be reasonable arguments on both sides. I suspect that we have here an example of a philosophical debate which might continue indefinitely.

The Problem of the Two Truths

In what is perhaps the most famous passage of the *MMK*, Nāgārjuna proclaims that the Buddhas' teaching of the *dharma* (*buddhānāṃ dharmadeśanā*) depends upon two truths – the truth of worldly convention (*lokasaṃvṛtisatya*) and the truth (*satya*) from the ultimate point of view (*paramārthataḥ*). The distinction (*vibhāga*) between these two truths must be understood if the Buddhas' teaching is to be comprehended.[10]

I do not want here to enter into the complex and perennial debate about the precise meaning or meanings of this declaration. However, it is clear that one sense at least of 'conventional truth' is the various non-definitive teachings which are employed in order to realize the ultimate truth, i.e. reality. Nāgārjuna must be saying, at least, that it is necessary to rely on these teachings in order to come to know the ultimate truth.

If, however, the ultimate truth is, as interpretation (1) maintains, unconceptualizable, how is it that reliance on conceptual conventional truths will be efficacious in bringing about the realization of this ultimate truth? The relationship between an unconceptualizable ultimate truth and the conceptual, conventional truths of Buddhist doctrine is very problematic. Once the breach between the unconceptualizable ultimate truth and the conceptualizable conventional truth has been created, it seems to be impossible to bridge the chasm.

How is it that some concepts – i.e. the various teachings which are conventional truths – can be relied on to produce a non-conceptual knowledge of an unconceptualizable ultimate truth? Any explanation would of course involve conceptualization, which would seem to compromise the unconceptualizable nature of the ultimate truth. An explanation would have to state precisely what it is about the (supposedly) unconceptualizable, inexpressible ultimate truth which reliance on the conventional truths of Buddhism helps one to realize. However, without such an explanation, the claim that Buddhist teachings are efficacious cannot be justified. Without such justification, the notion that certain concepts are to be relied upon in order to realize the unconceptualizable ultimate truth will remain an assertion which cannot be substantiated.

Interpretation (1) in fact entails, it appears, epistemological (and ethical) relativism. If no conceptual formulations can be justified as 'closer' to the unconceptualizable reality than others, then no conceptual formulation can be demonstrated to be any better (or worse) than any other. But if, on the contrary, some conceptual formulations are shown to be 'closer' to the unconceptualizable reality than others, then the unconceptualizable reality is not in fact unconceptualizable.

It might be objected that for interpretation (1) in fact the ultimate truth is only unconceptualizable in one of its aspects, i.e. $reality_2$. $Reality_1$ – the mundane ultimate truth – is accessible to conceptualization. It can be specified. That is, it is the absence of *svabhāva* of entities. In which case it can be demonstrated that the various conceptual, conventional teachings of Buddhism are efficacious in bringing about the realization of this conceptualizable ultimate truth.

But this solution just pushes the problem one step back, because it prompts the apparently unanswerable question how is the (mundane) ultimate truth which is conceptualizable – i.e. the absence of *svabhāva* of entities – related to the unconceptualizable (trans-mundane) ultimate truth, i.e. reality_2?

Why should it be that the realization of the conceptualizable ultimate truth should have any bearing on the realization of the unconceptualizable ultimate truth? How can a conceptualizable mundane ultimate truth be any 'closer' to the unconceptualizable trans-mundane ultimate truth than any other conceptualization? The intractable problem is, in this case, the relationship between the two aspects of the ultimate truth.

Of course, the proponent of interpretation (1) will claim that although reality_2 is unconceptualizable, some concepts are indicative of this reality whereas others are not. One thinks here of the Zen image of the finger pointing at the moon. Just as the finger directs one towards the moon, the conceptual truths of Buddhism direct one towards the unconceptualizable ultimate truth. And just as the finger pointing at the moon is not the moon which it directs one towards, so too the conceptual truths of Buddhism are not the ultimate truth – at least in its final, unconceptualizable aspect – which they direct one towards. Candrakīrti might perhaps be interpreted to be making this point in his commentary to *MMK* XXIV, 9,

> *atrāha – yadi tarhi paramārtho niṣprapañcasvabhāvaḥ sa evāstu, tatkimanayā aparayā skandhadhātvāyatanāryasatya-pratītyasamutpādādideśanayā prayojanamaparamārthayā, atattvaṃ hi parityājyam/ yacca parityājyaṃ kiṃ tenopadiṣṭena, ucyate/ satyametadevam/ kiṃ tu laukikaṃ vyavahāramanabhyupagamya abhidhānābidheyajñānajñeyā-dilakṣaṇam, aśakya eva paramārtho deśayitum, adeśitaśca na śakyo 'dhigantum, anadhigamyaca paramārthaṃ na śakyaṃ nirvāṇamadhigantumiti ...*
>
> Here it is objected [by an opponent]: If then the ultimate [truth] is an intrinsic existent which is without conceptual

> diffusion, let that be so! In that case, what is the purpose of this inferior teaching – which is not the ultimate [truth] – of the aggregates, elements, sense-fields, noble truths, dependent origination, etc? Surely what is not true should be rejected; and what is [accomplished] by means of that teaching to be rejected?
>
> It is replied [by Candrakīrti]: This is certainly true. However, without assenting to ordinary conventions – characterized by naming and named object, knowledge and object of knowledge, etc – it is simply not possible to teach the ultimate [truth]. And [if the ultimate truth is] not taught, it cannot be realized. And without realizing the ultimate [truth], it is not possible to realize *nirvāṇa*. (*PP* 494).

But, interpreted in this way, Candrakīrti's reply does not really come to terms with the force of the opponent's objection. The opponent is surely right that if the ultimate truth is *niṣprapañca*, and if this means that reality is in fact unconceptualizable, it must be that all conceptual expressions of this ultimate truth are simply false *qua* expressions of the ultimate truth. The notion that some concepts, viz. the conceptual formulations of Buddhism, 'indicate' the unconceptualizable ultimate truth is incoherent. It appears to be an attempt to have one's cake and eat it. To indicate is to point out, and to point out is to discriminate – i.e. conceptualize – what is pointed out, in this case the (supposedly) unconceptualizable ultimate truth. It is irrational that reality is both: (i) unconceptualizable and (ii) indicated conceptually. (i) and (ii) are incompatible. The Mādhyamika must give up either (i) or (ii). If the Mādhyamika wants to preserve the justification for Buddhist theory and practice, it is (i) which must be abandoned.

Perhaps, however, the proponent of interpretation (1) can address the problem of the two truths more satisfactorily in another way. He may say that, for the Mādhyamika, the absence of *svabhāva* of entities is the conceptualizable ultimate truth that all entities lack inherent existence. Here entities' 'lack of inherent existence' means that they are one and all conceptually constructed (see here chapter 4 for a thorough discussion of this point). The various conventional, non-definitive teachings of Buddhism (such as impermanence) are intended gradually to help one realize this conceptualizable ultimate truth that entities are merely conceptual constructs. The eventually achieved knowledge, the proponent of interpretation (1) might say, that entities have a conceptually constructed nature might induce one to stop the proliferation of concepts. As a result, the ineffable, unconceptualizable reality which underlies (according to interpretation (1)) the conceptually constructed entities might become visible, whereas previously it was obscured. To use the familiar analogy, previously the unconceptualizable reality was like a mirror covered by dust. With the dust removed the mirror can be seen unimpeded. The dust in this case is the conceptually constructed entities. Realizing the ultimate truth about them (i.e. that they *are* conceptually constructed) might enable one to wipe the dust from the mirror.

Understood in this way, then, the ultimate truth that entities lack *svabhāva* is the conceptualizable ultimate truth – it is indeed what is actually the case about entities. Entities really are conceptual constructs. Seeing this ultimate truth makes possible – it is the *sine qua non* for – the manifestation of the ineffable, unconceptualizable substratum underlying the conceptually constructed entities which the proliferation of conceptually constructed entities normally conceals. In this case, the relation between $reality_1$ and $reality_2$ is made clear. It is by thorough knowledge of the conceptualizable $reality_1$ – brought about gradually by means of the conventional truths of Buddhism – that one stops constructing $reality_1$, thus enabling the unconceptualizable $reality_2$ to shine forth, as it were.

I have a final reflection on this notion of an unconceptualizable substratum. I suppose that – in accordance with the Buddhist notion of universal transience – this substratum might be understood by the proponent of interpretation (1) as an ineffable flow of pure change/becoming, rather than as static/unchanging. Thus, independently of conceptualization reality is pure 'entity-free' becoming/change, upon which the conceptualizing mind imposes the variety of conceptually constructed entities. The substratum – the pure process of change – is prior to and independent of the conceptual discrimination (*vikalpa*) and conceptual diffusion (*prapañca*) which fabricates the world of entities on the basis of this pristine process of change.

There are at least two philosophical objections to this proposal, however. First, it can be argued that the idea of 'change' always presupposes *something* which is changing. Change is arguably always a possession of an entity. Change is necessarily change of entity *x*. The notion of change without an entity of which it is the change is perhaps incomprehensible. In other words, the idea that there is an unconceptualizable entity-free substratum of change, upon which conceptually constructed entities are imposed, may be incoherent. Second, if the unconceptualizable substratum is a process of pure change it has, surely, been conceptualized – namely, *as a process of pure change*! To be consistent interpretation (1) should not say that the ineffable/unconceptualizable reality is *either* static/unchanging *or* changing.

The Night in Which All Cows are Black

Hegel, in his *Phenomenology of Spirit*, criticizes Schelling's notion that reality is without specifications and determinateness. He comments that such a reality would be contentless and singularly uninteresting, 'as the night in which, as the saying goes, all cows are black – this is cognition naively reduced to vacuity.'[11] Hegel's criticism can also be applied to interpretation (1), in its advocacy of an unconceptualizable reality, apprehended by non-conceptual knowledge.

It is my contention that possession of a concept is what enables one to pick out or discriminate *x* (including the discrimination that *x* is *y*). See here Dummett's comment, concerning the concept of a square, that 'at the very least' to grasp the concept 'is to discriminate between things that are square and those that are not.'[12] Thus,

(a) an entity which is conceptualizable is an entity which can be discriminated, and an entity which is unconceptualizable is an entity which cannot be discriminated. An entity which can be discriminated can be known (for knowledge involves the discrimination of entities), but an entity which cannot be discriminated cannot be known. It is not possible that an entity cannot be discriminated and is knowable. In which case, an unconceptualizable reality, i.e. a reality which cannot be discriminated, and which can be known is a contradiction.

(b) knowledge which is non-conceptual is knowledge which cannot discriminate anything. But knowledge which cannot discriminate anything is not knowledge. There cannot be, therefore, non-conceptual knowledge.

In fact, the notion of non-conceptuality, as I am employing it here, is perhaps incompatible with consciousness *per se*. For consciousness is arguably always consciousness of x. In order for consciousness to be consciousness of x, x must be picked out, i.e. discriminated, from other entities. As I have explained, it is the possession of a concept that enables one to discriminate x. Without concepts there would be no discrimination of x at all. And without the discrimination of x, there would be no consciousness of x, and hence no consciousness. A non-conceptual consciousness is thus impossible.[13]

It appears to me, then, that the advocate of a non-conceptual knowledge of an unconceptualizable reality truly must be proposing a 'night in which all cows are black.' For his position entails that a reality which cannot be discriminated is apprehended (if this is the right word) by a knowledge which does not discriminate anything! How is this distinguishable from total blankness?

There are at least two possible objections to my account. I have argued that there can be no unconceptualizable reality which can be known because (i) all knowledge involves discrimination, and (ii) it is only concepts which discriminate. An opponent might question either (i) or (ii).

If (i) is rejected, the opponent must claim that there is a special form of knowledge which does not discriminate, i.e. does not pick out x or x is y. This special non-discriminatory knowledge apprehends the unconceptualizable reality.

But surely it is contradictory to claim that knowledge can *apprehend* without *discriminating*. I do not think that I can make sense of knowledge which does not discriminate anything. Such a knowledge would be contentless, and would thus would not be a case of knowledge.

If (ii) is opposed, the opponent must claim that not all discrimination occurs via concepts. There is a special form of discrimination which does not occur by conceptual means. It is this special form of discrimination, i.e. a non-conceptual knowledge, which apprehends the unconceptualizable reality.

But the claim that there is such a non-conceptual discrimination of reality seems rather strange to me. This special non-conceptual knowledge must discriminate reality without picking out x or x is y (for if this knowledge picked out x or x is y it would be, by my definition at least,[14] conceptual). But what can it possibly mean to discriminate reality without picking out x or x is y? No answer is forthcoming. The opponent might say, of course, that there *can be* no answer because I am asking for a conceptual explanation of a non-conceptual knowledge. But I can surely with equal justification say that there *can be* no answer because such a non-conceptual knowledge does not exist. (That is, if no such answer is forthcoming, I have no reason to believe that there is such a non-conceptual knowledge of an unconceptualizable reality). Maybe here we reach the limits of the discussion!

S. Katz, etc on Non-Conceptual Religious Knowledge

The notion of non-conceptual religious knowledge has been the subject of some debate in recent years amongst scholars. Much of the discussion has focussed on the work of S. Katz concerning the nature of mystical experiences.[15] Katz argues against the notion that there are pure, unmediated, i.e. non-conceptual, mystical experiences. He rejects the theory that there are such non-conceptual experiences, which only become subject to conceptualization after the event, i.e. when the mystic begins to reflect on and communicate what he has non-conceptually realized. On the contrary, Katz claims, the mystical experience itself must be conceptually-laden, even if the mystic himself does not realize that this is the case. Katz says, much as I have just argued, that 'the notion of unmediated experience seems, if not self-contradictory, at least empty.'[16] Conceptualization must be intrinsic to a mystical experience if this experience is to be meaningful, i.e. if it is to be an experience of anything at all.

M. Bagger,[17] who appears to be in agreement with Katz, makes some important and related points:

(i) If there were non-conceptual experiences then they would be contentless. In which case, the mystic should not be able to remember the experience which he has had (for there would literally be nothing to remember). Yet mystics do claim to remember – often in a very vivid manner – the supposedly non-conceptual experiences which they have had. Insofar as they remember something, then, the original experience must have involved discrimination, and, hence, must have been conceptual.

(ii) The mystic might well be unaware of the conceptualization which takes place in his supposedly non-conceptual experience. Nevertheless, the conceptualization must be present if the experience is to occur. Conceptualization might well take place on a 'sub–conscious' level, as when one identifies a familiar object – the sun for example – without reflecting that 'there is the sun'.

I shall have more to say about this later, for it provides a key to an alternative interpretation (i.e. interpretation (2)) to interpretation (1) concerning the meaning of non-conceptual knowledge in Nāgārjuna's writings.

(iii) Even if there were non-conceptual experiences – pure consciousness events, as Bagger calls them – it is difficult to see what religious significance they might have. Such an experience would be akin to deep sleep, and would surely not yield any information about the nature of reality. What truth could be conveyed by such an experience, and what bearing could it possibly have on life?

I think that these points raise some very serious difficulties for interpretation (1), given its claim that there is non-conceptual knowledge of unconceptualizable $reality_2$. Which is not to say, I must emphasize, that therefore Nāgārjuna does not hold a version of interpretation (1). Rather, it is simply to say that if Nāgārjuna (or anyone else, for that matter) upholds a version of interpretation (1), then it seems difficult to make sense of their position.

Concluding Philosophical Reflections on Interpretation (1)

My conclusion is, therefore, that interpretation (1) entails some serious philosophical problems. If Nāgārjuna upholds a version of interpretation (1), then he is open to the criticisms which I have made.

Those Mādhyamikas who advocate an unconceptualizable reality, apprehended by non-conceptual knowledge, will argue that I have become stuck in conceptual difficulties, and I am thus blind to the higher perspective of a non-conceptual knowledge of an unconceptualizable reality. To this I reply that I can make no sense of such an unconceptualizable reality, nor, consequently, of the non-conceptual knowledge of it. No doubt opponents will counter that this simply supports their point; I am unable to make sense of an unconceptualizable reality, accessible to a non-conceptual knowledge, because my perspective is limited by my stubborn adherence to concepts. Of course, they will say, you cannot make sense of a reality which can be discriminated only non-conceptually; this is because the only tools which you permit for 'making sense' are conceptual! But what other tools are there, I ask?

Or else, my opponents might say, you place too much emphasis on 'making sense'; the unconceptualizable reality is apprehended by a non-conceptual experience which does not have a 'justification'. That attempts to make sense of this position entail paradoxes and insoluble difficulties just proves that the nature of reality is in fact unconceptualizable.

But, while I am certainly open to the possibility that there are higher perspectives than the one for which I have argued here, this suggestion by the advocate of interpretation (1) seems to me to point towards irrationalism and relativism. A reality which is not ascertainable by conceptual means, and is apprehended by some other mysterious method which cannot be communicated, seems to me to be irrevocably subjective as well as philosophically and religiously/spiritually barren.

Note, finally, the possible ethical and political implications of such a doctrine. A leader or teacher who has supposedly realized an unconceptualizable reality need not be accountable for his utterances and actions. When questioned about his reasons or motives, he might simply say that his statements and actions cannot be explained, because they stem from his non-conceptual, inexpressible realization of reality. This is surely a recipe for despotism.

Interpretation (2): The Non-Conceptual Meditative Knowledge-Experience of Emptiness

As I have explained, Nāgārjuna states that there is conceptual knowledge of reality – namely, 'all entities are without *svabhāva*' – and also that reality is free from conceptual diffusion, signless etc. The resolution of the apparent contradiction by means of an equivocation in the term 'reality', so that one sense of 'reality' is conceptualizable and another is unconceptualizable, leads to apparently unacceptable philosophical consequences. The notion of an 'unconceptualizable reality', apprehended by non-conceptual knowledge, seems to be unintelligible. Interpretation (1), then, would appear to be a philosophical dead-end.

Let me suggest another interpretation (i.e. interpretation (2)) which, unlike interpretation (1), does not advocate an unconceptualizable reality, apprehended by non-conceptual knowledge.

There are, in Nāgārjuna's texts, some (though, admittedly, not many) explicit references to meditation (*bhāvanā*). See, for example, *MMK* XXIV, 24, and the following verse from the *LS*,

āryairniṣevitāmenāmanāgamya hi bhāvanām/
nānimittaṃ hi vijñānaṃ bhavatīha kathaṃ cana//

Certainly, without entering that meditation practised by the *āryan*-s, of course the signless consciousness will not occur here in any way. (*LS* 26).

Furthermore, given that Nāgārjuna was a Buddhist monk, and meditation is central to Buddhist practice, it seems reasonable to think that some of his other statements may be about meditative states, even though he does not explicitly say so.

According to interpretation (2), when Nāgārjuna says that reality is *niṣprapañca*, *nirvikalpa*, etc this is not actually a description of reality. (In other words, Nāgārjuna's way of expressing himself is imprecise, even inaccurate). Rather, it is a description of the nature of the *experience* of knowing reality, i.e. the absence of *svabhāva* of entities, as this experience occurs in a meditative context.

This is not to say that the meditative experience of knowing reality is in all senses non-conceptual. On the contrary, the meditative experience of knowing reality must be conceptual, in the specific sense that such a meditative experience discriminates the absence of *svabhāva* of entities. That is, the meditative experience is the experience of something. Otherwise it would not be a case of knowledge, for nothing would be known when having this experience.

Nevertheless, there are other senses of the term 'non-conceptual' and it is in these senses that a meditative experience of reality might appropriately be called 'non-conceptual'. In other words, interpretation (2) depends on an equivocation in the meaning of the term 'conceptual'. Given that the meditative experience of reality does discriminate the true nature of entities as its object, the meditative experience can be characterized as 'conceptual'. But the term 'conceptual' can have other meanings as well (I shall identify three other meanings). It is in these senses that the meditative experience of reality might acceptably be called 'non-conceptual'. Thus, according to interpretation (2),

The meditative knowledge-experience of reality is conceptual in $sense_1$ of 'conceptual', and is not conceptual in $sense_2$, $sense_3$, and $sense_4$ of 'conceptual'.

But all of this requires further explanation and clarification, which I shall now attempt to give.

Knowledge of Reality Versus the Reality Which is Known

There is clearly a difference between reality and the knowledge of reality. It is, according to the Mādhyamika, always the case that all entities are without *svabhāva*, whether or not it is known that this is the case. Thus, Candrakīrti, for example, quotes with approval the canonical statement to the effect that the *tathāgata*-s (who know the true nature (*dharmatā*) of *dharma*-s), may either arise or not arise but the *dharmatā* of *dharma*-s remains.[18] The *dharmatā*, i.e. the true nature of entities (their absence of *svabhāva*) is always the case, although the knowledge of it may be present or absent. Knowledge of reality is dependent for its existence upon the reality which is known, but reality is not dependent for its existence upon the knowledge of it. Which is to say that all entities have a conceptually constructed existence, and are thus marked by emptiness, whether or not any cognizer knows that this is so.

(Notice, however, that (for the Mādhyamika) – although the true nature of entities is not dependent on the knowledge of it – this true nature of entities *is* dependent on the mind's activity of conceptual construction. Entities are in their true nature empty of *svabhāva*, i.e. they have conceptually constructed existence. If the mind's activity of conceptual construction did not occur, there would be no entities, and hence no true nature *of* entities. I suspect that this is the meaning of Candrakīrti's declaration, in the *MA*, of the 'emptiness of emptiness' (*stong nyid stong nyid=śūnyatāśūnyatā*). As Candrakīrti says, the teaching of the emptiness of emptiness opposes (*bzlog*) the (wrong) apprehension of emptiness as a *dngos po* (=*bhāva*) – a *dngos po* being, in my judgement, here a 'mind-independent existent').[19]

See here Bhāvaviveka's explanation, in the *TJv*, of the compound '*paramārtha*'. Bhāvaviveka explains that, taken as a *karmadhāraya* compound, the expression '*paramārtha*' means 'the object which is ultimate'. The object (*artha*) is reality/the true natue of things, which is qualified by the adjective 'ultimate' (*parama*). But, understood as a genitive *tatpuruṣa* compound, the expression '*paramārtha*' means 'the object of the ultimate'.[20] The ultimate (*parama*) is here a noun, standing for 'ultimate knowledge' (*paramajñāna*), which possesses as its object (*artha*) reality/the true nature of entities. Thus,

Bhāvaviveka's analysis of the compound in these two ways makes the distinction between reality, and the knowledge which apprehends this reality.

Knowledge of Reality is an Experience

'Knowledge', it must be recognized, is both of something and for someone. There is no knowledge without something which is known. But, equally, there is no knowledge which occurs abstracted from a subject who is knowing. It is not simply that 'there is knowledge of *x*'; it is also that 'for subject *a* there is knowledge of *x*'. It is non-sensical to speak of something being known without anyone who possesses the knowledge. I cannot intelligibly say that it is known that there is a red apple on the table and yet there is no one who has the knowledge that there is a red apple on the table. '*X* is known' permits the question '*x* is known by whom?' Insofar as knowledge is not only of something but also for someone, it is the case that knowledge is *an experience.*

In which case, knowledge of reality in the context of meditation, as a species of knowledge-in-general, is not simply knowledge of something, it is also knowledge for someone. There is both something which is known, viz. reality, and a subject who knows it. The meditative knowledge of reality is an experience.

I do not want here to explore in detail the problematic notion of 'experience'. The essential point for my present purpose is that many[21] experiences have, to borrow a distinction made in contemporary epistemology, both a content and a character. M. Pendlebury has defined the content of an experience as the properties which the experience represents, whereas the character of the experience is the properties which the experience possesses.[22]

Take for instance my experience of a sunset. It is true to say that my experience represents a sunset. There is a content, viz. the sunset, of which the experience is an experience. However, it is not correct to attribute the properties of the sunset to the experience itself. That my experience is of a sunset does not mean that my experience is a sunset! The sunset has properties – such as its orange and red colour, its location in the sky, it is several miles long etc – which my experience of the sunset most certainly does not have. My experience is not an orange and red colour, nor is it located in the sky, and it is certainly not several miles long.

My experience of the sunset does of course itself possess properties – which constitute the character of the experience – but these are not the properties represented by the experience. For example, the experience of the sunset will possess an emotional property or emotional properties. The experience will feel a certain way – perhaps happy, sad, exciting, boring, etc. Just as the properties of the sunset which are represented by the experience are not possessed by the experience, so too the properties possessed by the experience of the sunset are not properties of the sunset which is represented by the experience. The sunset is not happy or sad, exciting, boring etc.

In other words, many experiences have a subjective pole and an objective pole. Both the subjective pole and the objective pole have a variety of properties. But it is simply a confusion to attribute to the objective pole properties which belong to the subjective pole, or *vice versa*:

> Experience= experience [characterized by properties *a*, *b*, *c*] of an object [with properties *x*, *y*, *z*].

I shall argue that three of the properties which characterize the meditative knowledge-experience of reality (as opposed to the properties which characterize the reality which is experienced) might plausibly be called 'non-conceptual'. That is, the meditative knowledge-experience of reality possesses the properties of: (1) acquaintance with its object, (2) absence of explicit conceptualization, and (3) focussed conceptualization.

A Short Digression: The Private Nature of Experience

But it is also arguable that there is a sense in which *all* experience (and not just the meditative experience of reality) has a non-conceptual and inexpressible character. Unlike trees, tables, and other physical entities, an experience is not a public object. There is an irrevocably private dimension to experience. You cannot have my experiences, and I cannot have your experiences. This does not mean, however, that one cannot give an account of one's experiences. Nor does it mean that any such account is necessarily inaccurate. In fact, it is possible to give an accurate account of one's experience. Nevertheless, the account – even if it is an accurate account – is not the experience of which it is the account.

Suppose, for instance, that I have an experience of a sunset. I might describe to you the nature of my experience. I might say what the sunset which I experienced was like. For example, the sunset was bright red and tinged with yellow, several miles long, etc. I might also describe to you how it felt for me to experience this sunset. I felt absorbed, peaceful, delighted, etc. This account of my experience might be either inaccurate or accurate. Perhaps I have remembered incorrectly. In fact, the sunset was not tinged with yellow, and I felt sad, not delighted. Or else it might be that my account of my experience is entirely accurate. That is, the sunset which I experienced was in fact bright red and tinged with yellow, several miles long, etc, and it might be entirely true that I felt absorbed, peaceful, delighted, etc. Nevertheless, if I relate this accurate description of my experience to you, you do not have my experience, though my accurate description might enable you to understand, and empathize with, my experience. Perhaps you have had a similar experience in the past, and you now recollect it, and think, 'what David has experienced must be just like what I experienced at that time'. Further, even if we experience the same sunset at the same time, and both feel the same way when doing so, your experience is not mine, and neither is my experience yours.

Thus, any description, any conceptualization, of an experience – though it might be accurate – remains simply a description/conceptualization, and is not the experience itself. One might say that experience has a 'lived', first person character. It is this which is untranslatable into concepts and words. Nagel[23] famously comments that the subjective nature of an experience, 'what-it-is-like-to-be a particular subject', is only accessible from the point of view of the subject himself. See also Pivcevic who writes,

> That experiences ... occur biographically accounts for the exclusively 'private ownership' of experiences and distinguishes experiences from public objects ... We can, of course, and do, make objectifying references to our own and other people's experiences, reflect upon them, analyze them, discuss them. Moreover we are able to analyze to some extent, as well as report about, our own experiences while they are actually happening. Provided I am articulate enough, I can give a running commentary on my own mental states and attitudes and describe them in minute detail, possibly just as vividly and as acurately as any 'external object'. But none of this

> diminishes the difference in ontological status between experiences and intersubjectively accessible public items. My experiences are slices of my own lived time and are, in this sense, inalienably mine, as no 'external' object can be.[24]

One's meditative experience of reality is (if one admits the existence of such a phenomenon), like all other experiences, a first-person occurrence. I might describe my meditative experience of reality to you. I might say that I experienced the absence of *svabhāva* of entities, that I felt calm, at one with the object of meditation (like water poured into water, as the Tibetans say), etc. This might in fact be an accurate description of my experience. This is actually what was experienced, and how it felt to be having the experience. Nevertheless, the description is not the experience. And if you too have had at the same time as myself a meditative experience that all entities are without *svabhāva*, and you also felt calm, at one with the object of meditation, etc this does not mean that your experience is mine, or that my experience is yours. Any account of a meditative experience of reality must necessarily leave out the lived-nature, the first person perspective, of the experience, which is not translatable into concepts and words.

While I think that this is a philosophically respectable sense in which experience – including the meditative experience of reality – might be termed 'non-conceptual' (and 'inexpressible'), it must be acknowledged that there is no indication in Nāgārjuna's writings that this is what he in fact means. But this is not surprising given that the first-person nature of experience – it appears to me – has only been systematically explicated in modern, western philosophy, especially by philosophers influenced by phenomenology and existentialism. This interpretation, then, reads Nāgārjuna in the light of a modern theory of experience. This modern theory of experience is no doubt worthy in its own right of serious philosophical study, but it would be anachronistic to suggest that Nāgārjuna intends his claims that (the experience of) reality is non-conceptual to be understood in this way. Furthermore, if Nāgārjuna's statements that (the experience of) reality is *niṣprapañca*, *nirvikalpa*, and so on were meant to communicate that the meditative experience of reality has an untranslatable first person character, then, given that all experiences have an untranslatable first person character, Nāgārjuna would have to admit that all experiences are *niṣprapañca*, *nirvikalpa*, etc! But, in fact, Nāgārjuna describes only the experience of reality in these terms.

Let me turn, then, to the three other ways mentioned above (see p. 70) in which the meditative knowledge-experience of reality might be more plausibly read to be non-conceptual for Nāgārjuna.

(1) Knowledge by Acquaintance

'Conceptual knowledge' can have the sense of a theoretical knowledge, which is unacquainted with the object described. I have knowledge of the Bengal tiger because I have been informed about the nature of the Bengal tiger. The Bengal tiger has been described to me, and I have understood the description. But I have never come across a Bengal tiger in the flesh, as it were. In this sense I have a conceptual, i.e. theoretical, knowledge. When I come across the Bengal tiger (of which, perhaps, I have had previously a theoretical knowledge), then I have what might be termed a non-conceptual knowledge by acquaintance of the Bengal tiger. (But note that both the theoretical knowledge and the knowledge by acquaintance are conceptual in the different sense that they both involve discrimination of the object 'Bengal tiger'.)

Similarly, interpretation (2) suggests, there is a distinction between a theoretical knowledge of reality – i.e. that all entities are without *svabhāva* – and an acquaintance with this reality. The meditative experience which Nāgārjuna describes as without conceptualization has the character of direct acquaintance as opposed to being merely theoretical. It is in this sense non-conceptual. The theoretical knowledge of reality is, one might say, the knowledge of the fact that all entities lack *svabhāva*. By contrast, in the context of meditative experience, one might come face-to-face with the emptiness (*śūnyatā*) of entities itself.

In dGe lugs pa Madhyamaka exegesis, it is explained that emptiness (or, better, an emptiness), i.e the very absence (*med pa*) of *svabhāva* itself, is an (albeit negative) characteristic or quality of each entity. As Napper comments, for Tsong kha pa, 'emptiness is not seen as a unitary Absolute, but rather as multiple. There are as many emptinesses as there are phenomena. Each and every phenomenon has its own emptiness, and the emptiness of one is not the emptiness of another.'[25] However, though (an) emptiness characterizes each entity, ordinary people (*mu stegs can*) fail to perceive it.[26] Through a meditative training – consisting of repeated analysis demonstrating the absence of *svabhāva* of entities, coupled with *śamatha* meditation (which makes one's mind calm, concentrated and potent) – it is said that one comes to perceive emptiness(es).[27] One has a personal realization of, becomes directly acquainted with, the quality which is the absence of *svabhāva* in the meditative object. One sees it for oneself, as it were. (See here the traditional Buddhist formulation of the three levels of wisdom (*prajñā*), according to which meditative wisdom (*bhāvanāmayīprajñā*) occurs after, and as the result of, the wisdom of hearing (*śrutamayīprajñā*) and the wisdom of reflection (*cintāmayīprajñā*). There is a process of learning about and deepening one's understanding of the nature of reality. This culminates in a personal realization. One no longer simply knows that reality is such and such. One is now directly acquainted with this reality).[28]

Candrakīrti's comments on Nāgārjuna's statement, at *MMK* XVIII, 9, that reality (*tattva*) is not dependent on another (*aparapratyaya*) are pertinent. Candrakīrti explains that *tattva* is not dependent on another in the sense that one who realizes *tattva*, i.e. the truth that all things lack *svabhāva*, must do so by himself, i.e. by direct personal experience rather than by the instruction of another:

> *paropadeśāgamyam/ svayamevādhigantavyamityarthaḥ/*
>
> The meaning [of *aparapratyaya*] is that [*tattva*] is not to be understood by means of the teaching of another. It is to be understood by oneself alone. (*PP* 373).

I understand this to mean that in effect Candrakīrti takes Nāgārjuna's statement to be about the character of the experience of reality, rather than about the reality which is experienced. One must experience reality personally, and the theoretical knowledge which one gains from others is no substitute for this direct perception.

Candrakīrti proceeds to give the famous analogy of people with eye-disease (*taimirika*) who mistakenly (*vitatham*) see hair (*keśa*), gnats (*maśaka*), and flies (*makṣikā*), etc. People with this eye-disease can be taught by another person without eye-disease (*vitimira*) that their vision of hair, gnats, flies, etc is false. And it might be described to the people with eye-disease how it would be to have vision without the false seeing of hair, gnats, etc. In a sense, people with eye-disease might understand. They could even describe accurately that they have eye-disease, that it causes them mistakenly to see hair, gnats, flies, etc, and they might be able to describe accurately what it would be like to see without the eye-disease influencing their vision. Nevertheless, their knowledge remains theoretical, for, despite their knowledge of the fact that there are no gnats, flies, hairs, they still see the gnats, flies, hairs, etc. Their actual vision has not been changed, no matter how eloquently and thoroughly they might be able to describe what it would be like to be without the eye-disease.

Similarly, Candrakīrti says, the teaching of emptiness might be taught by another, and this teaching might be understood. Yet one would still fail to see emptiness. One's understanding would be theoretical rather than by acquaintance. One would still fail to perceive the absence of *svabhāva* of entities, even though one would understand that in fact the absence of *svabhāva* is the true nature of entities. One's knowledge would be, then, merely conceptual, in the sense that it had not yet transformed one's perception. One has yet to have the correct vision of emptiness (*aviparitaśūnyatādarśana*) for oneself, a face-to-face encounter with reality, which takes place, I suggest, in the context of a meditative experience.[29]

But there is surely a distinction between a meditative perception of emptiness, and the perception of this emptiness in the context of one's life as a whole. (Though there is no mention of this distinction in Nāgārjuna's writings. He is simply silent on the matter). It does not follow that because one has had a face-to-face encounter with emptiness in meditation, therefore in one's post-meditative experience of entities one will perceive their emptiness. The meditative experience of emptiness is more like a remission of the eye disease, rather than a permanent cure. The permanent post-meditative perception of emptiness would be analogous to actually permanently curing the eye disease, rather than simply having theoretical knowledge of what it would be like to be without the eye-disease, and having occasional periods of remission.

However, knowledge by acquaintance of emptiness in the context of meditation is presumably intended to be a step towards a knowledge by acquaintance of entities as empty in one's life as a whole. A face-to-face encounter with emptiness in meditation is perhaps a necessary condition for one's post-meditative perceptual experience to be (eventually) brought into permanent accord with one's theoretical understanding that all entities are without *svabhāva*. When entities are perceived in everyday life to be without *svabhāva*, one would no longer, presumably, become attached to them. (See here, for example, *YṢ* 29 in which Nāgārjuna says that, unlike the people of the world (*'jig rten*), who – blinded by ignorance (*ma rig ldongs gyur pa*) – are followers of the stream of desire (*sred pa rgyun gyi rjes 'brangs*), the wise man (*mkhas pa*) is free from desire (*sred pa dang bral ba*)).The idea is, I suppose, that if one actually saw entities to be lacking *svabhāva*, one would become thoroughly convinced that they are unworthy of attachment. One would thus no longer covet these entities. It is a first principle of Buddhist teaching that it is attachment/desire which causes suffering (*duḥkha*), and the absence of attachment entails the cessation of suffering. Thus, the soteriological implication of meditative knowledge by acquaintance of emptiness would be (according to the Mādhyamika) to facilitate the eventual total freedom from attachment, and hence the eradication of suffering.

(Note, however, that there seems to be no *a priori* reason why one might not still get attached to entities, even if one always perceives that they are empty. It is perhaps possible that one might get attached to an entity even though one sees that this entity is a mental fabrication. The Mādhyamika might say, of course, that one *ought* not get attached to entities, because they have a tenuous, merely conceptually constructed existence, and one's attachment will only bring one suffering. But this does not necessarily mean that one *will* not be attached, despite the Mādhyamika advice. Still, it does seem reasonable to think that, if one always saw entities to be simply conceptual constructs (especially if this seeing were complemented by a training in Buddhist ethics (*śīla*), which is intended – among other things – to promote non-attachment), one's attachment to and desire for these entities might be weakened or even eradicated. This claim would need to be tested empirically, however).

There is a final point. As I have explained in the previous chapter, at *MMK* XIII, 8 Nāgārjuna says that those who hold emptiness to be a view are incurable. Perhaps emptiness is an incurable view if one merely correctly understands it (as the absence of *svabhāva* in all entities) in a theoretical way, without having any inclination to achieve the corresponding perception of emptiness, i.e. the mere absence of *svabhāva* of entities, in meditation and, finally, in one's life as a whole. The theoretical teaching of emptiness is simply a medicine, it is a means to an end. If the means is mistaken for the end one will be incapable of actually perceiving the emptiness of entities. Without the direct encounter with the absence of inherent existence of entities one will remain attached to them, and thus one will continue to suffer. Read in this way, then, Nāgārjuna's proclamation is a warning that emptiness will be effective as a cure against suffering only if one's understanding of emptiness is transformed from a view (*dṛṣṭi*) into a vision (*darśana*).[30]

(2) Lack of Explicit Conceptualization

I have argued that all knowledge must be characterized by conceptuality, insofar as knowledge involves discrimination. There cannot be knowledge which does not have something of which it is the knowledge. There cannot be, therefore, knowledge which is non-conceptual in the sense of 'non-discriminative'.

Nevertheless, it is arguable that much knowledge by acquaintance occurs without any explicit conceptualization. I have been discriminating the various computer-keys for several hours. However, it is only in the past minute that I have made this discrimination explicit. That is, I have only noticed my activity of discriminating the computer-keys in the past minute. Before that, there was obviously discrimination of the computer-keys – for I have been effectively employing my computer – even though I had not thought 'there are the computer-keys!' The conceptualization of the computer-keys which has been taking place for several hours has only in the past minute become explicit.

It would seem to be true, in fact, that, although all knowledge-experiences are conceptual (in the sense that they discriminate something), most of one's knowledge by acquaintance is of a non-explicitly conceptual nature. I am reminded here of Heidegger's explication of this point. For the most part, he contends, one is engaged in the everyday world in a way which does not involve judgements about the entities with which one engages. One generally uses a hammer, for instance, without standing back from the activity and reflecting, 'this is a hammer'. Nevertheless, one does discriminate the hammer, for one is able to employ it quite effectively. In fact, Heidegger contends, entities tend to be explicitly conceptualized when they no longer function in the way in which one expects. If the hammer breaks, it is at this point that I am most likely to explicitly conceptualize about the hammer. The hammer which I have been discriminating in a non-explicit way will suddenly stand-out to me as a hammer. I am likely to judge that 'this is a hammer, and it is broken.' As long as the hammer fulfills its function, however, I am unlikely to make my conceptualization of it explicit.[31]

Another situation in which conceptualization is likely to be explicit is when one is learning, and has not yet mastered, some skill. While learning a piano-sonata, for example, the pianist must explicitly conceptualize the musical directions which enable him to play the music. But as he becomes more familiar with the music – with practice – he will think less and less in this explicitly conceptual way. When he has perfected his playing, I suspect that there is very little explicit conceptualization which takes place. This is not to say that the pianist's experience becomes non-conceptual (i.e. in the sense of 'not discriminating anything'), for he certainly does discriminate the music which he plays. But the pianist is unlikely on the whole to be aware of the conceptualization which occurs. He simply plays, naturally and without noticing the various notes which he is discriminating.

Interpretation (2) wants to argue, then, that when Nāgārjuna says that reality is *niṣprapañca*, etc. a philosophically plausible way to interpret this statement is that the experience of knowing reality, as it occurs in meditation, is without any explicit conceptualization. The knowledge-experience must discriminate something, to be sure, and in this sense it is undoubtedly conceptual. There is the face-to-face discrimination of the quality of emptiness possessed by entities. It is just that, at the time of the meditation, the meditator, due to his absorption in his experience of emptiness, does not reflect 'this is emptiness', nor does he proclaim 'this is emptiness'. He does not stand-back from the experience in which he is immersed. He is simply absorbed in the experience, like the pianist who is totally familiar with the music which he plays. In this sense, then, the meditator on reality also does not have a view, a position, or a thesis. He does not formulate or express a proposition that entities lack *svabhāva*, although he is undoubtedly discriminating, in a face-to-face encounter, this lack of *svabhāva*.

But this in no way inhibits, I would suggest, the ability of the meditator to make the conceptualization which occurs during his meditation explicit, during his post-meditative experience (just like the pianist, if required, can relate the various steps he takes in playing the mastered sonata). At the time of the meditation, he might be simply absorbed in his experience of emptiness. But afterwards he might well think and say that 'I experienced the absence of *svabhāva* of entities.' This conceptualization and statement would, further, be a perfectly accurate description of what he discriminates in his meditative experience of reality. The Mādhyamika would, on the basis of his meditative experience, be able to say and conceptualize that the ultimate truth about entities is that they lack *svabhāva*. The Mādhyamika might not have a thesis/position/view at the time of meditation on reality, but this is entirely compatible with his having an accurate thesis/position/view later on.

(3) Focussed Conceptualization

I must stress again, however, that such knowledge by acquaintance of emptiness must still be conceptual in the sense that something is discriminated, viz. the absence of *svabhāva* of entities. If something were not discriminated, there would in fact be nothing with which one would be acquainted in the meditative experience.

But, interpretation (2) suggests, the meditative experience of reality is conceptual in a very focussed fashion. It has only one object, that is, the true nature of all entities (emptiness). Such a meditative experience takes the true nature of all entities as its sole object. The conceptualization which occurs is a case of one-pointed concentration (*samādhi*), and one is undistracted by the usual stream of mental activity which normally occurs in (primarily non-meditative) experience. It is this undistracted, focussed nature of the meditative experience of reality which produces the state of calm (*śānta*) which Nāgārjuna describes (at *MMK* XVIII, 9; see pp. 45–46) as a characteristic of reality. Perhaps it would be more accurate to say that both the meditative experience of emptiness and emptiness itself, as a mere absence, are calm. In fact, it is the mind which experiences reality, as well as the reality which is experienced, which are calm. The mind is no longer caught up in the normal conceptual diffusion (*prapañca*) of (primarily non-meditative) experience.[32]

When Nāgārjuna describes – also at *MMK* XVIII, 9 – reality (*tattva*) as 'without diversity' (*anānārtha*) this might be a description of both reality as the single characteristic possessed by all entities, i.e. their true nature which is their lack of *svabhāva*, and the nature of a meditative experience which focusses on this single characteristic possessed by all entities. Such an experience does not have diverse objects, but rather is the experience of only the common nature of all things. Which is not to say that entities do not have other characteristics. It is simply that the meditative experience focusses on one of their characteristics – viz. their lack of *svabhāva* – to the exclusion of all others. (Like, for example, when one focusses on the redness of a rose to the exclusion of the rose's other characteristics – its shape, size, smell, etc. The rose does not cease to have these characteristics when one's awareness is focussed only on the redness of the rose).

In this case, the meditator on reality, aware only of the common nature of all things, cannot, at the time of his meditation, perceive entities in their particularity. The following statement from the *YṢ* might be interpreted in this way,

> *'di 'am de 'o zhes gang du/*
> *rnam par dpyad nas mi dmigs na/*
> *rtsod pas 'di 'am de bden zhes/*
> *mkhas pa su zhig smra bar 'gyur//*
>
> Which wise man will assert, by means of a dispute, that 'this or that is true', when, as a result of sustained thought, he does not perceive anywhere 'this or that'? (*YṢ* 42).

'Sustained thought' is here a translation of *rnam par dpyad*, which Lindtner re-constructs as *vicāra*.[33] *Vicāra* is traditionally said to be present – along with 'initial thought' (*vitarka*) – in the first *dhyāna*, or meditative absorption.[34] This might suggest, then, that Nāgārjuna is here adverting to a meditative state in which the meditator, having analyzed/reflected on the true nature of entities in a concentrated, probing fashion in the first *dhyāna*, becomes absorbed in the reality common to all entities, without any perception of their particularity as 'this or that' (*'di 'am de*).

It is perhaps relevant that Nāgārjuna sometimes describes reality as isolated or separated (*vivikta*).[35] According to the Pāli tradition, *viveka* is separation from the five hindrances (*nīvaraṇa*) to meditation, and is especially associated with the first *jhāna*.[36] When the mind becomes separated from the five hindrances, one achieves the first *jhāna*. Perhaps Nāgārjuna means, not that reality is isolated, but that there is a meditative experience – which occurs in the first *dhyāna* – in which the mind focusses on emptiness to the exclusion of, i.e. isolated or separated from, all other matters. One is aware totally and only of the absence of *svabhāva* of entities. All other conceptualization has fallen away.

Concluding Remarks on and Criticisms of Interpretation (2)

I have explained three ways in which, according to interpretation (2), a meditative experience of reality might be called 'non-conceptual' without meaning that the experience does not discriminate anything at all. Such an experience might be itself characterized, in the ways which I have suggested, as non-conceptual – i.e. it is a focussed, undistracted knowledge by acquaintance without explicit conceptualization – while still being conceptual in the sense that it discriminates an object, i.e. the absence of *svabhāva* (emptiness) which is the true nature of entities.

Perhaps, then, interpretation (2) offers a different way to understand Bhāvaviveka's teaching that the ultimate (*don dam pa*) has two aspects (*rnam pa*). Bhāvaviveka's supramundane (*'jig rten las 'das pa*) ultimate, without impurity (*zag pa med pa*) and without conceptual diffusion (*spros pa med pa*) might correspond to this focussed meditative knowledge by acquaintance, without explicit conceptualization, of emptiness. The second aspect of the ultimate, which Bhāvaviveka describes as pure mundane knowledge (*dag pa 'jig rten pa'i ye shes*), and having conceptual diffusion (*spros pa dang bcas pa*), might correspond to the theoretical, factual knowledge that all entities lack *svabhāva*. It is this second aspect of the ultimate, it may be recollected, which Bhāvaviveka says is expressed by his thesis (*dam bca'*) or position (*phyogs*) that all entities are without *svabhāva*. (Reality is, furthermore, beyond the extremes (*mtha'*) of existence and non-existence – not in the sense that reality transcends all conceptualization (as the proponent of interpretation (1) (such as Mi pham) claims) but rather – in the sense that the true nature of entities is their existence without *svabhāva*, rather than existence with *svabhāva* or total non-existence).

As I have said already, interpretation (2) is, in my judgement, the most plausible reading of Nāgārjuna's texts. The dominant concern of his writings is that the ultimate truth/true nature of entities is their absence of *svabhāva*. (See here chapters 2 and 4 for textual evidence). It seems advisable, therefore, to interpret those uncommon passages which use the language of non-conceptuality to be describing a particular way of experiencing this absence of *svabhāva*, rather than as asserting a distinct unconceptualizable reality. But let me, in conclusion, suggest two serious philosophical difficulties with interpretation (2).

The Problem of Emptiness as a Mere Absence

I have explained that, according to interpretation (2), the meditative experience of reality has as its sole object the absence of *svabhāva* itself, i.e. emptiness. Meditation on emptiness is thus conceptual, in the sense that it discriminates something. But what can it possibly mean to discriminate a mere absence? Can the discrimination of an absence in fact be distinguished from the discrimination of nothing at all? It is arguable, then, that the meditation on emptiness, after all, involves a complete cessation of conceptualization – i.e. it does not discriminate anything – akin to the already-mentioned *saṃjñāvedayitanirodha/nirodhasamāpatti* of the Abhidharma.[37]

But in this case the meditation on emptiness is not actually a state of consciousness (and certainly not a state of knowledge). For, as I have explained, consciousness is always consciousness of something. Unless Nāgārjuna were to view liberation as the annihilation of all mental activity whatsoever (which would undeniably entail the cessation of all suffering (*duḥkha*)), it is difficult to see what soteriological benefit could be derived from such a meditation (assuming, indeed, that it is even psychologically possible).

The unanswered question is, of course, whether Nāgārjuna *intends* the meditation on emptiness to be such a state of complete mental inactivity. According to interpretation (2), Nāgārjuna's intention, no matter how problematic, is that emptiness is something (a mere absence) which is known in meditation. Meditation on emptiness is therefore intended by him to be, in the sense that something is discriminated, conceptual. I concede, however, that Nāgārjuna's intention might be different. It is possible, I suppose, that the meditation on emptiness for Nāgārjuna might be a 'paranormal' state, induced by the realization that all entities are merely conceptual constructs (i.e. they are without *svabhāva*), in which one simply stops all of one's conceptual constructing. Meditation on emptiness would be, in this case, simply the complete eradication of conceptual construction.

As all experience is entirely conceptually constructed for Nāgārjuna, meditation on emptiness would thus be a total shutting down of the mind (rather than a state of knowledge), though why the attainment of such mental blankness would be desirable I cannot understand.

Interpretation (2) and the Question of Nihilism

I will argue in the next chapter that Nāgārjuna's philosophy, understood as an assertion of universal absence of *svabhāva,* is tantamount to nihilism, despite Nāgārjuna's advocacy of the Middle Path. Interpretation (2), as I have explained, sees emptiness as a quality, albeit a negative quality, of entities. It is this quality alone of entities, their ultimate truth, which is discriminated by the meditative knowledge by acquaintance of emptiness. But if Nāgārjuna's philosophy entails nihilism, then there can *be* no entities which have emptiness as their quality and there can *be* no emptiness which is the quality of entities. There can thus be no meditative knowledge by acquaintance of emptiness. The nihilistic implications (probably unintended by Nāgārjuna) of Nāgārjuna's philosophy therefore make interpretation (2) philosophically untenable. It is this problem of nihilism to which I shall now turn my attention.

Notes

1 Evans (1982), p. 74.
2 See especially *AS* 52 and *ŚS* 68–69a.
3 See *TJv* 96, 27, 4–8, 96, 28, 1–1 (Iida (1980), p. 86, 88). See also *MS* 2–3, 5–6.
4 See Swanson (1989), p. 90.
5 Cabezón (1992), pp. 147, 442–443.
6 Williams (1998b), pp. 98–99.
7 See Griffiths (1994), p. 149.
8 Lang (1983), p. 154.
9 See Robinson (1953), pp. 1–4.
10 *MMK* XXIV, 8–10.
11 *Phenomenology of Spirit* (trans. Findlay, 1977), p. 9.
12 Cited in Peacocke (1989), p. 10.
13 See here the Abhidharma account of *saṃjñā*, which can be translated as 'conceptualization'. *Saṃjñā* is the mental factor (*caitta*) which enables consciousness (*citta*) to identify/recognize the distinctive characteristic (*nimitta*) of its object. Significantly, *saṃjñā* must be present in all states of consciousness. See Nyanaponika Thera (1976), pp. 45–48, 70, Williams (1980), pp. 14 *ff.* It

would appear, then, that for the Abhidharma there are no non-conceptual states of consciousness. It might be objected, however, that the Abhidharma does recognize the 'cessation of sensation and conceptualization' (*saṃjñāvedayita-nirodha/saṃjñāveditanirodha*, also known as the *nirodhasamāpatti*), a meditative attainment (*samāpatti*) and non-associated compositional factor (*cittaviprayuktasaṃskāra*) which follows after the *naivasaṃjñānāsaṃjñāyatana*, the fourth and highest of the *ārupyadhyāna*-s. It is achieved, apparently, only by Āryans. There is a comparable meditative factor, called the *asaṃjñisamāpatti*, which is said to be achieved at the level of the fourth *dhyāna* by non-Āryans (*pṛthagjana*). Both of these meditative states are, it is claimed, characterized by the absence of *saṃjñā*. See *AKBh* II, 43–44, III, 6b. In which case it is wrong, it might be objected, to say, as I have, that the Abhidharma does not accept non-conceptual states of consciousness. In reply, I say that in these meditative states, according to the Abhidharma, the practitioner possesses nothing but very basic physical functions, described as the 'life principle' (*jīvita*). See *AKBh* II, 45a–b. In what sense, I wonder, then, can these meditative conditions be labelled 'states of consciousness'? In fact, these absorptions are described as 'interruptions' of the mind. See *AKBh* II, 44e, Griffiths (1986), p. xiv, 10, etc, and Ruegg (1989), 193–198. The practitioner's mental continuum is entirely absent or dormant. Thus, for the Abhidharma, a state without conceptualization (*asaṃjñā*) would be not a special form of consciousness but rather an absence of any mental activity.

14 I suppose here someone might object that my use of the term 'conceptual' is too broad. Perhaps there is a pre-conceptual form of consciousness, in which one discriminates x or that x is y without possessing a concept. (For example, arguably in the course of my everyday work I might discriminate the keys of my computer keyboard without possessing a concept of these keys). But this does not appear to me to be a substantial objection in the present context. As a pre-conceptual cognition (what I will prefer to call, later in this chapter (see interpretation (2)), a 'non-explicitly conceptual cognition') discriminates x or that x is y, it is always potentially convertible into a conceptual cognition. (I arguably may not possess a concept of the keys of my computer at present, but insofar as I am pre-conceptually discriminating the keys, I have the capacity to form the concept of them). A pre-conceptual cognition, if one admits the existence of such a phenomenon, is thus not an *unconceptualizable* cognition, which is what the proponent of interpretation (1) must argue for.

15 See, for example, Katz (1978), pp. 22–74, and Katz (1992), pp. 3–41.

16 Katz (1978), p. 26.

17 See Bagger (1991), p. 407.

18 *PP* 40. See also *MA* VI, 222a–c, and *MABh* 182, in Tauscher (trans) (1981), p. 69. For an early canonical source for this idea, see the *Saṃyuttanikāya* II.25, 17*ff* (Quoted in Tauscher (1981), p. 130.)

19 *MA* VI, 186.

20 *Tjv* 96, 27, 3–1(Iida (1980), pp. 82–83).

21 I intentionally say that 'many', rather than 'all', experiences have both a character and a content. This is because there are some experiences – for example, experiences of bodily sensations such as pain – which simply feel a certain way but in which nothing more than this feeling is discriminated. The distinction between content and character does not seem to obtain in these cases.

22 Pendlebury (1992), pp. 125–127.
23 Nagel (1974), pp. 435–450.
24 Pivcevic (1986), pp. 151–152.
25 Napper (1989), p. 94.
26 See Napper (1989), p. 85.
27 See Hopkins (1996), p. 91 *ff*, Klein (1986), p. 16, Williams (1989a), pp. 72–74.
28 For a very early, non-Mahāyāna reference to the three levels of wisdom, see the *Sangītisutta*, *DN* III, 220 (trans. Walshe (1987), p. 486. Pagel (1995), p. 199, 242 *ff* notes that the three levels of wisdom feature in the *Samādhirājasūtra* and the *Bodhisattvapiṭaka*. Lopez (1988), pp. 7–8 quotes *Saṃdhinirmocanasūtra* VIII, 24, which is about the three levels of wisdom. See also *AkBh* II, 72b, VI, 5c–d, VII, 18c–d, and *BK* (trans. in Beyer (1974), pp. 104–105.) I am not aware of any direct reference by Nāgārjuna to the three levels of wisdom.
29 *PP* 373.
30 Interestingly, at *YṢV* 23, Candrakīrti contrasts the *darśana* (*mthong ba*) of emptiness, which is benign, with the *dṛṣṭi* (*lta ba*) of emptiness, which is malign.
31 See *Being and Time* (trans. Macquarrie and Robinson (1962)), pp. 98, 102–107. Heidegger's explication of the pre-theoretical apprehension of entities takes place in the context of his complex ontological speculations, with which I am not here concerned.
32 Note, however, that presumably even many of the preliminary meditative practices which lead to the focussed, direct apprehension of emptiness in meditation involve conceptual diffusion. According to the dGe lugs account at least, the meditator must engage in sustained, careful rational analysis, surveying various arguments which demonstrate (supposedly) that all entities lack *svabhāva*. It is only on this basis, and together with much practice in *śamatha* meditation, that the meditator is said to gain the direct apprehension of emptiness, without conceptual diffusion. See here Williams (1989a), pp. 72–74.
33 Lindtner (1982), p. 113.
34 See Nyanaponika Thera (1976), p. 56. See also, for example, *DN* I, 73 (trans. Walshe (1987), p. 102).
35 See *VVC* 29, *YṢ* 25, 30, 56, 59.
36 See Gethin (1992), p. 165. See also Scherrer-Schaub (1991), p. 244. *Vivikta* is also traditionally used to denote the physical isolation of the monk who is seeking liberation. Thus, it is in the physical isolation of the forest hermitage, etc that the monk strives to achieve the meditative isolation (in *jhāna/dhyāna*) from distractions and hindrances. The principle is, no doubt, that such physical conditions are most conducive to the attainment of *jhāna/dhyāna*. See Gethin (1992), p. 170, Scherrer-Schaub (1991), pp. 218–219, Ray (1994), pp. 63–64.
37 See note 13. It is perhaps significant in this respect that the *Chung-lun*, commenting on *MMK* XVIII, declares that the *samādhi* of cessation (of feeling and conceptions) (*nirodhasamāpatti*) is regarded as the highest *samādhi*, insofar as it entails the cessation of all mental activities. This is evidence, then, of both the acknowledgement of the existence such a meditative state, and a valuing of it, within early Madhyamaka thought. See Bocking (trans.) (1995), p. 281.

CHAPTER FOUR

The Problem of Nihilism[1]

Introduction: The Charge of Nihilism and Nāgārjuna's Response

In Nāgārjuna's texts his opponents not infrequently object that if the ultimate truth is, as Nāgārjuna says, the emptiness (*śūnyatā*) of all entities, then Nāgārjuna's teaching in fact destroys all entities.[2] Nāgārjuna's position entails, in other words, nihilism – the view that nothing exists at all. Nāgārjuna's response to this criticism is invariably that, on the contrary, it is emptiness which makes possible all entities.[3] His opponents have, he claims, misunderstood the meaning of emptiness.[4] Emptiness does not entail the non-existence of the various entities of which it is the emptiness. On the contrary, emptiness means that these entities exist as dependent arisings, without *svabhāva*. Emptiness is, Nāgārjuna claims, the famous Buddhist Middle Way between eternalism and nihilism.[5] Entities exist, it is true, but they exist only in dependence upon conditions. Entities are thus empty of independent existence. Nāgārjuna turns the opponents' argument on its head, claiming that in fact it is the rejection, rather than the acceptance, of the teaching of emptiness which destroys all entities.[6] Entities arise and perish in dependence upon conditions. To deny emptiness is to deny that there are such dependently arising entities. It is, therefore, emptiness which explains the existence of all entities.

When one first reads Nāgārjuna's explanations of the compatibility of emptiness and the existence of all entities they perhaps seem entirely convincing. *Of course* emptiness is compatible with the existence of the various entities of the world, for emptiness is precisely, as Nāgārjuna so often reiterates, the absence of *svabhāva* of all entities. And Nāgārjuna sometimes describes *svabhāva* as existence which is independent of causes and conditions. This is clearly stated, for example, in the *MMK*:

na saṃbhavaḥ svabhāvasya yuktaḥ pratyayahetubhiḥ/
hetupratyayasaṃbhūtaḥ svabhāvaḥ kṛtako bhavet//
svabhāvaḥ kṛtako nāma bhaviṣyati punaḥ katham/
akṛtrimaḥ svabhāvo hi nirapekṣaḥ paratra ca//

The occurrence of *svabhāva* is not appropriate by means of conditions and causes.
Svabhāva produced by causes and conditions would be created.
But indeed, how could *svabhāva* be created?
For *svabhāva* is uncreated, and is independent of another. (*MMK* XV, 1–2).

In fact, Nāgārjuna says, no entity (*bhāva*) has *svabhāva*. All entities are therefore empty (*śūnya*), i.e. they are empty of *svabhāva*. They are, in other words, dependently arisen (*pratītya-samutpanna*):

dngos po thams cad rang bzhin gyis/
stong pa yin pas dngos rnams kyi/
rten 'byung de ni de bzhin gshegs/
mtshungs pa med pas nye bar bstan//

Since all entities are empty of *svabhāva*, the unequalled
tathāgata taught the dependent arising of entities. (*ŚS* 68)

This includes even the *dharma*-s out of which, according to Abhidharma philosophy, macroscopic entities are formed:

apratītyasamutpanno dharmaḥ kaścinna vidyate/
yasmāttasmādaśūnyo hi dharmaḥ kaścinna vidyate//

Since a *dharma* not dependently arisen does not exist,
therefore a non-empty *dharma* certainly does not exist.
(*MMK* XXIV, 19).

One is tempted to think, then, that Nāgārjuna is certainly right, and that his opponents have simply misunderstood the ultimate truth which he expounds. For Nāgārjuna denies, it would seem, only that entities have an independent, uncreated existence, and there is obviously no incompatibility between this ultimate truth, and the manifold world of entities. The ultimate truth provides, in fact, the explanation of the interrelationships between, and the coming-to-be and passing away of, the various entities which constitute the world. Entities – be they animate, inanimate, mental, physical, small, big, etc – share the common characteristic (their ultimate truth) that they lack *svabhāva*, i.e. they exist in dependence upon conditions. Who could seriously argue with this? (Or, at least, even if one would oppose – as would many of Nāgārjuna's non-Buddhist opponents (with their advocacy of a permanent *ātman/puruṣa/jīva*, etc) – the view that dependent origination is universal, it would nevertheless be obviously wrong to equate the teaching of universal dependent origination with nihilism).

However, it is my contention that Nāgārjuna's claim that ultimate truth, i.e. emptiness, and the existence of entities are compatible – in fact that the ultimate truth is that which makes possible the existence of entities – is not as self-evidently correct as it perhaps appears. The opponents' objections, i.e.their accusations that Nāgārjuna's philosophy of emptiness is nihilistic, have more bite to them than Nāgārjuna's easy reply might suggest.

This might explain why the charge of nihilism was frequently levelled against Nāgārjuna and later Mādhyamikas, despite the (superficially convincing) Mādhyamika protestations. It is perhaps not simply that Nāgārjuna, and others were consistently misunderstood by a series of rather dull-witted opponents. For if the opponents of Madhyamaka philosophy simply failed to see that emptiness meant dependent origination, and repeatedly took it to mean non-existence – despite the reiterated Mādhyamika declarations that dependent origination and emptiness are synonyms – then they surely must have been very stupid! If one is to take the persistent objections to Madhyamaka seriously, one must suspect that there is a more substantial philosophical disagreement to be uncovered.

The purpose of the present chapter is, then, to examine critically Nāgārjuna's claim that it is emptiness, i.e. the absence of *svabhāva* of all entities, which makes the existence of entities possible. My argument will be that, seen in the context of Abhidharma principles (in the context of which Nāgārjuna was certainly working), Nāgārjuna's claim that emptiness is the absence of *svabhāva* of all entities entails considerably more than simply that entities are dependently originating. In fact, seen in the light of Abhidharma philosophy, there would appear to be a strong argument that Nāgārjuna's assertion that all entities lack *svabhāva* does destroy – contrary to Nāgārjuna's intention – the manifold world of entities. Nāgārjuna may be, unwittingly, a nihilist. Nāgārjuna might think that he treads the Middle Way, but perhaps in fact he has taken a wrong turning.

My interpretation here should be distinguished from that of T. Wood.[7] Wood argues that Nāgārjuna is self-avowedly a nihilist. I claim, by contrast, that Nāgārjuna probably did not see himself as a nihilist, but that it is arguable that, given the principles of his philosophy, he was a nihilist nevertheless. And, certainly, given the pre-suppositions of Abhidharma philosophy, his thinking would have been understood by many of his fellow Buddhists to result in nihilism.

The Abhidharma Notion of *svabhāva*

Nāgārjuna says, I have explained, that the dependent origination of entities is incompatible with their possession of *svabhāva*. Taken at face-value, this means simply that all entities dependently arise, and therefore they do not have independent existence. However – and this is a crucial point – in Abhidharma philosophy the dependent origination of some entities, i.e. *saṃskṛta dharma*-s, is said to be actually compatible with their possession of *svabhāva*. In other words, according to Abhidharma thought, possession of *svabhāva* does *not* entail independent existence.[8]

For the Ābhidharmika,[9] *svabhāva* is attributed to *dharma*-s because *dharma*-s are independent of causes and conditions *in a specific sense. Dharma*-s are not dependent upon parts for their existence. The *dharma*-s are the foundational components of the world. They are not further analyzable into constituents,[10] and they are the constituents of all other entities. These *dharma*-s are, for the Ābhidharmikas, 'ultimate truths' (*paramārthasatya*), and have 'substantial' or primary existence (*dravyasat*).[11]

There are innumerable instances of these *dharma*-s, but these innumerable instances are classified, by the Ābhidharmikas, into a finite number of categories. In the Vaibhāṣika Abhidharma at least, there are four categories of conditioned (*saṃskṛta*) *dharma*-s – form (*rūpa*), consciousness (*citta*), consciousness-factors (*caitta*), and conditioned factors dissociated from consciousness (*cittaviprayuktasaṃskāra*) – and one category of unconditioned (*asaṃskṛta*) *dharma*-s. In the *AKBh*, each category is further subdivided (except *citta*, which has only one member), so that in total seventy-five types of *dharma*-s are enumerated.[12] Each type of *dharma* has a self-characteristic (*svalakṣaṇa*), i.e. a definable nature, an own-nature (*svabhāva*),[13] which distinguishes it in the taxonomy from the other types of *dharma*-s. There are, according to this classification, eleven *rūpa dharma*-s, one *citta dharma*, forty-six *caitta dharma*-s, fourteen *cittaviprayuktasaṃskāra dharma*-s, and three *asaṃskṛta dharma*-s.[14] There are disagreements between Abhidharma/Abhidhamma traditions – and within the same tradition in different texts and at different stages in the tradition's development – about the details of this taxonomy, but these need not detain us here.

Saṃskṛta dharma-s are – it must be emphasized – subject to dependent origination (*pratītyasamutpāda*).[15] Thus, the *saṃskṛta dharma*-s have the general characteristics (*sāmānyalakṣaṇa*) of birth (*jāti*), duration (*sthiti*), and impermanence (*anityatā*). Often, decay (*jarā*) is also included in this list.[16] In fact, complex theories of conditionality were developed to explain the arising, duration, decay, and impermanence of *saṃskṛta dharma*-s.[17] These *saṃskṛta dharma*-s are, furthermore, each said to remain only for a moment (*kṣaṇa*).[18] There is a causally connected flow of these momentary atomic events.

The complex, analyzable entities constructed out of the *svabhāva*-endowed ultimate truths (the *dharma*-s) have a derivative or conceptually constructed existence (*prajñaptisat*) and are conventional truths (*saṃvṛtisatya*).[19] These are the entities of the commonly experienced world – i.e. the world of trees, mountains, houses, and people.

Saṅghabhadra and, later, Pūrṇavardhana make a further distinction between 'first-order' and 'second-order' *prajñaptisat* entities. First-order *prajñaptisat* entities are those which are constructed directly on the basis of *dravyasat* entities whereas second-order *prajñaptisat* entities are constructed on the basis of other *prajñaptisat* entities. A pot, for example, is constructed out of various parts, such as its sides, bottom, handle, which are not themselves *dravyasat*. A forest, to take another example, is constituted by a number of trees, which are themselves constituted by their various parts. And so on. There can, then, be very complex conceptual construction – with entities being constructed on the basis of entities which are themselves constructed, etc. However, even second-order *prajñaptisat* entities must finally have a *dravyasat* basis. All construction – no matter how complex – is finally based on an unconstructed reality.[20]

Conventional truths are, for the Abhidharma, entities which are conceptual constructs in the sense that they are the product of the mind's synthesizing activity on the basis of the various *dharma*-s. In which case, it appears that for the Abhidharma, conventional truths originate in dependence upon two factors: (i) the constituents, i.e. *dharma*-s which form the basis of construction, and (ii) the constructing activity of the mind. Without the presence of both of these elements, there can be no conventional truths.[21]

Nāgārjuna's Notion of *niḥsvabhāva* Understood in the Abhidharma Context

Thus, for Abhidharma philosophy, it is incorrect to say that the possession of *svabhāva*, i.e. the nature/characteristic possessed by the unanalyzable *dharma*, entails that a *dharma* is independent of causes and conditions. All *dharma*-s possess *svabhāva* and most of these *svabhāva*-possessing *dharma*-s, i.e. all of the *saṃskṛta dharma*-s, also dependently originate. By contrast, Nāgārjuna seems to say that an entity with *svabhāva* would have independent, uncreated existence.

A Terminological Difference?

It might be argued, therefore, that Nāgārjuna has simply *defined svabhāva* differently than the Ābhidharmikas. Which would be to say that the *svabhāva* which Nāgārjuna rejects is not the *svabhāva* which the Ābhidharmika upholds. Whereas Nāgārjuna defines *svabhāva* as independent existence, the Ābhidharmika defines *svabhāva* as unanalyzable, more-than-conceptual existence, i.e. *dravyasat*.

In this case, it might be argued, Nāgārjuna and the Ābhidharmika agree that there are dependently originating, unanalyzable, and more-than-conceptual (*dravyasat*) *saṃskṛta dharma*-s. But whereas for Nāgārjuna the dependent origination of these *saṃskṛta dharma*-s means that they do not have *svabhāva* (= independent existence), for the Ābhidharmika these dependently originating *saṃskṛta dharma*-s do have *svabhāva* (=unanalyzable, more-than-conceptual existence). With regards to *saṃskṛta dharma*-s, Nāgārjuna and the Ābhidharmikas are in *philosophical* agreement but *terminological* disagreement. (But note that if Nāgārjuna is claiming that *all* entities lack *svabhāva* (= independent existence), then this would seem to imply that for him, unlike for the Ābhidharmikas, there are at least no *asaṃskṛta dharma*-s[22]).

Universal Absence of *svabhāva* as Equivalent to *prajñaptimātra*

There is a strong argument, however, that in fact the disagreement with regards to *svabhāva* is not about terminology. One must remember that Nāgārjuna is, after all, a second century Indian Buddhist. The *lingua franca* of ancient Indian Buddhist philosophy was the language of the Abhidharma. It is improbable, it can be argued, that Nāgārjuna would simply begin to employ, without notification, a key term of the Abhidharma philosophy in an entirely innovative way. It is more plausible that Nāgārjuna considers the notion of *svabhāva* which he refutes to be that employed within the Abhidharma context in which he operates. (It certainly appears from Nāgārjuna's texts that he thought that he had a point of substantial disagreement to make).

In this case, when he claims that *all* entities lack *svabhāva*, Nāgārjuna probably means, not simply that no entities originate independently of conditions but also, that no entities originate independently of the constructing activity of the mind. There are no basic, unanalyzable existents out of which the *prajñaptisat* world is formed. Thus, all entities whatsoever are, for Nāgārjuna, simply conceptual constructs. When Nāgārjuna says that entities with *svabhāva* would be uncreated and independent he must mean, in fact, that such entities would be uncreated by and independent of *the constructing mind*. Nāgārjuna's denial of *svabhāva* is not in fact a statement of the truism that all entities dependently originate, but is rather an assertion that all entities originate in dependence upon the constructing mind.

It is arguable, however, that Nāgārjuna's general tendency to equate lack of *svabhāva* with dependence on causes and conditions, rather than specifically with dependence on parts, indicates a subtle shift or broadening in the meaning of *svabhāva*.

As I have explained, the Ābhidharmikas had argued that entities which can be analyzed into their parts are simply conceptual constructs, i.e. they lack *svabhāva*. But *dharma*-s, though in most cases dependently originating, are partless and thus are not conceptually constructed, i.e. they have *svabhāva*.

Perhaps by contrast Nāgārjuna is claiming that any entity which originates in dependence upon causes – *be these causes the parts of the entity or external to the entity* – can be analyzed into these causes, and is thus simply a conceptual construct imposed on the concatenation of causes. Thus, for Nāgārjuna, even if there were partless *saṃskṛta dharma*-s as the Ābhidharmika says (though, as I show below, Nāgārjuna himself occasionally seems to deny the existence of partless entities), because these *dharma*-s are dependently originating, as the Ābhidharmika claims, they can be analyzed into – and are thus (according to Nāgārjuna) conceptually constructed on the basis of – their causes. *Svabhāva* and dependent origination are – contrary to the Ābhidharmika understanding – incompatible. According to Nāgārjuna, if the Ābhidharmika persists in attributing *svabhāva* to the *dharma*-s, he cannot also say that they dependently originate. To be dependently originated is to be conceptually constructed.

So Nāgārjuna arrives at his often stated position that any entity which is posited as having *svabhāva* must also be independent of causes, i.e. permanent (despite what the Ābhidharmikas maintain). And there are, of course, no such independent, permanent entities for Nāgārjuna.

* * *

If this interpretation is correct, the ultimate truth is for Nāgārjuna that there are no ultimate truths in the Abhidharma sense. By this Nāgārjuna does not mean simply that there are no independent, permanent entities. Nāgārjuna means, in addition, that there are no unanalyzable, more-than-conceptually constructed entities.[23] In the language of later Madhyamaka philosophy,[24] no entity whatsoever is found under analysis. Whatsoever entity one examines, one finds, according to the Mādhyamika, that it is simply a concept (or name) attributed by the mind to a concatenation of causes. If the causes are themselves examined, they are themselves found to be simply concepts attributed by the mind on the basis of their own causes. And so on. There are no foundational more-than-conceptually constructed entities. Nāgārjuna's advocacy of universal absence of *svabhāva* is thus equivalent to the notion that everything is just conceptual construction (*prajñaptimātra*).

I think that the evidence which I have collated below demonstrates that Nāgārjuna does indeed employ the Abhidharma notion of *svabhāva*, and his denial that any entities have *svabhāva* does entail, for him, that all entities are *prajñaptisat*. In which case, Nāgārjuna's claim that emptiness does not entail nihilism, because emptiness means simply that entities lack independent existence, is untenable. Nāgārjuna's superficially convincing argument completely fails to address the real criticism which his opponents are making of his philosophy. Nāgārjuna does not in fact deny *only* that there are independently existing entities. Nāgārjuna denies *also* that there are any entities which arise independently of conceptual construction. Nāgārjuna's opponents do not think that the universal dependent origination of entities would result in nihilism. But they do consider that, if all entities were to have, as Nāgārjuna contends, conceptually constructed existence, then nihilism would indeed be entailed. As I shall explain later in this chapter, I think that they are right.

Evidence for *prajñaptimātra* in Nāgārjuna's Writings

At no point of which I am aware does Nāgārjuna explicitly and unambiguously state that all entities are *prajñaptisat*, at least in the works which I consider to be most reliably attributable to him.[25] The question is, therefore, what other indirect textual evidence is there that Nāgārjuna does in fact think that all entities lack *svabhāva* – in the sense that they are analyzable, and hence conceptual constructs? I shall examine the evidence, which, I think, is plentiful.

Dependence on Parts

There do not appear to be many places in Nāgārjuna's writings where he makes explicit that he means that all entities originate in dependence upon their parts. He does not seem to say often that entities lack *svabhāva* in the sense that they are dependent on their parts for their existence. On the contrary, as I have already explained, he usually describes *svabhāva* more broadly as independence from causes and conditions, and he claims that all entities lack *svabhāva* because they originate in dependence upon causes and conditions – be these causes and conditions the entities' parts or external to the entities. There are, however, the following statements in the *RV*:

naiko 'nekapradeśatvānnāpradeśaśca kaścana/

On account of many parts, there is not one, and there is nothing without parts ... (*RV* I, 71a–b).

skyes bu khams drug 'dus pa'i phyir/
yang dag ma yin ji lta ba/
de bzhin khaṃs ni re re la 'ang/
'dus phyir yang dag nyid du min//

Just as the person is not real, because it is a composite of the six elements, likewise also each element is not a reality, because it is a composite. (*RV* I, 81).[26]

'*Saṃvṛti*' and '*sāṃvṛta*' in the *AS*

The terms '*saṃvṛti*' and '*sāṃvṛta*' (which, I think, are synonyms[27]) are used in Nāgārjuna's *AS* to denote the dependently originating entities of which the universe is constituted[28]:

... *pratyayajaṃ viśvaṃ tvayoktaṃ nātha sāṃvṛtam//*

... everything born out of conditions is declared by you, Oh Protector, to be *sāṃvṛta*. (*AS* 6c–d).

hetupratyayasaṃbhūtā paratantrā ca saṃvṛtiḥ/

Saṃvṛti arises from causes and conditions and is dependent. (*AS* 44a–b).

As I have explained already, in Abhidharma philosophy *saṃvṛtisatya* denotes an entity which has *prajñaptisat* status. It seems plausible that Nāgārjuna's description of all dependently originating entities as '*saṃvṛti*' and '*sāṃvṛta*' – bearing in mind the Abhidharma use of the term '*saṃvṛtisatya*' – is meant to communicate that all entities have a conceptually constructed existence. Entities are conventions, that is, in the sense that they do not exist independently of the constructing mind.

'*Saṃvṛti*' and '*vyavahāra*' in *MMK* XXIV

The term '*saṃvṛti*' appears also at *MMK* XXIV, 8 as a member of the compound '*lokasaṃvṛtisatya*'. Nāgārjuna proclaims that the Buddhas' teaching of the *dharma* is based upon two truths – the truth of worldly convention (*lokasaṃvṛtisatya*) and the truth from the ultimate perspective (*paramārthataḥ*). Then, at *MMK* XXIV, 10 Nāgārjuna employs the term '*vyavahāra*', which is here, I believe, a synonym for *lokasaṃvṛtisatya* in verse 8. He says that without depending on convention (*vyavahāra*), the ultimate (*paramārtha*) is not taught. Without understanding the ultimate, *nirvāṇa* is not attained.

One way of reading these verses[29] is as saying that the ultimate truth is the ultimate truth about the various entities which make up the world. These entities are one and all conventions. That is, they are merely conceptual constructs. As the ultimate truth is not independent of entities, and these entities are conventions (= conceptual constructs), the ultimate truth can only be taught in dependence upon conventions. And the ultimate truth is precisely that entities are simply conventions/conceptual constructs. *Nirvāṇa* is attained only when one understands entities in their ultimate truth. (See here *YṢ* 9c–d, 'just thorough knowledge of cyclic existence is declared to be *nirvāṇa*' (*parijñānaṃ bhavasyaiva nirvānaṃ iti kathyate*)). *Nirvāṇa* occurs, in other words, when one apprehends that entities are simply conventions/conceptual constructs. (The implication here is, of course, that ordinary, unenlightened people have not attained *nirvāṇa* precisely because they have failed to see the ultimate truth about entities. The conventional/conceptually constructed nature of all entities is not seen by the unenlightened. On the contrary, unenlightened people wrongly believe entities in many cases to have a mind-independent existence).

Synonyms for *prajñaptimātra*

Furthermore, Nāgārjuna sometimes describes all entities as the product of *kalpanā*, *vikalpa*, and *parikalpa*, terms which might be synonyms for *prajñapti*. He also sometimes refers to all entities as '*nāmamātra*', which might be equivalent to saying that all entities have conceptually constructed existence. Thus, Nāgārjuna declares that,

> *atastvayā jagadidaṃ parikalpasamudbhavam/*
> *parijñātamasadbhūtamanutpannaṃ na naśyati//*

> Therefore, you [the Buddha] have fully understood that this world is produced from *parikalpa*. It is unreal, unarisen [and] is not destroyed. (*LS* 19)

kalpanāmātramityasmātsarvadharmāḥ prakāśitāḥ/

Therefore, all *dharma*-s have been made manifest [by the Buddha] to be 'only *kalpanā*' ... (*AS* 36a–b)

'jig rten ma rig rkyen can du/
gang phyir sangs rgyas rnams gsungs pa/
'di yi phyir na 'jig rten 'di/
rnam rtog yin zhes cis mi 'thad//

Since the Buddhas speak of the world as having the [causal] condition which is ignorance, therefore why not accept that this world is *vikalpa*? (*YṢ* 37)

nāmamātraṃ jagatsarvamityuccairbhāṣitaṃ tvayā/

You [the Buddha] sonorously declare that the whole world is only *nāma*. (*AS* 35a–b).

The Non-Origination of Dependently Originating Entities

Also, it is perhaps significant in this respect that Nāgārjuna does not simply say that entities dependently originate. He often declares that in reality there is no origination of dependently originating entities:

pratītyajātaṃ cājātamāha tattvavidāṃ varaḥ//

... and the best of knowers of reality said the dependently arisen is not arisen. (*YṢ* 48c–d).

This might be read as a statement that dependently originating entities do not originate with *svabhāva*. See here *YṢV* 48 in which Candrakīrti claims that this is the meaning of Nāgārjuna's statement. Thus Candrakīrti comments that 'the dependently arisen is not arisen with *svabhāva*'. (*rten cing 'brel par 'byung ba ngo bo nyid kyis ma skyes pa*). Candrakīrti's interpretation is corroborated by *YṢ* 19 in which Nāgārjuna states that:

tattat prāpya yadutpannaṃ notpannaṃ tatsvabhāvataḥ/
svabhāvena yannotpannamutpannaṃ nāma tatkatham//

That which is arisen depending on this and that is not arisen in accordance with *svabhāva*.
How can that which is not arisen by means of *svabhāva* be called 'arisen'? (*YṢ* 19).

Presumably Nāgārjuna's statements that the dependently arisen is unarisen with *svabhāva* are intended as more than simply declarations of the truism that a dependently arisen entity is not independent. His declarations are surely, it seems to me, meant to communicate something more significant than this!

It can be argued, therefore, that Nāgārjuna means that dependently arisen entities do not have *svabhāva* in the Abhidharma sense, i.e. they are not *dravyasat*. Which is to say that they are *prajñaptisat*. (In Abhidharma terms these are the only possible categories. Whatever is not *dravyasat* must be *prajñaptisat*). This would explain why the dependently arisen entity which arises without *svabhāva* cannot be called 'arisen'. That is, there are no real, *dravya*, dependently arising entities. All dependently arising entities are conceptually constructed (*prajñapti*), and in this sense their arising is unreal.

Comparisons with Dreams, Illusions, etc

Hence, perhaps, Nāgārjuna's frequent comparisons of dependently originating entities to dreams, illusions, and other fabricated entities. Dependently originating entities have, like a dream or an illusion, an existence which depends solely on the constructing activity of the mind. (Perhaps also dependently arising entities are said to be like a dream, illusion, etc because – like a dream or illusion – they often appear one way to the deluded mind, i.e. as having more than conceptual existence, yet exist in another way, i.e. as merely conceptual constructs):

> *utpanno 'pi na cotpanno yadvanmāyāgajo mataḥ/*
> *utpannaṃ ca tathā viśvamanutpannaṃ ca tattvataḥ//*
>
> Just as an illusory elephant is considered to be, although arisen, in addition unarisen, so everything is both arisen and in reality unarisen. (*AS* 30).
>
> *yathā mayā yathā svapno gandharvanagaraṃ yathā/*
> *tathotpādastathā sthānaṃ tathā bhaṅga udāhṛtam//*
>
> Arising, duration, and cessation are declared to be like an illusion, a dream, [and] a city of *gandharva*-s. (*MMK* VII, 34)
>
> *yathā māyāgajo naiti kutaścidyāti na kva cit/*
> *cittamohanamātratvādbhāvatvena na tiṣṭhati//*

tathā māyopamo loko naiti yāti na kutracit/
cittamohanamātratvādbhāvatvena na tiṣṭhati//

Just as an illusory elephant – because it is simply a delusion of the mind – does not come from anywhere, goes nowhere, [and] does not endure really, so too the world, which is like an illusion, does not come [from anywhere], goes nowhere, [and] does not endure really, because it is simply a delusion of the mind. (*RV* II, 12–13).

An especially interesting passage occurs in the *AS*,

yadvacchabdaṃ pratītyeha pratiśabdasamudbhavaḥ/
māyāmarīcivaccāpi tathā bhavasamudbhavaḥ/
māyāmarīcigandharvanagarapratibimbakāḥ/
yadyajātāḥ saha svapnairna syāttaddarśanādikam//

Like here [in this world] an echo arises depending on a sound, and also like an illusion and a mirage [arise], so too cyclic existence arises. If the illusion, the mirage, the *gandharva*-s' city, the reflection, as well as dreams, were not born, there would not be perception, etc of them. (*AS* 4–5).

This passage shows not only that cyclic existence (*bhava*) has an ontological status comparable with illusions, etc. In addition, illusions, etc, Nāgārjuna says, are perceived – i.e. they appear, they are not nothing – which entails that they do exist (they are born (*jāta*), as Nāgārjuna puts it). The implication would seem to be that, for Nāgārjuna, cyclic existence too is not merely nothing; it too is perceived, etc, and hence must exist, no matter how tenuously. Nāgārjuna seems to claim that entities are mere appearances to the mind, but this entails, he wants to say, that they have a 'mere appearance' type of existence. *Prajñaptisat* is still for Nāgārjuna a form of '*sat*'. (Though I will argue later in this chapter that the *unintended* consequence of Nāgārjuna's position that all entities are *prajñaptisat* must be that in fact entities do not exist *at all*). Tola and Dragonetti, in their explanation of these verses, express Nāgārjuna's point very well,

the magical illusion, the mirage, etc have a certain form of existence, an illusory one. This form of existence is the same form of existence of the empirical reality. It is this form of existence which allows the perception of the magical illusion etc and of the empirical reality.[30]

MMK XXIV, 18: An Analysis

Finally, there is also the extremely important but variously-interpreted *MMK* XXIV, 18, in which Nāgārjuna says that dependent origination (*pratītyasamutpāda*) is emptiness (*śūnyatā*), and emptiness is *prajñaptirupādāya* (and the Middle Path (*madhyamā pratipat*)).[31]

The phrase '*prajñaptirupādāya*', or, as it is usually expressed, '*upādāyaprajñapti*' means, literally, 'concept based upon' or 'concept depending upon'. (See here also the Tibetan translation '*brten nas gdags pa*').[32] As Warder explains, the commentary on the *Kathāvatthu* says that the term '*upādāya*' means 'conditioned by' (*paṭicca*), 'depending on' (*āgamma*), 'not without that' (*na vinā taṃ*).[33] The Pāli equivalent of *upādāyaprajñapti*, i.e. *upādāyapaññatti* or *upādāpaññatti*, is used, for example, in the *Kathāvatthu*, in a section entitled 'Examination of the "Concept Depending Upon"' (*Upādāpaññattānuyoga*). Here it is explained that the person (*puggala*) is a concept (*paññatti*) which is not a real entity. If the person were a real entity (rather than a concept) it would be identifiable with its really occurring constituents – identified in the text as the *khandha*-s, *dhātu*-s and so on – either individually or collectively. But the person cannot be so identified. The person is, then, a concept (created by the mind) depending upon its really occurring constituents, but itself not a really occurring entity.[34] See here also Candrakīrti's commentary on *MMK* XVIII, 1, in which he explains that non-Buddhists (*tīrthika*), because they do not understand *upādāyaprajñapti*-s, do not realize (because of fear (*trāsa*)) that the self (*ātman*) is merely a name (*nāmamātrakam*).[35]

It seems likely that Nāgārjuna means that an entity which is a *prajñaptirupādāya* is one which is a concept (*prajñapti*) depending on (*upādāya*) its parts. (Though, of course, for the Mādhyamika, unlike for the Ābhidharmika, the parts out of which an entity is constituted are themselves inevitably *prajñaptirupādāya*-s). In this case, *MMK* XXIV, 18 could plausibly mean that what is dependently originating (i.e. each and every entity) is empty (of *svabhāva*), and a dependently originating entity, empty of *svabhāva*, is simply a concept depending upon its parts. Seen in the light of emptiness, i.e. universal absence of *svabhāva*, then, the dependent origination of all entities means that all entities originate in dependence upon the mind.

★ ★ ★

It might be objected, however, that a *prajñapti* (in the compound *prajñaptirupādāya*) is a concept, and not a conceptually constructed entity to which a concept might refer. A concept of a chariot (to use a traditional example) is obviously not the same as an actual (though conceptually constructed) chariot. I have a concept of a chariot which I have now brought to mind, but I nevertheless certainly do not have a chariot. Even if Nāgārjuna claims that all entities are *prajñaptisat*, he clearly upholds the distinction between concepts and their conceptually constructed referents. As Nāgārjuna says,

> *saṃjñārthayorananyatve mukhaṃ dahyeta vahninā/*
>
> If there were identity of the concept and [its] object, the mouth would be burned by the [concept] fire. (*LS* 7a–b).
>
> ... *gal te bum pa mngon par brjod pa dang/ bum pa gcig nyid yin na bum pa brjod pa bzhin du phyi rol yang 'jim pa'i gong bu dang/ 'khor lo dang/ chu la sogs pa 'dus pa la ma ltos par grub par 'gyur te/ bum pa la sogs pa mngon par rtogs nas bum pa la sogs pa 'grub par 'gyur ro/ bum pa zhes brjod pa na kha gang bar 'gyur la me zhes brjod pa na mchu 'tshig par 'gyur te de ltar 'dod pa yang ma yin no/*
>
> ... if the word 'pot' and the pot were identical, [then] just as the word 'pot' comes into existence even externally, not depending on the assemblage of the lump of clay, the [potter's] wheel, the water, etc, [likewise], having clearly comprehended [the word] pot, the pot, etc would come into existence. When uttering 'pot', the mouth would become full, and when uttering 'fire' the lips would burn. And this cannot be accepted. (*VaidC* 52).

However, although it is clear from these passages that Nāgārjuna does want to uphold the distinction between concepts which refer to conceptually constructed entities and the conceptually constructed referents, this does not mean that he uses the term '*prajñaptirupādāya*' to denote the concepts which refer to conceptually constructed entities, rather than the conceptually constructed referents. As Warder has shown,[36] there is a long tradition (albeit only fully developed long after Nāgārjuna's time) in Abhidhamma thought of using the term '*paññatti*' both to denote concepts which refer to conceptually constructed entities and also to denote the conceptually constructed referents. ('*Paññatti*' also denotes those concepts which refer to *dharma*-s, non-conceptually constructed entities, (though, of course, *paññatti* does not denote the *dharma*-s themselves) but that is not relevant here).

In other words, for the Abhidhamma, it is not correct to assert that conceptually constructed entities are not *paññatti*-s. Which is not to say that concepts which refer to conceptually constructed entities and the conceptually constructed referents are conflated, but rather that the term '*paññatti*' has two distinct senses – i.e. *paññatti*-s which refer to conceptually constructed entities, and *paññatti*-s which are the conceptually constructed entities.[37] And, significantly, perhaps, the term '*upādāyapaññatti*' (as distinct from '*paññatti*') is sometimes used *only* to denote the *paññatti*-s which are the conceptually constructed referents and not the *paññatti*-s which refer to conceptually constructed referents.[38]

Thus, it is quite possible that Nāgārjuna is here using the term '*prajñaptirupādāya*' to denote conceptually constructed existents, i.e. the referents of concepts. Which is to say that a *prajñaptir-upādāya* is the chariot, for example, itself, and not the concept which has the chariot as its referent.

* * *

Candrakīrti seems to understand *MMK* XXIV, 18 in the way that I have suggested, for he writes, in his commentary on this verse, that emptiness and *upādāyaprajñapti* (and the Middle Path) are 'different names' (*viśeṣasaṃjñā*), i.e. synonyms, for dependent origination (*pratītyasamutpāda*). Candrakīrti gives the traditional example of the chariot (*ratha*). He says that, the *prajñapti* of the chariot which occurs depending on (*upādāya*) the parts (*aṅgāni*) of the chariot is not produced with *svabhāva*. Non-production with *svabhāva* (*svabhāvenānutpatti*), Candrakīrti says, is emptiness (*śūnyatā*).[39] In other words, the chariot is dependently originating = is empty (of *svabhāva*) = is a *prajñapti* dependently originating on the basis of its parts.[40]

It seems clear that Candrakīrti here intends the example of the chariot to illustrate what is the case about all entities. All entities are dependently originating, which means that they are empty of *svabhāva*, which means that they are *prajñapti*-s, i.e. conceptually constructed entities, depending upon parts.

Candrakīrti at least is therefore unequivocal, it seems to me, in his assertion of the universally conceptually constructed nature of entities. Thus, in the *YṢV* he criticizes his fellow Buddhists (*rang gi sde pa*) – whom he identifies as the Vaibhāṣikas (*bye brag tu smra ba*), Sautrāntikas (*mdo sde pa*), and Vijñānavādins (*rnam par shes pa tsam du smra ba*) – for asserting that (some) dependently arising entities have *dravyasat* (*rdzas su yod pa nyid*), i.e. *svarūpa* (*rang gi ngo bo*), here a synonym for *svabhāva*. He compares them, rather unkindly, to a wild horse (*rta dmu rgod*) which imitates the behaviour of an ass (*bong bu*)! (The implication being, of course, that the Mādhyamika, because he rejects that any dependently originating entity has *dravyasat*, is the thoroughbred!) [41]

Prajñaptimātra and *karma*

There is very strong evidence, then, for the interpretation that Nāgārjuna advocates that all entities have conceptually constructed existence. However, it does not follow that because Nāgārjuna says that everything is a conceptual construct, therefore the world, i.e. the manifold of conventions, is, for Nāgārjuna, under one's control. One needs to resist here, I think, the notion that the manner in which one conceptually constructs is, according to Nāgārjuna, generally a matter of choice. On the contrary, it is presumably the case that one's world is largely, in Nāgārjuna's view, a conceptual construction on the basis of previous actions (*karma/karman*), so that one is subject to it, rather than in control of it. The way in which the world manifests is the inevitable consequence of past deeds (*karmavipāka*). Nāgārjuna's acceptance of the law of *karma* is clear:

> *las rnams 'bras bu bcas nyid dang/*
> *'gro ba dag kyang yang dag bshad/*
>
> Actions having consequences and also the states of existence have been correctly explained [by the Buddha]. (*YṢ* 32a–b).
>
> *aśubhātsarvaduḥkhāni sarvā durgatayastathā/*
> *śubhātsugatayaḥ sarvāḥ sarvajanmasukhāni ca//*
>
> All sufferings and bad migrations result from vices.
> All good migrations and the pleasures in all [re-]births result from virtues. (*RV* I, 21).[42]

It must be granted, however, that Nāgārjuna never explicitly states that the world one is born into is a conceptual construct as a result of *karma*.[43] He might simply mean that the fact that one is born into a particular sort of world and particular circumstances is a product of *karma*. But if *karma* is the most significant conditioning force on the mind for Nāgārjuna – which, given that he is a Buddhist, it clearly is – and if everything is according to Nāgārjuna entirely a conceptual construct, it follows that it is *karma* which fundamentally produces the conceptually constructed world in which one exists.

I think that this is a very important point to stress, because it shows that, if in Nāgārjuna's view the world is a conceptual construct, nevertheless to a great extent for Nāgārjuna one is subject to, rather than master of, it. Conventions (*saṃvṛti*) are, therefore, often not entities which one can decide whether or not to construct in the way in which one does. On the contrary, conventions usually force themselves upon one; the way in which one constructs them has already been decided, as it were, by the law of *karma*.

In many cases, particularly I suppose concerning entities of the natural world, if there is consensus or agreement about conventions – for example, if we agree that the river is flowing with water – it is presumably the case that we agree because of common *karmavipāka*, rather than because we have each 'decided' to construct a river flowing with water! Our common *karmavipāka* compels us both to construct a river flowing with water. Human beings inhabit a generally similar conventional world because their common *karmavipāka* obliges them to construct the world in a generally similar sort of fashion. The *preta* might see the river as flowing with pus, and he might be in agreement with other *preta*-s in this matter, but this too is presumably because of common *karmavipāka*, rather than through any personal choice. *Preta*-s and humans might disagree on whether there is a river of pus or a river of water, but this is because their *karmavipāka* is different, so that the conventions differ which they are compelled to construct. (But note that, in this example, as both humans and *preta*-s see *a river*, their *karmavipāka* must to some degree be similar). *Preta*-s, I imagine, cannot decide to construct rivers of water in place of their conceptually constructed rivers of pus just as human beings (excepting great *yogin*-s, perhaps) cannot choose to construct rivers of pus in place of their rivers of water.

This explanation also suggests, incidentally, that for Nāgārjuna it is not one's culture or linguistic community which primarily determines the conventions which one constructs, contrary to some modern interpretations of Madhyamaka.[44] Rather, it is one's *karma* which is the most fundamental cause of the conceptual constructs to which one is subject. The root cause of my experiencing the world in the way in which I do – with its trees, mountains, rivers, etc – is that my *karma* has matured in such a way as to subject me to this sort of conceptual construction. That we both have similar experiences is presumably primarily because our *karma* is maturing in similar ways, not because we originate from a common culture or share a language, etc.

It will undoubtedly be the case that the culture or linguistic community in which one exists will affect to some extent the way in which conceptual construction will occur. For example, artifacts, institutions and values are obviously at least in part a matter of culturally determined conceptual construction. (Whether Nāgārjuna himself was aware of this point, I do not know. References in his works to socio-linguistic communities as forces of conditioning are conspicuous by their absence! References to *karma*, however, are common). However, it is worth noting that the specific culture and linguistic community in which one exists is itself presumably largely a conceptual construction as a result of *karma*. The primary cause of conceptual construction is, then, *karma*, rather than cultural or linguistic conditioning.

I must add, however, that Nāgārjuna's view that natural entities are the product of conceptual construction governed primarily by *karma* seems pretty implausible to me. I think that I can perhaps accept that I exist in the sort of world, in the sort of circumstances, in which I find myself as a result of *karma*, but it seems incredible to believe that the world in which I find myself is itself actually a product of *karma*. Am I really to believe that the world of trees, mountains, rivers, etc (and even the constituents of these entities) is entirely a conceptual construct which only comes into existence because of my past actions? This seems no less bizarre (perhaps more bizarre), surely, than the claim that trees, mountains, rivers, etc (and their constituents) somehow exist because of the cultural or linguistic conditioning to which one is subject.

It seems far more likely, then, that so-called conventions, i.e. the manifold entities of the world, are in fact, in many cases (for example, the entire natural world), not essentially a result of conceptual construction, i.e. they are not actually conventions. I suggest that there is a world – of complex natural entities – which exists prior to and independent of conceptual construction, be the conceptual construction a result of *karma*, cultural conditioning, or of any other form. Yet, if Nāgārjuna is advocating *prajñaptimātra*, he cannot admit that this is the case.

And there is another (and, I think, fatal) problem with Nāgārjuna's explanation here. He might want to advocate that the laws of *karma* govern the conceptual constructions which take place, but I do not think that in fact he can consistently uphold this position as well as the notion of *prajñaptimātra*. For if the laws of *karma* govern conceptual construction, then it must follow that the laws of *karma* are not themselves conceptual constructs. That the conceptually constructed world is a result of *karma* entails, I think, that the various laws which (supposedly) determine how one conceptually constructs the world on the basis of previous actions are not themselves part of the conceptually constructed world. Nāgārjuna's advocacy of the law of *karma* appears to compromise his position that everything is conceptually constructed.

Prajñaptimātra and the Possibility of a Public World

This is just the beginning of Nāgārjuna's difficulties, however. I contend that the *very intelligibility* of much of one's experience depends on the assumption that many of our cognitions do in fact apprehend mind-independent realities.[45] Even if Nāgārjuna were right, and there is not a mind-independent world which our cognitions apprehend, we must take for granted this mind-independent world nonetheless.

For example, if I trust my cognition of a pool of water, I trust that the pool of water which I cognize is accessible to the cognitions of other people (and, indeed, that these other people exist independently of my mind). I trust that they too can perceive the water, that it will quench their thirst, etc. And I trust that the water is there to be cognized by others not because we engage in a collective fantasy of thirst-quenching water, but because there is a mind-independent pool of water to be cognized. This is what it means to trust that one's cognition of the water is correct. I cannot trust that my cognition of the pool of water is correct, yet think that there is no mind-independent pool of water to be apprehended, by myself and others. And I do and in fact must – if I am to act at all and to participate in public reality – trust my cognition in this way.

Searle[46] makes the point that much human communication presupposes the mind-independent existence of many of the entities which are communicated about. This is a condition for the possibility of communication, and the fact that one does take part in such communication proves that one assumes that such entities do actually exist independently of one's mind. Such communication also, of course, assumes that the people with whom one communicates exist independently of one's mind. If I am to say to you that I am going to bathe in the pool of water, I must assume that the pool of water which I am planning to bathe in is accessible to your cognitions, as well as to mine. I also must assume that this pool of water is not simply a shared conceptual construct which we both have, but that there is an actual, i.e. mind-independent, pool of water which I (and you too) may bathe in (provided it is large and deep enough!). What could it mean, I wonder, to believe that one is going to bathe in a conceptually constructed pool of water (and, perhaps, with a conceptually constructed friend)?! So, a difficult problem for Nāgārjuna is how, if everything is a conceptual construct, a public world would be possible.

Nāgārjuna would of course admit that the unenlightened person believes that (many) entities have *svabhāva*, i.e. are more-than-conceptually constructed, even though this is not, according to Nāgārjuna, a correct belief. Unenlightened people do not *know* that the world which they conceptually construct is a conceptual construction. On the contrary, unenlightened people erroneously perceive and erroneously believe the conceptually constructed world to be (largely) mind-independent. As Candrakīrti says,[47] entities, though in fact conceptually constructed, 'exist [as mind-independent entities] from the perspective of the consensus of the world'. (*'jig rten grags pa'i sgo nas yod pa yin*). This 'perspective of the consensus of the world' is, of course, wrong, deluded. The true nature of entities is hidden, not apparent, for unenlightened people.

Thus, perhaps Nāgārjuna would claim, it is the false belief in more-than-conceptually constructed entities which allows the unenlightened person to participate in a public world. But, then, it is not really that there is a public world which the unenlightened person participates in, but rather a world which he falsely believes to be public (but which is really his conceptual construction)!

And this reasoning has the peculiar consequence that, if one came to know and perceive that all entities are in fact without *svabhāva*, i.e. are conceptual constructs, then the false belief and perception which enables one to participate in an (apparently) public world would be destroyed. The enlightened Mādhyamika would see not only that all objects of the supposedly public world are conceptual constructs but also that the very people with whom he might share the publicly accessible world are themselves his own conceptual constructs. There are in fact no other people who have similar *karmavipāka* to oneself and with whom one might therefore participate in a commonly acknowledged conceptually constructed world! The enlightened Mādhyamika must surely be a solipsist (which seems to me to be a peculiar sort of enlightenment).

It is difficult to see how, in this condition, the bodhisattva ideal – which is a fundamental pillar of Mahāyāna (and hence Madhyamaka[48]) spirituality – could be enacted. It does, after all, seem to be a real paradox (and by this I mean a non-sensical statement, a contradiction) that the bodhisattva saves all sentient beings yet there are no sentient beings to be saved (for they are all the bodhisattva's own conceptual constructs). The realization of emptiness – i.e. of the conceptually constructed nature of everything, including all sentient beings – would seem to be incompatible with the ideal of compassion. The bodhisattva who holds together knowledge of emptiness and compassion is not so much extraordinary as deeply puzzling.

The Nihilistic Consequences of *prajñaptimātra*

But it is not just that the notion that all entities are conceptual constructs precludes the possibility of a public world, and hence of compassionate activity. In addition, it would appear that Nāgārjuna's opponents are right, after all, to accuse Nāgārjuna of nihilism. For Nāgārjuna is not merely saying – despite his apparent claims to the contrary – that entities are *dependently originating*, but further that all entities are entirely *conceptually constructed*. But if *all* entities are entirely conceptually constructed, then there can be nothing unconstructed out of which conceptually constructed entities can be constructed. And if there is nothing unconstructed out of which the conceptually constructed entities are constructed, then these conceptually constructed entities cannot exist. Conceptually constructed entity *z* might be constructed on the basis of *y*. *Y* might also be constructed on the basis of *x*. And so on. But at some point this regress must stop. Not everything can be a product of conceptual construction, because 'conceptual construction' requires a basis or material which is not itself conceptually constructed.[49] To claim otherwise would be to advocate that the entire world is created *ex nihilo*! One can see here, perhaps, the cause of the Abhidharma (and the Yogācāra[50]) objection to Madhyamaka philosophy.

Also, the notion of conceptual construction would appear to entail – not only something foundational on the basis of which constructed entities can be constructed, but also – someone or something foundational who or which is doing the constructing. If it is contended that all entities are conceptually constructed, this would seem to necessitate an answer to the question, conceptually constructed by whom? If it is then said, as a consistent Mādhyamika presumably must say, that whoever conceptually constructs is himself conceptually constructed,[51] an infinite regress results. I don't think that I can make sense of the idea that even the agent (be it the self, the mind, or the flow of impermanent *citta*-s) which conceptually constructs entities is itself a conceptual construction. The explanation that the agent is itself a conceptual construction begs the question, for such a conceptual construction would itself require an agent to do the constructing. The meaning of 'conceptual construction' presupposes an agent which is a perpetrator of, and is logically prior to, the conceptual construction.

This in no way contradicts the important psychological/spiritual point that, in many respects, one's views about one's self and the world *are* conceptual constructs (e.g. as a result of upbringing, habit, education, and, arguably, *karma*). I am simply making the compatible philosophical point that in order to have conceptually constructed views about who one is and how the world is, there must be someone/something itself unconstructed which *has* the views, or is *doing the viewing*.

The very idea of conceptual construction seems to imply, then, both some material, itself unconstructed, which is the basis of construction, and also some agent who is the constructor of what is constructed. Yet, according to the interpretation which I have presented, in his assertion that all entities are conventions, i.e. *prajñaptisat*, Nāgārjuna precludes the possibility of either of these necessary requirements for conceptual construction. If, therefore, as Nāgārjuna seems to say, the ultimate truth is that all entities are conventional truths in the Abhidharma sense, then it seems to follow that – unwelcome as the conclusion might be to Nāgārjuna himself – in fact nothing whatsoever exists at all. Nāgārjuna is, as his opponents contend, a nihilist.

If my reasoning here is correct, then it can be concluded, in addition, that Nāgārjuna falls into the paradox of nihilism, of which the opponent at *VV* 1 accuses him. For his statement that 'all entities are empty of *svabhāva*' does indeed, it would seem, entail that nothing whatsoever exists. In this case, absurdly, Nāgārjuna cannot actually utter the statement or establish that 'everything is empty' – for the statement and the proof are themselves non-existent!

An Alternative Reading

Is there any way out of this conundrum for the interpreter of Nāgārjuna? Can Nāgārjuna be saved from nihilism (and solipsism)? Let me suggest an alternative interpretation.[52]

According to this alternative interpretation, the true object of Nāgārjuna's critique of *svabhāva* is actually the position, propounded by the Vaibhāṣika Abhidharma, that (*saṃskṛta*) *dharma*-s, insofar as they exist 'with *svabhāva* only' (*sasvabhāvamātra*) are permanent. In which case the Abhidharma notion of *svabhāva* which Nāgārjuna attacks is not *svabhāva* as denoting unanalyzable and thus more-than-conceptually constructed existence. Rather, he attacks the Vaibhāṣika theory that the possession of *svabhāva* by the (*saṃskṛta*) *dharma*-s entails that the (*saṃskṛta*) *dharma*-s exist (with *svabhāva* only) in all three times, i.e. permanently.

For the Vaibhāṣika Abhidharma, the present existence of (*saṃskṛta*) *dharma*-s (in which they are endowed with – together with *svabhāva* – activity (*kāritra*)) is dependently originating, indeed momentary. However, these (*saṃskṛta*) *dharma*-s – possessing *svabhāva* but without activity – are said to exist also in the past and the future. (*Saṃskṛta*) *dharma*-s are (with *svabhāva* only) permanent.

The permanent existence of the (*saṃskṛta*) *dharma*-s (with *svabhāva* only) is what enables (*saṃskṛta*) *dharma*-s to have various capacities (*sāmarthya*) even when the (*saṃskṛta*) *dharma*-s are not presently existent, i.e. even when the (*saṃskṛta*) *dharma*-s do not have activity (*kāritra*). For example, the (*saṃskṛta*) *dharma*-s' permanent existence (with *svabhāva* only) is meant to explain how (*saṃskṛta*) *dharma*-s may be cognized (e.g. by memory or imagination) even when they are past or future, and also how past (*saṃskṛta*) *dharma*-s may have causal efficacy (e.g. the karmic effects of past skilful and unskilful mental (*saṃskṛta*) *dharma*-s). Thus, when one remembers or imagines a (*saṃskṛta*) *dharma*, it is the (*saṃskṛta*) *dharma* existing with *svabhāva* only which is one's object of cognition. If one suffers pain because of a previous unskilful (*saṃskṛta*) *dharma* it is the (*saṃskṛta*) *dharma* existing with *svabhāva* only which affects one's present mental continuum, producing the present mental (*saṃskṛta*) *dharma*.[53]

I make no comment here on the cogency of this Vaibhāṣika explanation. The important point in the present context is that such an explanation was, the Vaibhāṣikas thought, necessitated by various philosophical problems which arise from the position that (*saṃskṛta*) *dharma*-s dependently originate in a momentary fashion (for how can a momentary (*saṃskṛta*) *dharma* be an object of cognition if it is no longer or not yet existent, and how can such a momentary (*saṃskṛta*) *dharma* have causal efficacy if it has ceased?) The notion that the (*saṃskṛta*) *dharma*-s, existing *sasvabhāvamātra*, are permanent is not then intended as a denial of, but rather is an attempt to solve the theoretical problems posed by, this momentary dependent origination of (*saṃskṛta*) *dharma*-s.

But Nāgārjuna might argue that the Vaibhāṣika theory that the (*saṃskṛta*) *dharma*-s exist permanently (with *svabhāva* only) compromises the notion that (*saṃskṛta*) *dharma*-s are dependently originating. In effect, the Vaibhāṣika theory entails that there is a permanent essential nature of dependently originating (*saṃskṛta*) *dharma*-s which remains independent of the process of arising and cessation. For the Vaibhāṣika Abhidharma, then, dependent origination of (*saṃskṛta*) *dharma*-s is not dependent origination through and through – there is an essential nature which is untouched by *pratītyasamutpāda*.

According to this interpretation, Nāgārjuna's philosophy would not entail nihilism. Nāgārjuna does not reject (*saṃskṛta*) *dharma*-s, understood as the foundational (though dependently originating) existents upon which the world of complex entities is constructed. He does not assert that everything is a conceptual construct. There are foundational (*saṃskṛta*) *dharma*-s, Nāgārjuna might be saying, but, contrary to the Vaibhāṣika theory, they do not possess a permanent existence (with *svabhāva* only). Which is to say that the foundational (*saṃskṛta*) *dharma*-s in no respect are other than dependently originating.

Textual Difficulties

However, although I would not completely discount this interpretation, it seems to me to be somewhat implausible. I think that for Nāgārjuna, and later Mādhyamikas, it is far more likely that it is the Abhidharma theory of *dharma*-s with *svabhāva* as unanalyzable (and, hence, as more-than-conceptually constructed) existents – rather than the specifically Vaibhāṣika theory of (*saṃskṛta*) *dharma*-s (with *svabhāva* only) as existing permanently – which is the (principal) object of attack. This is for three reasons:

(i) As I have already commented (see note 9), it is not at all clear that the Abhidharma philosophy with which Nāgārjuna was familiar was in fact that of the Vaibhāṣika school, who upheld the notion that (*saṃskṛta*) *dharma*-s exist permanently *sasvabhāvamātra*. And Nāgārjuna at no point explicitly mentions the Vaibhāṣika doctrine, which is surely strange if it is the principal object of his attack.

(ii) As I have explained in detail in this chapter, there is very strong evidence in Nāgārjuna's texts that his fundamental objection is to the notion that any dependent originating entity has more than a conventional, conceptually constructed status. Thus, it does not seem that, even if Nāgārjuna were criticizing the Vaibhāṣika doctrine of permanent (*saṃskṛta*) *dharma*-s existing with *svabhāva* only, it is the primary object of his critique of *svabhāva*. That is, a large body of textual evidence (reviewed above) suggests that, even if (*saṃskṛta*) *dharma*-s with *svabhāva* were posited as in all respects impermanent or momentary – i.e. as being through and through dependently originating – Nāgārjuna, etc would object to them, on the grounds that the possession of such a *svabhāva* would entail unanalyzable (and, hence, more-than-conceptual) existence.

(iii) Finally, it is clear that later Mādhyamikas, such as Candrakīrti (see *YṢV* 40–41) criticize the notion of *svabhāva* not only as it appears in the Vaibhāṣika Abhidharma, but also as it occurs in the Sautrāntika and Vijñānavāda[54] schools, neither of which accept the Vaibhāṣika theory of permanent (*saṃskṛta*) *dharma*-s (with *svabhāva* only). (In fact, the Sautrāntikas were vigorous opponents of this Vaibhāṣika theory. They assert the complete momentariness of (*saṃskṛta*) *dharma*-s with *svabhāva*[55]). What all three of these schools have in common is an acceptance – contrary to Madhyamaka – of some foundational, more-than-conceptually constructed form of existence (*dravyasat*). Candrakīrti makes clear that his objection is to the notion of *dravyasat* as it occurs in all three of these schools. He does not say that his objection is to the Vaibhāṣika theory that (*saṃskṛta*) *dharma*-s *sasvabhāvamātra* exist permanently.

A Philosophical Problem

But even if Nāgārjuna were saved from nihilism by means of this alternative interpretation, this would not be the end of his philosophical difficulties. Even if Nāgārjuna accepts that there are simple, more-than-conceptually constructed *dharma*-s (albeit, in all respects dependently originating), he will still accept, with the Abhidharma, that all non-atomic (analyzable) entities are conceptual constructs on the basis of these really existing *dharma*-s.

But it seems to me that this way of drawing the distinction between conceptually constructed and more-than-conceptually constructed existents is philosophically dubious. I find it implausible that analyzable entities, i.e. entities which have parts, must always be conceptually constructed. Is it actually the case that the various commonly experienced analyzable entities of the natural world, for example, are conceptually constructed on the basis of numerous atomic particles? Is a tree or a mountain, for instance, really a conceptually constructed entity – all that exists in a non-conceptually constructed way being various *dharma*-s, which the mind uses as its basis of construction? It seems far more plausible that analyzable entities such as mountains and trees, etc exist with parts but also independently of conceptual construction.

Granted, many of the functions that one attributes to these analyzable natural entities are mind-dependent (e.g. the tree is for fire-wood, the tree is for shelter, the tree is beautiful) but this is very different from saying that the analyzable natural entities to which one attributes functions are themselves conceptually constructed. Such entities acquire a value within the realm of human purposes, even if this position or value is 'useless'. But this emphatically does not mean that these entities are reducible to the values which are assigned to them.[56]

One might also argue that some of the characteristics (for example, perhaps colour) attributed to analyzable natural entities do not actually inhere in these entities, and are thus attributions by the mind. This would be to introduce a Lockean-type of distinction between primary and secondary qualities. Of course, it is a moot point precisely which qualities of a natural entity are inherent and which qualities are not. But it seems very likely that not all characteristics of analyzable, natural entities are attributions by the mind.

Thus, a fundamental philosophical mistake, perhaps, in the Abhidharma and Madhyamaka philosophies alike, is that they equate analyzable existence with conceptually constructed existence. My contention is that it seems more plausible that many analyzable entities have in fact mind-independent existence.

No doubt one must accept that analyzable entities – such as trees and mountains – cannot exist without their (essential) parts, but it does not follow that such entities are conceptually constructed on the basis of their (essential) parts. That a tree, for example, cannot exist without dependence upon its (essential) constituents – the roots, trunk, branches, etc – does not entail that the tree is a conceptual construction. It just means that one of the conditions which must exist in order for the entity 'tree' to occur is that its various (essential) constituents be present. Analyzable entities have that type of existence which is dependent upon (essential) parts, but it seems quite plausible that such an entity might still have a mind-independent existence.[57]

Of course, some entities, it might be conceded, are entirely conventional, i.e. entirely the product of conceptual construction. For example, institutional facts such as laws and the rules of games are completely dependent on consensus or custom for their existence. If human beings and human societies did not create laws and the rules of games, they simply would not exist at all. It is arguable that artifacts, such as cars and tables, are also conventions/conceptual constructions insofar as they are designed by minds and only exist in relation to human purposes. (Although such artifacts are always made of (analyzable) natural materials, i.e. non-artifacts, which, though certainly dependently originating, are not dependent on conceptual construction for their existence. The wooden table may only exist in dependence upon the human mind (for tables only exist in the context of human conventions), but the wood at least (without its 'tableness') has a mind-independent existence).[58]

Conclusion

Thus, on one reading (for which there is a considerable amount of textual evidence), Nāgārjuna declares that everything is simply a conceptual construct, and he is thereby condemned, contrary to his intentions, to nihilism. On another reading (for which there is far less textual support), Nāgārjuna attacks only the Vaibhāṣika theory that *dharma*-s exist permanently *sasvabhāvamātra*. According to this latter reading, Nāgārjuna is right to declare that he is no nihilist, for he claims only that *dharma*-s are in all respects dependently originating, and not that even *dharma*-s are conceptual constructs. There is thus a foundation, not itself conceptually constructed, on the basis of which conceptual construction may take place. However, even according to this interpretation, Nāgārjuna advocates the dubious position that all analyzable entities (non-*dharma*-s) have conceptually constructed existence (*prajñaptisat*). Even if Nāgārjuna's philosophy does not entail nihilism, Nāgārjuna is probably guilty (along with the Ābhidharmikas and other Buddhist thinkers[59] who reject the more-than-conceptual existence of analyzable entities) of excessive ontological parsimony.

In fact, the tendency throughout Buddhist philosophy is to regard analyzable entities with great suspicion. No doubt this is at least partly for religious/spiritual reasons. It is blatantly obvious that it is the analyzable entities to which one tends to get attached (rather than their atomic constituents!). One is more likely to be attached to one's car, for example, than to the molecules of metals, etc which are its microscopic parts. It is also obvious (though this somehow does not stop our folly) that we suffer when these analyzable entities to which we are attached dissolve into their parts, as they must eventually. Hence the Buddhist tendency to stress the unreality of these analyzable entities may be seen as a means to stop one coveting them, which would put an end to suffering. But, while it is undoubtedly true that analyzable entities are liable to dissolution into their parts – and one would thus be wise not to get attached to these analyzable entities if one wants to avoid suffering – it does not follow that these analyzable entities are conceptual constructed on the basis of their parts.

Notes

1 I would like to acknowledge my debt in what follows to Professor P. Williams, especially Williams (manuscript 2), pp. 12–29. Many of the points which I make in this chapter have been inspired by Williams' interpretation of Madhyamaka, with his emphasis on the need to view Madhyamaka philosophy in the context of Abhidharma thought.

2 See especially *VV/VVC* 1–20, and *MMK* XXIV, 6, spoken by an opponent. See also the opponent's criticism at *ŚS* 15.

3 See *MMK* XXIV, 14, and *VV/VVC* 70.

4 *MMK* XXIV, 7.

5 See, for example, *MMK* XXIV, 18a–b, *VV* 22, *VVC* 70, *LS* 22, *AS* 40a–b. See also Candrakīrti's *PP* 368 for a particularly clear statement of this point.

6 See *MMK* XXIV, 36.

7 See Wood (1994).

8 Mention must also be made of the unconditioned (*asaṃskṛta*) *dharma*-s which, according to Vaibhāṣika Abhidharma, are *ākāśa*, *pratisaṃkhyānirodha*, and *apratisaṃkhyānirodha*. They both have *svabhāva* and do not dependently originate. See *AKBh* I, 5–6. See also Griffiths (1986), p. 168. It would appear, then, that – although for the Abhidharma possession of *svabhāva* does not *entail* independent existence – possession of *svabhāva* is *compatible* with independent existence. Some entities which have *svabhāva* (the *saṃskṛta dharma*-s) dependently originate; some entities which have *svabhāva* (the *asaṃskṛta dharma*-ṣ) do not dependently originate.

9 In the following analysis of Abhidharma philosophy, I primarily rely on Vasubandhu's *Abhidharmakośabhāṣya* and accounts of Saṅghabhadra's **Nyāyānusāra*. It should be noted, however, that these works post-date Nāgārjuna's writings by several centuries. Further, despite what some interpreters say (see, for example, Kalupahana (1986)), it is not clear that the Abhidharma with which Nāgārjuna was familiar was that of the Vaibhāṣika/Sarvāstivāda. For example, when in the *VVC* 7 Nāgārjuna provides a list of *dharma*-s, it does not seem to correspond to the traditional Vaibhāṣika taxonomy. See Bhattacharya (1990), p. 100 for a brief discussion of this issue. (It is clear, however, that Candrakīrti was familiar with both the Vaibhāṣika and the Sautrāntika schools, for he refers to them by name. See *YṢV* 40.)

10 *AKBh* VI, 4. See Cox (1995), pp. 138–139. See also Matilal (1986), pp. 246–248.

11 See Williams (1981), p. 238, and Cox (1995), pp. 138–139. See also *AKBh* II, 22, II, 62c, VI, 4.

12 See Cox (1995), p. 12.

13 See *AKBh* VI, 14c–d. See also Griffiths (1986), p. 167, Cox (1995) p. 139.

14 See Cox (1995), p. 12.

15 See *AKBh* III, 24d, III, 27.

16 See Cox (1995), pp. 146–149. Griffiths (1986), p. 52, Karunadasa (1967), pp. 79–90. On the *svalakṣaṇa* and the *sāmānyalakṣaṇa* see, for example, *AKBh* VI, 14c–d.

17 See Karunadasa (1986), pp. 126–141.

18 See *AKBh* III, 11a–b, III, 85b–c.
19 On the distinction between conventional truths and ultimate truths, see *AKBh* VI, 4.
20 See Williams (1981), p. 238, Buescher (1982), pp. 153–154.
21 See, for example, *AKBh* IX.
22 See here *MMK* XXV, 5, which might be interpreted to support this reading.
23 As Williams (manuscript 2), p. 27 notes, there are thus two distinct senses in which the term 'ultimate truth' (*paramārthasatya*) is employed in Madhyamaka. Ultimate truth can mean: (1) ultimate truth in the Abhidharma sense of unanalyzable and more-than-conceptually constructed existence, and (2) ultimate truth in the sense of 'how things actually are', i.e. the true nature of things. For the Mādhyamika, then, there is no ultimate truth in sense (1), but there is ultimate truth in sense (2). In fact, the ultimate truth in sense (2) is that there is no ultimate truth in sense (1).

It might reasonably be objected, however, that the Mādhyamika is caught here in a paradox, similar to the liar's paradox. If the ultimate truth is that *everything* has conceptually constructed existence, does not this entail that the ultimate truth (in sense 2) itself is simply a conceptual construct, i.e. a convention? In which case the ultimate truth (in sense 2) is not actually ultimately true, i.e. it is not the way things actually are. If it is true that everything is a conceptual construct, then it is false that everything is a conceptual construct. Might one not have to say, then, that the ultimate truth is that there are no ultimate truths *except* the ultimate truth that there are no ultimate truths? But in this case Nāgārjuna's position of *prajñaptimātra* has certainly been compromised.

Nāgārjuna, it seems to me, does not deal with this problem. The most ingenious attempted solution which I have come across is provided by the dGe lugs pas. The dGe lugs pas say that the ultimate truth, i.e. emptiness, is true (*dben pa yin pa*) but that this ultimate truth/emptiness does not truly exist (*bden par ma grub pa*). In other words, the ultimate truth/emptiness is the ultimate *truth* but it, like everything else, has a merely conventional *existence*. As I understand this point, the dGe lugs pas mean that the ultimate truth/emptiness exists as the ultimate truth/emptiness *of* entities. It does not and cannot exist apart from the entities of which it is the ultimate truth/emptiness. Entities one and all have conceptually constructed existence – they do not have 'existence from their own side' (*rang ngos nas grub pa*) and are 'mere imputations by thought' (*rtog pas btags tsam*). Therefore, the ultimate truth/emptiness, which depends for its existence upon these entities, also has a conceptually constructed existence. (Hence emptiness is itself empty). But despite the fact that the ultimate truth/emptiness does not truly exist, it is nevertheless the ultimate truth – i.e. it is what is actually the case about all entities. See here Cabezón (1992), p. 477, Newland (1992), p. 15, 87, 93.

Clearly, then, the dGe lugs pas have here given the ultimate truth/emptiness a special status (as they must do in order to avoid the above-mentioned paradox). It seems to me that the dGe lug pas are saying, in effect, that in one way the ultimate truth is *not* a conceptual construct (for it is what is actually the case about entities) and yet in another way the ultimate truth *is* a conceptual construct (for it only exists in dependence upon the conceptually constructed entities of which it is the ultimate truth).
24 See, for example, Hopkins (1996), pp. 410–411.

25 I mean the *MMK*, *ŚS*, *VV/VVC*, *YṢ*, *RV*, and *CS*.

The **Vyavahārasiddhi* (*Tha snyad grub pa*) 5 a–b states that all of the twelve members of cyclic existence are *tha snyad kyis ni gdags pa*, which Lindtner (1982), p. 99 reconstructs as *vyavahārataḥ prajñapti*, which he translates as 'conventional designations.' The **Vyavahārasiddhi* is attributed to Nāgārjuna by Śāntarakṣita (see Lindtner (1982), p. 94), but, despite Lindtner's confidence that the work is by Nāgārjuna, the attribution is surely quite doubtful (given the lack of other evidence). P. Williams informs me of a passage in the *Pratītyasamutpādavyākhyāna* (attributed to Nāgārjuna) which states that '*btags pa tsam du yod pa de ni rdzas su yod par mi rung ngo*.' It is a moot point whether this text is actually by Nāgārjuna. For some discussion of the attribution of this text to Nāgārjuna see Lindtner (1982), pp. 170–171. If this text is by Nāgārjuna, this passage is an explicit statement of his recognition of the *prajñaptisat-dravyasat* distinction, although it does not show that he considers *all* entities to be *prajñaptisat*.

26 See also Āryadeva's *CŚ* XIV, 19a–b. In addition, especially noteworthy is the *Hastavālanāmaprakaraṇa*, attributed by the Tibetan translations to Āryadeva (although it is attributed to Dignāga by the Chinese translations). See Tola and Dragonetti (1995b), pp. 2–5 for a discussion of the authorship of this text. (They favour the attribution to Āryadeva). The Tibetan translation refers to this short work as the 'Commentary of the Treatise which is called "The Parts of the Constituents"' (*cha shas kyi yan lag ces bya ba'i rab tu byed pa'i 'grel pa*). Indeed, the main theme of the work is that no entity is partless, and thus there are no unanalyzable atoms. All entities are said to be *prajñaptisat* (*btags yod pa*) in the sense that they exist dependent on sides, parts, etc (*ngos cha la sogs pa la ltos nas yod pa*). See *HV* 1–3. If the *HV* is by Āryadeva (which is very far from certain) this would prove that Nāgārjuna's direct disciple, at least, advocated that everything has conceptually constructed existence.

Many later Mādhyamikas clearly reject partless *dharma*-s, and this would seem to imply that, according to them, everything is *prajñaptisat*. Śāntarakṣita, for example, in the *Madhyamakālaṃkāra*, states that all entities have parts. See Tillemans (1983), pp. 305–320, and mKhas grub rje *sTong* 151–156 (Cabezón (trans) (1992), pp. 147–151). See also Śāntideva, who writes at *BC* 9, 86 that 'even the constituents can be analyzed down to atoms. The atom too can be divided according to the directions . . .' (trans. Crosby and Skilton (1996), p. 124).

27 Although Monier-Williams (1899) does not list '*sāṃvṛta*', '*saṃvṛta*' (p. 1116) is clearly very similar in meaning to '*saṃvṛti*'.

28 But the *AS* also uses the term '*saṃvṛti*' in a second sense, that is, to denote all of the Buddhist teachings other than the teaching of the ultimate truth, i.e. emptiness (*śūnyatā*). In this sense, emptiness is the teaching with definitive meaning (*nītārtha*) whereas *saṃvṛti* is the various Buddhist teachings of provisional meaning (*neyārtha*). See *AS* 56–57, 'The gift of the *dharma*, the ambrosia which is the teaching of the Buddhas, was proclaimed [by you, i.e. the Buddha]. It was declared to be the definitive meaning. It is, of course, just the emptiness of *dharma*-s. But the teaching of arising and ceasing, etc, beings and souls, etc, was declared by you, Oh Protector, to be just the provisional meaning, and is *saṃvṛti*.' (*dharmayautukamākhyātaṃ buddhānāṃ śāsanāmṛtam/ nītārthamiti nirdiṣṭaṃ dharmāṇāṃ śūnyataiva hi/ yā tūtpādanirodhādi-sattvajīvādideśanā/ neyārthā ca tvayā nātha bhāṣitā saṃvṛtiśca sā//*).

29 See my discussion in chapter 3 of the problem of the two truths for a quite different reading of these verses.

30 Tola and Dragonetti (1995b), p. 149.

31 *MMK* XXIV, 18, *yaḥ pratītyasamutpādaḥ śūnyatāṃ tāṃ pracakṣmahe/ sā prajñaptirupādāya pratipatsaiva madhyamā.*

32 See here Nagao (1991), pp. 190–192. I assume that *prajñaptirupādāya= upādāyaprajñapti*. Candrakīrti appears to think so, for his commentary on Nāgārjuna's phrase consistently employs the form '*upādāyaprajñapti*'. The Tibetan translators must also have considered the two phrases as synonyms, because they translate both Nāgārjuna's '*prajñaptirupādāya*' and Candrakīrti's '*upādāyaprajñapti*' as '*brten nas gdags pa.*'

33 Warder (1970a), p. 190.

34 *Kathāvatthu* (Aung and Rhys Davids (trans.) (1969)), pp. 33–39. See also Warder (1970a), p. 186.

35 *PP* 344.

36 Warder (1970a), pp. 181–196.

37 The distinction is between, in Abhidhamma terms, concepts (*paññatti*): 'requiring to be made understood (*paññāpetabba*)' (i.e. conceptually constructed entities), and 'making understood' (*paññāpana*) (i.e. the concepts which refer to conceptually constructed entities (and *dharma*-s)). Warder notes that Buddhadatta (5th century) makes this distinction in his *Abhidhammāvatāra*, as do later Abhidhamma thinkers. The most developed expression of this theory is in the *Paramatthavinicchaya* of Anuruddha II of Kāñcī (12th century). See Warder (1970a), pp. 190–196.

38 See Warder (1970a), p. 192.

39 *PP* 504.

40 See also *MA* VI, 150–165.

41 See *YṢV* 40–41.

42 See also *MMK* XVIII, 5, XXIV, 17; *VVC* 70.

43 It is, however, true that the *Bodhicittavivaraṇa* which is traditionally attributed to Nāgārjuna, states that 'convention arises from *karma* [produced by] defilement.' (*kun rdzob nyon mongs las las byung*) (*BV* 69a). This seems to state pretty explicitly that the conventional world, i.e. the entire world, actually exists as a consequence of *karma*. However, Williams (1984), p. 79 *ff* has argued persuasively that the *BV* is not by Nāgārjuna.

44 See, for example, Huntington (1989).

45 See Searle (1995), p. 184.

46 See Searle (1995), pp. 181–188.

47 See *MA* VI, 167.

48 For Nāgārjuna's advocacy of the bodhisattva ideal, see *RV* V. Some of the most striking Indian Mahāyāna works on the bodhisattva ideal are by Mādhyamikas. Most notably, there is Śāntideva's *BC* and Candrakīrti's *MA/MABh*.

49 See here Searle (1995), pp. 55–56.

50 Williams has argued that the Yogācāra is perhaps best understood as a response to what were felt to be the nihilistic implications of the Madhyamaka teaching of *prajñaptimātra*. Thus, the Yogācāra returns to the Abhidharma principle that there must be a *dravyasat* basis for *prajñaptisat* entities. For the Yogācāra, Williams argues, this *dravyasat* substratum is the flow of experiences, i.e. the *paratantrasvabhāva*, on the basis of which the world of objects is constructed. In other

words, the series of mental moments cannot be analyzed away (though it is, of course, dependently originating). Its foundational existence is presupposed if there is to be any conceptual construction at all. See Williams (manuscript 2), pp. 25–36.

51 See here *MA* VI, 71c–d and *BV* 55.

52 I suppose that one might try to solve the problem of nihilism by resorting to interpretation (1), considered in chapter 3. That is, Nāgārjuna is not a nihilist because he posits an ineffable, unconceptualizable reality which underlies *prajñaptisat* entities. But in this case one is confronted by the philosophical difficulties which I have explained in the previous chapter.

53 See *AKBh* V, 25c–27. See also Williams (1981), pp. 227–257. Cox (1995), pp. 134–137, 141.

54 For a more sustained attack by Candrakīrti on the Vijñānavādins, see *MA* VI, 45–97. The Vijñānavādins are presented as upholding that the *paratantrarūpa*, i.e. the dependently originating flow of experiences, is the basis or cause of *prajñaptisat* entities. It is this notion of a foundational *paratantrarūpa* which Candrakīrti refutes.

55 See *AKBh* V, 25c–27.

56 See here Searle (1995), p. 14 *ff*.

57 See Williams (1998b), pp. 119 *ff*.

58 For some reflections on this issue, see Searle (1995).

59 I think, for example, of Dharmakīrti. See Dreyfus (1997), pp. 55–59.

PART II

CHAPTER FIVE

The Purpose of Part II

In the first part of this study, I have examined and assessed the interpretation that Nāgārjuna's philosophy is a form of scepticism. I have concluded that Nāgārjuna is not a sceptic, for he claims to know that all entities lack *svabhāva*. I have, furthermore, investigated the notion of non-conceptual knowledge in Nāgārjuna's thought. Finally, I have argued that, though Nāgārjuna saw himself as treading the Middle Path between nihilism and eternalism – insofar as he asserts that entities do exist, but exist only without *svabhāva* – nevertheless it appears that, understood in the context of Abhidharma philosophy, his claim that all entities are without *svabhāva* is probably tantamount to nihilism.

I move now, in the second half of this study, to a different but related issue. Ancient Indian epistemology is discussed primarily in terms of (means of) knowledge,[1] and objects of knowledge (*pramāṇa* and *prameya*). Nāgārjuna states, in verse 30 of the *VV*, that he does not apprehend (*upa-√labh*) anything by way of any *pramāṇa*. He subsequently, in verses 31–51, presents an extensive critique of the *pramāṇa*-s. Another work attributed to Nāgārjuna, the *Vaid*, contains, in verses 2–20, a similarly extensive critique. The central concern of the second half of this study will be, in fact, to examine and assess these critiques.

If, however, one is to understand Nāgārjuna's critiques of the *pramāṇa*-s, one needs to do two things: (i) clarify the nature of the theory of *pramāṇa*-s at which the critiques are aimed, (ii) carefully study the content of the critiques of these *pramāṇa*-s, as found in the *VV*/*VVC* and the *Vaid*/*VaidC*. I will, therefore, begin by examining the (Nyāya) theory of *pramāṇa*-s, and will then explicate the structure and mechanics of the arguments which criticize this theory, as found in the two aforementioned works attributed to Nāgārjuna. I shall, furthermore, attempt to assess these critiques from a philosophical perspective.

A helpful study of the critique of the *pramāṇa*-s and *prameya*-s in the *VV/VVC* has been provided by M. Siderits.[2] F. Tola and C. Dragonetti have given a comprehensive commentary of the argument in the *Vaid/VaidC.*[3] However, to my knowledge no study to date has examined at length the two critiques together. This would, it seems to me, be a useful endeavour. The two critiques are in many aspects similar, and consequently can help to illumine one another. However, in some significant aspects, the two critiques are quite different from one another. Hence if they are studied together they will give a complete picture of Nāgārjuna's refutation of the *pramāṇa* theory. Furthermore, I believe that there is still much philosophical work to be done in understanding and evaluating the arguments presented in both critiques. My aim in what follows is, therefore, both to make use of both critiques in order to achieve as comprehensive an understanding as is possible of Nāgārjuna's attack on the *pramāṇa*-s, and to treat these critiques with as much philosophical sensitivity as I can muster!

Notes

1 As I shall explain in more detail later, '*pramāṇa*' in early Indian epistemology (i.e. as found in the *NS*) appears to refer to knowledge itself. In later Indian epistemology, however, '*pramāṇa*' came to denote the *means* of knowledge, whereas the knowledge thus arrived at is called '*pramā*'. '*Pramāṇa*' can thus mean either the means of knowledge or knowledge. (There is a similar dual-meaning of the English term 'perception', for example (perception (*pratyakṣa*) is, as we shall see, one of the *pramāṇa*-s). One may say either that one knows the tree *by means of* perception,. or that the knowledge of the tree *is* a perception).

2 See Siderits (1980), pp. 307–335.

3 See Tola and Dragonetti (1995a), pp. 99–114.

CHAPTER SIX

The Nyāya *Pramāṇa* Theory

Introduction

The issue of (the means of) knowledge (*pramāṇa*) preoccupied Indian philosophers from very early times. Speculation about knowledge developed with the gradual accumulation of various rules for practising the art of philosophical disputation. (The connection seems natural; philosophical disputation is concerned, after all, with gaining knowledge of the truth. The issue of the conditions for and nature of such knowledge must have arisen for these disputants). Practitioners of the art of philosophical disputation are mentioned, for example, in the early epic literature, and, disparagingly, in the Pāli Canon.[1]

These rules for disputation, and the accompanying speculations about knowledge, were not associated with a single philosophical school. On the contrary, they seem to have been developed, for example, by Naiyāyikas, Buddhists, Mīmāṃsakas, Vedāntins, etc. There are several early extant versions of the rules for disputation, both Brahmanical and Buddhist.[2]

It is not clear to what extent, if at all, the very early *pramāṇa* theorists considered their theories of knowledge to have spiritual or soteriological significance. Which is to say, we do not know whether they considered their reflections on *pramāṇa*-s as such to have a direct bearing on the issue of liberation.[3] But the connection is surely there to be exploited, for it is a commonplace of much Indian philosophy/spirituality that liberation (*mokṣa*) from suffering is achieved through the transcendence of ignorance.

It is not surprising, then, that *pramāṇa* theory came to be seen as the means by which ignorance could be replaced by truth, suffering could be overcome, and liberation could be achieved. The opening verse (*NS* I, 1, 1) of the *Nyāyasūtra*, an extremely important and relatively early work in *pramāṇa* theory, states that true cognition (*tattvajñāna*) of the sixteen epistemological categories (*padārtha*), the first and most important of which is *pramāṇa*, brings about the ultimate happiness (*niḥśreyasa*). The following verse (*NS* I, 1, 2) states that the primary cause of transmigration and suffering (*duḥkha*) is ignorance, or false cognition (*mithyājñāna*). Suffering results from (re-)birth (*janma*) (and death), i.e. the process of transmigration, which is itself caused by volitional activities (*pravṛtti*). These are in turn produced by the various faults (*doṣa*) which accrue from past actions. And these faulty past actions occurred because of ignorance (*mithyājñāna*). It is, therefore, by eradicating ignorance that the entire causal process which follows from it will be destroyed, and emancipation attained. Thus emancipation from transmigration and suffering (*apavarga*) is to be achieved by replacing ignorance by knowledge. It is for this reason that an investigation of the nature of knowledge and its objects is so important. The spiritual significance of the epistemological inquiry is paramount in the *NS*.[4]

The *pramāṇa* theory which is criticized in the *Vaid/VaidC* is, without a doubt, that of the Nyāya school, as found in some redaction of the *NS*. The *Vaid* begins by enumerating sixteen epistemological categories, the first two of which are *pramāṇa* and *prameya*, a list which is found, in exactly the same order in the already-mentioned first verse of the *NS*. Nāgārjuna (or whoever is the author of the *Vaid/VaidC*) says that, as a proponent of emptiness (*stong pa nyid du smra ba= śūnyatāvādin*), the purpose of his treatise is to remove the arrogance of those (*de yi nga rgyal spang ba*) who with the arrogance of [their] knowledge of logic/reasoning (*rtog shes pa'i nga rgyal gyis*) clearly wish for disputes (*rtsod par mngon 'dod pa*).[5] He shall, as the title of his work suggests, tear the Naiyāyika position into tiny pieces.[6] Furthermore, the *Vaid/VaidC*, in presenting the arguments of the opponent, contains numerous quotations from (preserved in Tibetan translation) and references to the *NS*.[7]

The identity of the opponent, or opponents, and hence which precise *pramāṇa* theory is being criticized, in the *VV/VVC* is, however, not quite so obvious. This issue has, indeed, been the subject of some modern scholarly controversy.

Bhattacharya thinks that the opponent is a Naiyāyika, whereas Lindtner suspects that the opponent is an Ābhidharmika (of some unknown variety) following the rules of debate, which include a *pramāṇa-prameya* theory, in a Buddhist logical treatise such as the *Upāyahṛdaya*. (However, it should be noted that Kajiyama[8] has argued at length that the *Upāyahṛdaya* – which is extant only in a Chinese translation – is actually *by* Nāgārjuna!)

There is evidence for both interpretations. Thus Bhattacharya cites several examples of Naiyāyika technical terms which are used in the course of the *VV*. Lindtner, for his part, points to various passages (such as *VVC* 54, 55 and 70) which appear to indicate (in fact, according to Lindtner, only make sense if) the opponent is a Buddhist. In addition, verse 7, along with the auto-commentary, seems to assume that the opponent accepts the listed 119 *kuśaladharma*-s, which are almost certainly a list from some (unknown to us) Abhidharma school or treatise. However, Bhattacharya thinks that it could be that a Naiyāyika opponent is using the standpoint of Buddhists against Nāgārjuna, who is himself a Buddhist. In other words, the opponent, a Naiyāyika, argues here in accordance with principles which Nāgārjuna, as a Buddhist, should accept. This would be a good debating tactic because the refutation becomes more powerful if it demonstrates that Nāgārjuna contradicts the religious tradition to which he belongs. Lindtner, furthermore, points to the repeated use of the Buddhist term *'āgama'* instead of the Naiyāyika term *'śabda'*, and also to the coherence of the *VV* with the *ŚS* and the *MMK*, which are both (according to Lindtner) directed against the Ābhidharmikas. He also argues that, as Nāgārjuna devoted a special work, viz. the *Vaid*, to the controversy with the Naiyāyikas, a second work would have been redundant. This last argument does not make sense, however, because Lindtner himself has acknowledged that Nāgārjuna did write two works directed against the Abhidharma, without one of them being considered by Lindtner to be redundant. According to Lindtner's reasoning, the *VV*, if it is a third critique of Abhidharma, would be *doubly* redundant! It seems to me that if Nāgārjuna wrote (at least) two works in criticism of Abhidharma, he may well have written two critiques of Nyāya philosophy.

Another possibility, which Johnston and Kunst suggest, is that Nāgārjuna in the *VV* has more than one opponent in mind. This seems to me to be a reasonable interpretation.[9] At any rate, what is clear is that, whoever the opponent is, he accepts a theory of the *pramāṇa*-s which is in its essential aspects similar to that of the early Naiyāyikas. For the purposes of this study, therefore, I will be content to refer to Nāgārjuna's opponent as a Naiyāyika. Let us look, then, at the Nyāya *pramāṇa* theory.

In commenting on the theory of the *pramāṇa*-s in the *NS*, one must be sensitive to the fact that this text is a rather cryptic (though fairly orderly) set of aphorisms. Matilal suggests that it may have been intended as a mnemonic device rather than a self-sufficient text.[10] The significance of what is stated by these aphorisms is often far from obvious, and it was the task of many commentators over many hundreds of years to explore their meaning and possible implications. Thus, for example, the definitions of the four *pramāṇa*-s at *NS* I, 1, 4–7 have been the subject of extensive commentary and dispute. Much of this discussion post-dates the final redaction of *NS*, and also Nāgārjuna's writings. One also needs to be aware that the Nyāya *pramāṇa* theory is not a monolithic set of ideas without development or diversity. The *NS* is in fact the foundation upon which the later theorists built.

Cognition (*jñāna*)

Knowledge (*pramāṇa* in the *NS* or, in later Nyāya, *pramā* (see below)), for the Naiyāyikas, is a type of cognition (*jñāna*), and a cognition is a mental event. It is more accurate, then, to speak with Matilal of 'knowledge-events' or 'knowledge-episodes'. (As Matilal says, this conception of knowledge as a temporary mental event is at odds with the dominant western philosophical understanding which, since Plato's *Meno* (according to which knowledge has the character of 'not running away'), has described knowledge as a permanent (or at least enduring) acquisition. If I say that I know that 2+2=4, I am likely to be referrring, not to a particular mental event of correct computation (the knowledge-episode that 2+2=4) but rather to my enduring possession of the knowledge that 2+2=4 (whether or not I am actually having a cognition, i.e. a knowledge-episode, that 2+2=4)).[11]

Cognition in the *NS*

The *NS* says that cognitions are transitory (*anavasthāyin*) qualities (*guṇa*) of the self (*ātman*).[12] What one would ordinarily call a single cognition of, for example, the pot is in fact a series of very similar cognitive events – cognition of the pot at t_1, pot at t_2, etc.

Each of these transitory cognitions is described as giving a distinct apprehension (*abhivyaktagrahaṇa*) of the object. The *NS* gives the analogy of the series of flashes of light from a lamp (*pradīpārci*).[13]

Clearly, also, cognition is intentional in nature. I use the term 'intentional' here in the general sense in which it is employed by Brentano and Husserl (a use which is itself derived from the Christian scholastic tradition). Whenever there is a cognition there is something of which it is the cognition.[14]

The *NS* does not provide a systematic taxonomy of cognitions, although one can detect the beginnings of a process of categorization. The *NS* distinguishes, for example, knowledge-episodes from doubt (*saṃśaya*),[15] and confutation (*tarka*)[16] (as we shall see, according to later Nyāya philosophy, confutation produces a cognition which is not a knowledge-episode). Some reference is also made to memory (*smṛti*).[17] And the notion of erroneous cognition, is implied in the *NS* by its identification of various fallacies which can occur in reasoning.[18]

The Developed Nyāya Theory of Cognition

The later Naiyāyika theorists[19] are more explicit and present a developed categorization of cognitions (see table 2[20]). First, they divide cognitions into non-memories (*anubhava*)[21] and memories (*smṛti*). Memories can be in accord with the object (*yathārtha*) recollected or not in accord with the object (*ayathārtha*) recollected.

However, memories, even when in accord with their object, are not knowledge-episodes (*pramā*). This is because a correct memory simply reproduces a previous knowledge-episode, rather than producing a new knowledge-episode. (This was, it is worth noting, a controversial point in Indian philosophy. Some schools argued that correct memory is in fact a type of knowledge).[22]

Unlike memory, non-memories cognize the object afresh, rather than mentally reproducing the object on the basis of previous non-memories. I might perceive a fire or infer that there is a fire because there is smoke. In both cases the phenomenon of the fire, previously uncognized by me, has been apprehended. Later I may remember the fire which I perceived or inferred, but this is, according to the Naiyāyikas, a mental reproduction of my previous knowledge-episode.[23]

Although all knowledge-episodes are non-memories, not all non-memories are knowledge-episodes, however. Such non-memories which are also not knowledge-episodes are generally classified as cognitions characterized by doubt (*saṃśaya*), error (*viparyaya*), and cognitions produced by confutation (*tarka*) (all three categories are often themselves sub-divided into various types). Thus, the category 'cognitions which are non-knowledge-episodes and non-memories' is wider than the category 'erroneous cognitions', because it includes also the phenomena of doubting and cognitions produced by confutation.

Whereas erroneous cognition is not a knowledge-episode (*apramā*) because it is simply wrong, i.e. it contradicts the real nature of its object, a doubting cognition is not a knowledge-episode because it fails to arrive at a definite and explicit judgement about its object. Doubting is a state of wavering judgment (*vimarśa*), a cognition which is not able to apprehend anything definite about the object towards which it is directed. As such it is neither true not false. If I am not sure whether or not the object I perceive is a tree-stump or a man, then I have not made a judgement which can be evaluated as true or false. This is by contrast with error, which apprehends something about the object, but gets it wrong. If I perceive the tree-stump as a man, then there is a definite judgement which is false.

Confutation (*tarka*) is a form of reasoning which may occur as a result of doubt (*saṃśaya*) about which of two contradictory qualities an entity actually possesses.[24] For example, there might be doubt about whether the body is eternal or non-eternal. One of the contradictory qualities is refuted by a demonstration that its acceptance would entail an absurd consequence. If x were $y \therefore z$; $\sim z$ $\therefore$ it is not the case that x is y. If the body were eternal, it would follow that the body does not decompose. But this is absurd, because the body does decompose. Therefore, it is not the case that the body is eternal. Confutation is akin, then, to the *reductio ad absurdum*. It is argument concerned solely with identifying the fallacies (*upādhi*) in positions.[25]

The Naiyāyikas clearly came to see *tarka* as supportive (*sahakārin*) in the production of knowledge-episodes, but not as productive by itself of knowledge-episodes.[26] Why exactly this is so is not, however, very clear.

It appears to be the case that confutation cannot produce knowledge for the Naiyāyikas because it is a type of reasoning that does not conform to the rules of inference (*anumāna*). It does not have the parts of the syllogism (*avayava*). There is not a thesis (*pratijñā*), reason (*hetu*), example (*udāharaṇa*), application (*upanaya*), and conclusion (*nigamana*).[27] But why, I wonder, must all reasoning have the form of the syllogism in order to produce knowledge?

Uddyotakara seems to argue that *tarka* is not a means of knowledge because, unlike inference, it does not establish concomitance between an subject (*pakṣa*) and its property to be proved (*sādhya*). It simply refutes that the subject has a particular property. The point seems to be, then, that *tarka* does not produce any new knowledge. Used on its own it is simply cavil (*vitaṇḍā*), i.e. argumentation for the sake of finding fault rather than establishing any position. But it could be objected, I think, that if it is established that an entity does not have a property, is this not a form of new knowledge?[28]

Matilal makes the point that, for the Naiyāyikas, knowledge-episodes must be based on empirical evidence. Thus, for instance, inference (*anumāna*) must have recourse to a previously perceived familiar example (*dṛṣṭānta*). By contrast, *tarka* employs solely *a priori* arguments to deduce the fallacies or paradoxes in philosophical positions. As such, it cannot be a means of knowledge.[29] However, surely an *a priori* argument that establishes the paradoxes in philosophical positions produces the knowledge that these positions are in fact paradoxical? Furthermore, it is not clear to me that a confutation is necessarily purely *a priori*. It may, for example, depend on the contradiction between the position under scrutiny and a commonly perceived fact. For example, take the (obviously absurd) position that the body is eternal. A confutation might proceed as follows: 'If the body were eternal it would not decompose. The body is commonly perceived to decompose. Therefore, it is not eternal.'

The Nyāya position that *tarka* does not produce knowledge is, then, rather puzzling (to me, at least!). It is not surprising, I think, that some Naiyāyikas, referred to by Uddyotakara with disapproval, claimed that *tarka* is a form of inference, and hence is actually productive of knowledge.[30] The notion of *tarka*, it seems to me, requires a separate, thorough study (which I shall not undertake here).

Pramāṇa-s

Finally, the later Naiyāyikas identify four means of knowledge (*pramāṇa*) by which knowledge-episodes (*pramā*) can occur. These

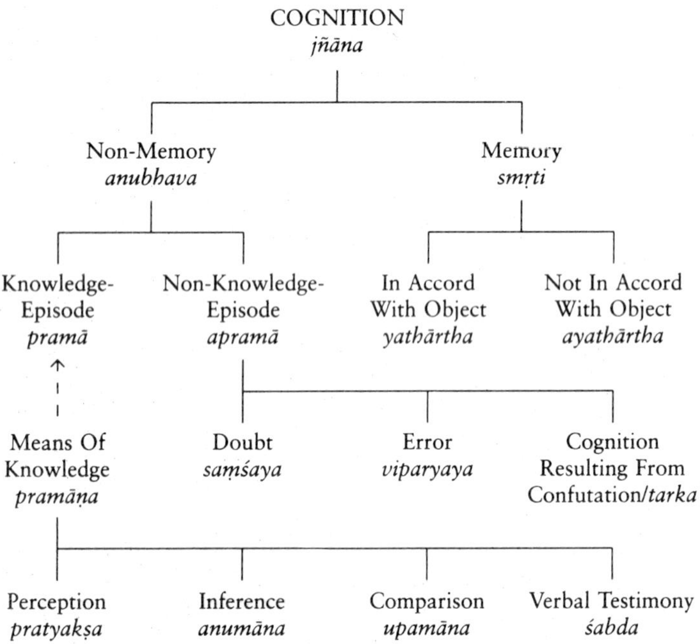

Table 2 The Developed Nyāya Theory of Cognition (*jñāna*)

means of knowledge are perception (*pratyakṣa*), inference (*anumāna*), comparison (*upamāna*), and verbal testimony (*śabda*).[31] Let me illustrate what is meant by means of a simple example.

Take the case of the platypus. How might one know the platypus? One may perceive the platypus. By means of perception one has a knowledge-episode of the platypus. One may infer that there is a platypus, because, although the platypus itself has not been perceived, certain signs of the platypus have been perceived (e.g. its tracks, its droppings, its home). By means of inference, one has a knowledge-episode of the platypus. One may know that there is a platypus on the basis of the testimony of a reliable witness. Perhaps the local platypus expert has seen the platypus, and tells one that it exists. By means of verbal testimony, one has a knowledge-episode of the platypus. Finally, one may never have perceived a platypus, but may have a knowledge-episode of it if a correct analogy is made between certain features of a familiar entity and the platypus (e.g. the platpyus has a beak like a duck, the platypus lays eggs like a chicken, etc). By means of comparison, one has a knowledge-episode of the platypus. (This is a rather simplified explanation of the four ways in which knowledge-episodes may occur, according to the Naiyāyikas, but it serves, I think, to illustrate their general point).

Note, however, that the distinction between *pramāṇa* and *pramā* is not present in the *NS*. The *NS* does not distinguish between the means of knowledge and the resulting knowledge. (It does not, for example, contrast perception in the sense of the process by which one arrives at knowledge, with the perception which is the result of such a perceptual process). A *pramāṇa*, according to the *NS*, is simply a knowledge-episode.[32] This point is especially important for the present study, because the *pramāṇa* theory which Nāgārjuna criticizes is that found in the *NS*. In explaining Nāgārjuna's critique, then, my translation of '*pramāṇa*' will generally be 'knowledge-episode'.

Prameya-s

When a cognition which is not a memory actually corresponds to its object, then it is a knowledge-episode (*pramāṇa* or, in later Nyāya, *pramā*). Knowledge-episodes might be described as truth-hitting (following Matilal[33]) non-memories. But what is it that these knowledge-episodes hit? What is the nature of the objects, i.e. the *prameya*-s, which are correctly apprehended by a knowledge-episode?

NS I, 1, 9 identifies various types of *prameya*-s (a very motley list, I might add), viz. the self (*ātman*), the body (*śarīra*), the senses (*indriya*), objects of the senses (*artha*), cognitions (*buddhi*), mind (*manas*), activity (*pravṛtti*), faults (*doṣa*), transmigration (*pretyabhāva*), consequences (*phala*), suffering (*duḥkha*), and emancipation (*apavarga*),[34] which are then explained individually.

Vātsyāyana, in his commentary on this verse, elaborates on this apparently peculiar collection. He says that the list is not exhaustive, and the items mentioned are those objects of knowledge-episodes which are most relevant to the pursuit of emancipation from transmigration. There are, Vātsyāyana says, many other examples or instances of *prameya*-s. And all objects of knowledge-episodes, Vātsyāyana continues, fall under the six ontological categories (*padārtha*) found in the *Vaiśeṣikasūtra*, viz. substance (*dravya*), quality (*guṇa*), motion (*karman*), universal (*sāmānya*, *jāti*), inherence (*samavāya*), and individuators/particulars (*viśeṣa*).[35] (There seems to have been, from early on, a close relationship between the Nyāya and Vaiśeṣika schools. Dreyfus[36] describes the Vaiśeṣika as a 'sister school' of the Nyāya. Potter[37] writes that 'although there were occasional points of disagreement, Nyāya and Vaiśeṣika have from the first considered themselves as mutually supportive, Nyāya specializing in epistemology and methodology, Vaiśeṣika in metaphysics.')

Objects of knowledge are substances, qualities, motions, particulars, universals, and inherence (or combinations of these six categories). This shows that for Vātsyāyana the *NS*'s epistemology of *pramāṇa*-s and *prameya*-s is to be understood in conjunction with the Vaiśeṣika metaphysics. And Vātsyāyana's commentary being the earliest which is extant, it seems reasonable to take him as authoritative on this point. The Nyāya *pramāṇa* theory, understood in the context of this Vaiśeṣika metaphysics, is a form of philosophical realism.

Nyāya Realism

'Realism', it must be admitted, is a notoriously vague and ambiguous term. As Dreyfus points out,[38] the Naiyāyikas are realists in three senses: (i) they accept the reality of external objects, i.e. objects which have existence independently of the cognition of them, (ii) they advocate the existence of universals which are not linguistic or mental objects. In other words, some of the external objects which exist independently of the cognition of them are universals, and (iii) they attempt to abide by the dictates of common-sense in their philosophical explanations. This appears to mean that the Naiyāyikas think that their philosophical theories should be compatible with ordinary beliefs, such as the belief that the external world exists, and that this world is knowable by means of perception and reasoning, etc.

I am employing the term 'realism' in the present context primarily in sense (i). The Naiyāyikas accept the mind-independent existence of many[39] of the entities which fall under the ontological categories of substance, qualities, motions, universals (making them realist in sense (ii)), inherence, and particulars. Thus, knowledge-episodes are cognitions of objects, be they substances, qualities, motions, etc (or combinations of these), which often exist independently of the mind, i.e. whether or not they are actually cognized.

The Nyāya epistemology's starting point is then, it is fair to say, the common-sense intuition that knowledge is a matter of the correct apprehension of objects which are independent from cognition. Thus, knowledge is a matter of cognitions mirroring, so to speak, a state of affairs.

A perception of an object, 'red pot', for example, is a perception of a quality 'red' in which inheres the universal 'redness', and a substance 'pot' in which inheres the universal 'potness'. These qualities, substances, universals, etc of external objects occur whether or not cognitions correctly apprehend them. Perceptual knowledge may therefore be described as an undistorted apprehension of its object as it is in itself.

Similarly, inference is the process of reasoning about the entities which have been perceived in order to draw correct conclusions about their imperceptible properties. I see smoke on the hill, and I know that smoke is invariably concomitant with fire. I therefore have a knowledge-episode that there is fire on the hill, even though I cannot perceive it. Again, the process is one of mirroring and accurate apprehension of what occurs independently of the cognition. There is a fire to be apprehended by an inference, and this fire exists as a substance, in which a universal 'fireness' inheres, with its qualities, in which inhere the appropriate universals (for example, 'hotness', 'brightness') whether or not the cogniton of it occurs. Reality is there to be contacted, as it were.

So too with verbal testimony and comparison. What is apprehended by relying on a reliable report by another person as well as the unfamiliar entity which is known by means of an accurate comparison with a familiar entity (*dṛṣṭānta*) exist independently of and undistorted by the knowing subject.

At *Vaid*/*VaidC* 5, the Naiyāyika opponent compares knowledge-episodes to a balance (*srang*). Just as the balance weighs its objects, so too the *pramāṇa*-s apprehend their objects. *NS* II,1,16 also compares the *pramāṇa* to the balance (*tulā*). This is a natural comparison to make in Sanskrit, given that the verbal root *pra-√mā*, from which the terms '*pramāṇa*' and '*prameya*' are derived, means both 'to measure' and 'to know'.[40] The Tibetan translation of *pramāṇa* (*tshad ma*, 'measure') and *prameya* (*gzhal bya*, 'what is to be weighed') is obviously intended to preserve the Sanskrit etymology.[41] Further, as Tola and Dragonetti note, the Sanskrit root *√tul*, from which the word '*tulā*' is derived means both 'to weigh' and 'to ponder' or 'to examine'.[42] There is, then, a strong semantic affinity between the words '*tulā*' and '*pramāṇa*'. Furthermore, it is evident that there is a definite similarity between the activity of weighing and that of knowing. In both cases there is an assessment of an object, and the issue of accuracy is of vital importance.

The analogy, I think, expresses the Nyāya realism. A balance is thought to be accurate when it records accurately the weight of the weighed object. And it is generally understood that to weigh the object accurately means that the balance in question has recorded the actual weight of the object, i.e. the weight of the object as it exists independently of the weighing process. The accurate balance in no way distorts the weight recorded. The weight recorded *corresponds* to the balance-independent weight of the object. Similarly, a knowledge-episode accurately apprehends the object known as it exists independently of the knowledge-episode. There is no distortion by the knowledge-episode of the object known. The knowledge-episode *corresponds* to the mind-independent nature of its object.

I shall argue that it is precisely this realism which is the principal object of Nāgārjuna's attack in his critiques of the *pramāṇa*-s and the *prameya*-s. Nāgārjuna is directly opposed to the Nyāya theory that there are knowledge-episodes which apprehend mind-independent objects. According to Nāgārjuna, given that all entities have conceptually constructed existence (*prajñaptisat*), there are no mind-independent entities for knowledge-episodes to apprehend. Let us turn now to Nāgārjuna's critiques.

Notes

1 See Matilal (1977), p. 76.

2 See Matilal (1977), pp. 76–77.

3 See Potter (1977), p. 20, Williams (1978) p. 280.

4 Potter (1977), p. 20 notes, however, that, unlike in later Naiyāyika writings, the epistemological and soteriological elements of the *NS* 'only sit uneasily side by side'. This suggests, then, that the integration of these elements was recent and incomplete.

5 *Vaid* 1.

6 The Sanskrit word '*vaidalya*' (Tibetan, *zhib mo rnam par 'thag pa*) means 'tearing to pieces', so that '*Vaidalyaprakaraṇa*' is a *karmadhāraya* compound meaning the 'Treatise (*prakaraṇa*, Tibetan, *rab tu byed pa*) which is the Tearing to Pieces'. What it tears to pieces are, of course, the epistemological categories of the Naiyāyikas. See Tola and Dragonetti (1995a), p. 4.

7 For a thorough study of the references to and quotations from the *NS* in the *Vaid* and *VaidC*, see Tola and Dragonetti (1995a), pp. 99–156, 179–201.
8 See Kajiyama (1991).
9 See Bhattacharya (1978), p. 89, 99–100, Lindtner (1982), p. 71, and Johnston and Kunst in Bhattacharya (1978), p. 40.
10 Matilal (1977), p. 53.
11 See Matilal (1986), pp. 97–101.
12 See, for example, *NS* III, 2, 20, in which an opponent objects to the Naiyāyika claim that cognition is a quality of the self (*ātmaguṇa*). For the transitoriness of cognitions, see *NS* III, 2, 44–45.
13 *NS*, III, 2, 43–45.
14 The equivalent term used in later Nyāya philosophy is *viśayatā*, which Monier-Williams (1899), p. 997 defines as 'the character or condition of being an object or having anything for an object, the relation between an object and the knowledge ot it'. See Matilal (1968), p. 8
15 *NS* I, 1, 23.
16 *NS* I, 1, 40.
17 *NS*, III, 2, 25.
18 See *NS* I, 2, and *NS* V, 2.
19 My account here of the 'later theorists' largely relies on Chatterjee (1978), pp. 20–48. His interpretation is based on texts (much later than the *NS*) such as the *Saptapadārthī*, the *Tarkasaṃgraha*, the *Tattvadīpikā*, the *Tarkabhāṣā*, the *Nyāyamañjarī*, etc. See also Potter (1977), pp. 154–156.
20 This table is inspired by Chatterjee (1978), p. 22, and Potter (1977), p. 154.
21 The term '*anubhava*' seems to be rather resistant to adequate translation in this context. Monier-Williams (1899), p. 36 gives 'perception, apprehension, fruition; understanding; impression on the mind not derived from memory; experience, knowledge derived from personal observation or experiment; result, consequence.' Chatterjee (1978), p. 20 translates the term as 'presentation'. Potter (1977), p. 154 prefers 'presentative apprehension.' I settle for 'non-memory' because the other alternatives seem rather obscure and/or inaccurate.
22 Chatterjee (1978), p. 27, says that the Vaiśeṣikas considered memory to be a distinct form of knowledge, as did the Jainas.
23 Chatterjee (1978), pp. 26–28.
24 See *NSBh* I, 1, 40, Jhā (trans.) (1984), p. 446.
25 See Potter (1977), pp. 203–207.
26 *NSBh* I, 1, 40, Jhā (trans.) (1984), p. 448. See Chatterjee (1978), pp. 44–45.
27 On the members of the Nyāya inference, see Potter (1977), pp. 179–189. Chatterjee (1978), pp. 274–277.
28 See *NSV* I, 1, 40, Jhā (trans.) (1984), pp. 454–458. On *vitaṇḍā* see Potter (1977), p. 208.
29 Matilal (1986), pp. 78–79.
30 *NSV* I, 1, 40, Jhā (trans.) (1984), p. 454. Matilal (1986), p. 79 notes that the Jainas accepted *tarka* as an independent means of knowledge.
31 Indian philosophers, of course, keenly debated the number and definitions of the *pramāṇa*-s. The Cārvākas, for example, admitted only perception as a *pramāṇa*. (In fact, the *Tattvopaplavasiṃha*, a Cārvāka text from the seventh or eighth century by Jayarāśi Bhaṭṭa, does not even accept that perception (*pratyakṣa*) is a means of knowledge. This appears to be a significant

epistemological shift from the early Cārvāka position. See Franco (1983), pp. 147–166). Some Buddhists, such as Dignāga, rejected comparison and verbal testimony as distinct *pramāṇa*-s. See Hayes (1988). Other schools added different, distinct *pramāṇa*-s (for example the disputed phenomenon of memory). On the number and types of *pramāṇa*-s accepted by the various schools of Indian philosophy, see Hattori (1968), pp. 78–79.

32 See Shastri (1964), pp. 424–427, and Williams (manuscript 1), p. 12.

33 Matilal (1986), pp. 135–140.

34 *NS*, I, 1, 9.

35 *NSBh*, I, 1, 9 (translation by Jhā (1984), p. 212). For the Vaiśeṣika ontological categories, see *VS*, 1. See also Potter (1977), pp. 43–145.

36 Dreyfus (1997), pp. 52–53

37 Potter (1977), p. 12.

38 Dreyfus (1997), p. 54.

39 While *many* of the entities which fall under these categories are said to have mind-independent reality, not *all* enitities have for the Naiyāyikas such mind-independent reality. For example, many qualities (*guṇa*), such as hatred, effort, pleasure, pain are of a mental nature. See Potter (1977), pp. 112–128. Also, as Potter notes, the Naiyāyikas 'adhere to certain parsimonious practices' with regard to universals. The category of universals was seen, by Śivāditya's time, to contain both mind-independent universals (*jāti*) and mind-imposed universals (*upādhi*). In order to qualify as mind-independent, a universal had to pass a number of tests. For example, a universal must have more than one instance. Further, a universal cannot be accepted as mind-independent if such acceptance would lead to an infinite regress (for example, the universal 'universalhood' is thereby ruled out). A number of other tests was also enumerated. See Potter (1977), pp. 135–136. However, it must be emphasized that these tests were only developed many centuries after the *NS*.

40 See Monier-Williams (1899), p. 685.

41 See Chandra Das (1970), p. 1023, 1079.

42 See Tola and Dragonetti (1995a), p. 181.

CHAPTER SEVEN

Nāgārjuna's Non-Apprehension of Entities

At *VV/VVC* 30, Nāgārjuna proclaims that he does not apprehend any entity by means of any *pramāṇa*. What does Nāgārjuna mean when he makes this claim? I shall, in the present chapter, offer an interpretation which understands Nāgārjuna's statement as a rejection of the Nyāya philosophical realism described in the previous chapter.

The Opponent's Objection at *VV/VVC* 5–6

Nāgārjuna's statement is actually a response to an objection raised by his opponent at *VV/VVC* 5–6. Nāgārjuna has stated, the opponent notes, that all entities are empty (*śūnyāḥ sarvabhāvāḥ*). But in order to attribute emptiness to entities, Nāgārjuna must first apprehend them by means of some knowledge-episode (*pramāṇa*), be it a perception (*pratyakṣa*), inference (*anumāna*), verbal testimony (*āgama*) or comparison (*upamāna*). However, the opponent continues, the knowledge-episode is itself an entity (*bhāva*) and is thus, according to Nāgārjuna's statement, itself empty. Therefore, there are for Nāgārjuna no *pramāṇa*-s by which entities to be negated, i.e. made known as empty, are apprehended. And thus his position that all entities are empty is not tenable.

Note that here the opponent is not arguing that the objects of a knowledge-episode must exist, i.e. be non-empty, in order to be negated (although he later, in a separate objection, makes this point too[1]). Nor is he making the point that the negation which makes known the emptiness of all entities itself is an entity and must, as empty, be unable to negate (although, again, he also makes this point in another objection[2]).

Rather, the opponent says that the entities to be negated must *first* (*tāvat*) be apprehended by a knowledge-episode in order subsequently to be negated. One cannot, for example, negate, i.e. make known the emptiness of, the pot unless one has correctly cognized the pot which one is going to negate (for otherwise one would not know what it is that one is to negate!). The knowledge-episode which apprehends the pot to be negated must itself exist. (A non-existent knowledge-episode cannot apprehend anything). But the implication of Nāgārjuna's own assertion of universal emptiness is, the opponent contends, that there can be no knowledge-episode which exists in order to apprehend the entities to be negated.

Nāgārjuna's Response at *VV/VVC* 30

It is obvious that the opponent has here taken Nāgārjuna's assertion of universal emptiness to mean that nothing whatsoever exists. Thus, if nothing whatsoever exists, then there can be no knowledge-episode which apprehends the entities of which non-existence (emptiness) is subsequently to be made known. However, it is clear that Nāgārjuna's response at other points in the text (for example, at *VV/VVC* 22) to this accusation of nihilism is that the opponent has misunderstood his assertion of universal emptiness. That all entities are empty does not entail that they do not exist; rather, it means that they have an existence without *svabhāva*.

It is in this context, I think, that Nāgārjuna's reply to the opponent's objection should perhaps be understood. Nāgārjuna responds, at *VV/VVC* 30, that the opponent's criticism (*upālambha*) would indeed be correct if Nāgārjuna claimed to apprehend (*upa-√labh*) any entity on the basis of which apprehension he affirmed (*pra-√vṛt*) or denied (*ni-√vṛt*) something about it. In fact, however, Nāgārjuna says that he does not apprehend anything by means of any *pramāṇa*, and thus he neither affirms nor denies anything about any entity. Therefore, the criticism does not apply to him.

Nāgārjuna's point here is certainly obscure. However, it seems plausible that Nāgārjuna means that he does not apprehend any *svabhāva*-endowed entity. Thus, he does not affirm the existence with *svabhāva* of entities. But neither does he deny that entities exist. 'Deny' here would thus have the meaning of asserting the contrary of existence with *svabhāva*, i.e. total non-existence. Nāgārjuna intends to tread the celebrated Middle Way (*madhyamā pratipat*) by advocating the existence without *svabhāva* of entities, as opposed to the extremes of affirmation of existence with *svabhāva* or denial, i.e. complete non-existence.[3]

In which case, according to Nāgārjuna, it is a knowledge-episode which exists but without *svabhāva* which apprehends entities which exist but without *svabhāva*. It is a negation (of the *svabhāva* of entities), which exists but without *svabhāva*, which makes known that these entities do not have *svabhāva*. This is the true implication of Nāgārjuna's teaching of universal emptiness.

If, by contrast, for Nāgārjuna there were an apprehension (by means of a knowledge-episode) of entities, and then there were a negation which makes known that entities do not exist at all, then the opponent's criticism would be correct. For how could a knowledge-episode – which, being itself an entity, would not exist at all – apprehend entities in order that they may subsequently be the object of such a negation? (Not to mention the problem of how entities which do not exist at all could be apprehended, and how a negation of the existence of all entities – which, being itself an entity, would not exist at all – could make known that entities do not exist at all).

This, then, is how I interpret Nāgārjuna's reply to his opponent. But what does Nāgārjuna mean when he says that all entities exist but without *svabhāva*? Here one must recollect my discussion in chapter 4. The absence of *svabhāva* of entities does not mean simply that entities dependently originate. On the contrary, seen in the context of the Abhidharma, the absence of *svabhāva* of entities means for Nāgārjuna that entities have conceptually constructed existence (*prajñaptisat*), i.e. they originate entirely in dependence upon the conceptualizing mind. Thus, there are not really any entities which dependently originate in a mind-independent way.

So, when Nāgārjuna says that he does not have any knowledge-episodes of entities with *svabhāva*, he means that he does not have any knowledge of entities which exist in a mind-independent, more-than-conceptually constructed, way. But this is not to say that Nāgārjuna means that he does not know whether or not there are entities which exist mind-independently (which would be a sceptical position). On the contrary, Nāgārjuna clearly means that he does not have knowledge-episodes of mind-independent entities because he knows that there *are* no mind-independent entities (see chapter 2 for further discussion of this point).

Understood in this way, then, Nāgārjuna's claim that he does not apprehend anything by means of any *pramāṇa* is essentially a rejection of Nyāya realism. For the Naiyāyika: (i) there is a mind-independent reality, and, furthermore, (ii) there are correct cognitions (*pramāṇa*-s, or, later, *pramā*-s) which apprehend this mind-independent reality. Nāgārjuna does not accept (i), and consequently he does not accept (ii) either.

Notes

1 See *VV/VVC* 11–12.
2 See *VV/VVC* 17–19.
3 For Nāgārjuna's advocacy of the Middle Way between existence (with *svabhāva*) and non-existence, see *MMK* XV, 7, XXIV, 18, *AS* 22.

CHAPTER EIGHT

Mutually Dependent Existence

Nāgārjuna's Position

In the *VaidC*, Nāgārjuna makes the following statement about the *pramāṇa*-s and *prameya*-s:

> ... *gzhal bya yod na tshad ma ni tshad ma nyid du 'gyur zhing/ tshad ma yod na yang gzhal bya ni gzhal bya nyid du 'gyur ro/*
>
> ... when the object of knowledge exists, the knowledge-episode occurs as the knowledge-episode, and, also, when the knowledge-episode exists, the object of the knowledge occurs as the object of knowledge. (*VaidC* 2).

Nāgārjuna's point, it seems, is that *pramāṇa* and *prameya* cannot exist independently of one another. The *VaidC* states here that the *pramāṇa* (*tshad ma*) can only exist (*yod*) when it has a *prameya* (*gzhal bya*) to know, and the *prameya* is only a *prameya* when there is a *pramāṇa* which apprehends it. *VaidC* 2 goes on to say that the *pramāṇa* and *prameya* thus establish (*grub pa*) one another's existence. They 'acquire their nature in mutual dependence' (*phan tshun ltos nas bdag nyid thob pa 'gyur pa*), Nāgārjuna says. The *pramāṇa* and the *prameya* are ontologically mutually dependent. Which is to say that the existence of the *pramāṇa* is by means of the *prameya*, and the existence of the *prameya* is by means of the *pramāṇa*. They are mutually established in the sense that they cannot exist without one another.

Mutual Dependence and *niḥsvabhāva*

But what precisely is being claimed in this case? It seems unproblematic that the *pramāṇa* and *prameya* are mutually dependent in one sense. A knowledge-episode is always intentional, i.e. it is always knowledge of something, and an object insofar as it is known is always the object of a knowledge-episode. It makes no sense to speak of knowledge without something known, and something known without knowledge of it! But, I am inclined to ask, so what? This observation on the part of Nāgārjuna seems to be an unremarkable truism.

Presumably, Nāgārjuna intends to establish something more significant than this. Thus, at *Vaid/VaidC* 3, Nāgārjuna argues that the mutually dependent existence of the *pramāṇa*-s and *prameya*-s is incompatible with their possession of *svabhāva* (*rang gi ngo bo*). *Pramāṇa*-s and *prameya*-s are, Nāgārjuna also says, not self-established (*rang las grub pa ma yin*), which is here, I think, the same as saying that they are *niḥsvabhāva*.[1]

Nāgārjuna makes what appears to be the same point, although employing the terms '*jñāna*' and '*jñeya*' (which I translate here as 'knowledge' and 'object of knowledge' (they might also be translated as 'cognition' and 'object of cognition', however)) rather than '*pramāṇa*' and '*prameya*', in the *LS*,

> *ajñāyamānaṃ na jñeyaṃ vijñānaṃ tadvinā na ca/*
> *tasmātsvabhāvato na sto jñānajñeye tvamūcivān//*

> There is no object of knowledge without [it] being known, and there is not knowledge without that [object of knowledge]. Therefore, you have said that knowledge and the object of knowledge do not exist with *svabhāva*. (*LS* 10)[2]

One finds the same claim – this time using the terms '*pramāṇa*' and '*prameya*' – also stated by Candrakīrti:

> *tāni ca parasparapekṣyā sidhyanti – satsu pramāṇeṣu prameyārthāḥ, satsu prameyeṣvartheṣu pramāṇāni/ no tu khalu svābhāvikī pramāṇaprameyayoḥ siddhiriti/*

> And those [*pramāṇa*-s and *prameya*-s] are established by means of mutual dependence. When there are *pramāṇa*-s there are objects which are *prameya*-s [and] when there are objects which are *prameya*-s there are *pramāṇa*-s. But

certainly there is not establishment by way of *svabhāva* of the *pramāṇa* and *prameya*. (*PP* 75).

One must recollect that, seen in the Abhidharma context, the absence of *svabhāva* of entities means that they have conceptually constructed existence (*prajñaptisat*). Perhaps, then, Nāgārjuna means that the object which is known (and not simply its 'being known') and the knowledge-episode of it have conceptually constructed existence – i.e. they exist without *svabhāva* – because of their mutual dependence. In which case Nāgārjuna's attack is on the Nyāya realism which I described in chapter 6. The Naiyāyikas claim that there is a mind-independent world of entities which can be correctly apprehended by cognitions (*pramāṇa*-s). It is precisely this contention which Nāgārjuna opposes with his assertion that *pramāṇa*-s and *prameya*-s do not have *svabhāva*.

A Critical Analysis of Nāgārjuna's Position

But, if this is Nāgārjuna's intention, then surely his argument is faulty. He has given no justification for the claim that the object which is known (as opposed to its 'being known') is dependent upon the knowledge-episode. It is certainly true that a tree, for example, in order to be known is dependent on a knowledge-episode. But from this it does not follow that the tree itself is dependent for its existence on the knowledge of it! It seems quite plausible, in fact, that objects of knowledge are (in many cases at least) mind-independent entities, i.e. entities which exist with *svabhāva*. Simply to assert that objects of knowledge (trees, tables, etc) are conceptual constructs – i.e. exist without *svabhāva*, because they are mind-dependent – is in no way to establish that they are conceptual constructs. The *prameya* – understood as the object of knowledge (rather than its 'being known') – is quite possibly (in many cases) not dependent for its existence upon the knowing mind.

Furthermore, if a knowledge-episode is dependent upon the object which is known (*prameya*), in the sense that the *pramāṇa* must have an intentional object, it does not follow that the knowledge-episode is a conceptual construct, i.e. exists without *svabhāva*. It is one thing to say that a knowledge-episode exists in dependence upon its object (which does seem to be true, in the sense that a knowledge-episode, in order to exist, must be knowledge of something); it is quite another thing to say that the knowledge-episode is a conceptual construct. But Nāgārjuna appears to argue that because the knowledge-episode is dependent for its existence upon its object, therefore the knowledge-episode is a conceptual construct, i.e. does not have *svabhāva*! The fallacy here, I think, is the move from dependently originating existence to existence without *svabhāva*. It does not follow that an entity which dependently originates must have conceptually constructed existence (*prajñaptisat*).[3]

At any rate, what could it possibly mean to say that a knowledge-episode is a conceptual construct? I think that I can at least make sense of the notion that objects of knowledge are conceptual constructs (although it seems like a pretty implausible theory to me). But how can a *pramāṇa* be a conceptual construct? I accept that a knowledge-episode which spans some time might be made up of a number of momentary knowledge-episodes (as the Naiyāyikas themselves admit, see chapter 6), and might, perhaps, be described as conceptually constructed out of these momentary knowledge-episodes. (Though I am not sure that one needs even to accept this. The knowledge-episode which spans some time might exist in dependence upon its parts – i.e. the momentary knowledge-episodes – without necessarily being a *conceptual construction* on the basis of these parts). But what might it mean to say that these momentary knowledge-episodes are themselves conceptually constructed? Conceptually constructed out of what and by whom? So, I find the notion that *pramāṇa*-s lack *svabhāva*, i.e. have conceptually constructed existence, rather puzzling.

There is, however, one way, by employing the notion of 'conceptual construct' in a different sense, in which I can perhaps make sense of Nāgārjuna's claim that the *pramāṇa* is a conceptual construct. If, as Nāgārjuna claims, the object of knowledge (and not just its 'being known') is a mind-dependent entity, i.e. is *niḥsvabhāva*, then it is not in fact the case that there are any knowledge-episodes which apprehend mind-independent entities. But the Naiyāyika position is that knowledge-episodes do apprehend entities as they exist mind-independently. In which case, given the dependence of the object of knowledge on the knowledge-episode which apprehends it, the *pramāṇa* – understood as a cognition which correctly apprehends a mind-independent state of affairs – is, according to Nāgārjuna, a *fiction* (i.e. a conceptual construct). There are in fact no such knowledge-episodes which apprehend mind-independent objects, because the objects of knowledge-episodes are dependent for their existence upon the knowledge-episodes of which they are the objects. Thus, it is not simply that the object of knowledge – construed as a mind-independent entity – does not exist, i.e. is a fiction; also the knowledge-episode – construed as apprehending such a mind-independent entity – is equally fictitious.

The problem with this explanation is, however, as I have already explained, that Nāgārjuna has given us no good reason to accept that objects of knowledge actually are not mind-independent entities. In which case, Nāgārjuna has given us no good reason to accept that knowledge-episodes which are thought to apprehend such mind-independent objects are simply fictions.

So, in summary, it is true that a *pramāṇa* is dependent for its existence upon the *prameya* (given that, in order to exist, the *pramāṇa* must have an object of which it is the knowledge-episode). But this certainly does not establish that the *pramāṇa* does not have *svabhāva*, i.e. has conceptually constructed existence (*prajñaptisat*). It is true that the *prameya* is dependent upon the *pramāṇa*, in the uninteresting sense that an object which is known is necessarily dependent for its 'being known' upon the knowledge of it! But (in many cases) it is far from clear that the object which is known (by contrast with its 'being known') is dependent for its existence upon the knowledge-episode of it. Nāgārjuna has not demonstrated his highly counter-intuitive claim that an object of knowledge lacks *svabhāva*, i.e. arises as a conceptual construct created by the mind. He has thus not demonstrated either that the knowledge-episode, construed (with the Naiyāyikas) as a cognition which correctly apprehends a mind-independent object, is a fiction.

Notes

1 Nāgārjuna goes on to argue, at *Vaid/VaidC* 4, that an entity which exists cannot possess dependence. I take Nāgārjuna's point to be that an entity which exists with *svabhāva* cannot be dependent. He gives the example of the pot (*bum pa*) which, if it existed (with *svabhāva*), could not be dependent on the clay (*'jim pa*) and so on for its existence. (Why not, I wonder? It seems quite plausible that a pot or whatever might exist with *svabhāva* (i.e. as more than a conceptual construct) and yet depend for its existence on other entities such as clay). Nāgārjuna then says that an entity which does not exist cannot be dependent. It is ridiculous to claim that a non-existent, like the hare's horn (*ri bong gi rwa*), can be dependent on anything! Finally, an entity which both exists (with

svabhāva) and does not exist could not be dependent because both faults (*nyes pa gnyi ga*) previously mentioned would apply to it. Presumably the purpose of this (very obscure and unconvincing) argument at *Vaid/VaidC* 4 is to establish that dependently originating entities exist but they exist without *svabhāva*. There is a pot, for example, which exists (it is not a non-existent like the hare's horn), and depends on the clay, etc, but this pot does not have *svabhāva*.

2 See also *AS* 50, 'Just as when there is knowledge [there is] the object of knowledge, so also when there is the object of knowledge [there is] knowledge. When it is understood that both do not arise [with *svabhāva*?], then what exists [with *svabhāva*?]?' (*jñāne sati yathā jñeyaṃ jñeye jñānaṃ tathā sati/ yatrobhayamanutpannamiti buddhaṃ tadāsti kim//*).

3 See here also *ŚS* 56–57b, 'Depending on inner and outer sense-bases (*āyatana*) [i.e. the sense organs and the sensed objects], consciousness arises. Therefore, consciousness does not exist. It is empty like a mirage, an illusion. Consciousness does not exist, because it arises depending on the object of consciousness ... ' (*nang dang phyi yi skye mched la/ brten nas rnam par shes pa 'byung/ de lta bas na rnam shes med/ smig rgyu sgyu ma bzhin du stong// rnam shes rnam shes bya brten nas/ 'byung bas yod min shes pa dang* ...). Again, however, I fail to see why the fact that consciousness (*rnam par shes pa*) depends on its objects (and sense organs) in order to exist should entail that consciousness is empty (of *svabhāva*), i.e. a conceptual construct.

CHAPTER NINE

The Attack on Validation: Introduction

Nāgārjuna's Challenge to the Realist

At *VV/VVC* 31 Nāgārjuna challenges his realist opponent. The opponent claims, Nāgārjuna says, that the establishment of the variety of objects (*teṣāṃ teṣāṃ prasiddhirarthānām*) occurs through knowledge-episodes (*pramāṇataḥ*). But, Nāgārjuna asks, how can there be for you (the opponent) the establishment (*prasiddhi*) of the knowledge-episodes themselves?

The word 'establishment' (*prasiddhi*), derived from the verbal root √*sidh*, here means 'validation' or 'proof'.[1] I take Nāgārjuna's point to be that the opponent claims that he has knowledge-episodes of *svabhāva*-endowed entities, i.e. he apprehends these entities by means of perception, inference, verbal testimony, and comparison. Nāgārjuna's question is, then, how can you prove that these knowledge-episodes really do apprehend entities with *svabhāva*? That is, Nāgārjuna is in effect saying, 'prove to me that knowledge-episodes really are knowledge-episodes of *svabhāva*-endowed entities!'

Nāgārjuna's challenge should perhaps be seen in the context of the Nyāya theory of validation which he is probably criticizing. For the Naiyāyikas, the validation of *pramāṇa*-s means proof that these *pramāṇa*-s do correctly apprehend the *prameya*-s. And to apprehend correctly the *prameya*-s means to apprehend them as they exist independently of the knowledge-episode which apprehends them. As I have explained, knowledge for the Naiyāyikas is a matter of a knowledge-episode mirroring a mind-independent state of affairs. Thus, to validate a *pramāṇa* means to prove that it actually does mirror such a mind-independent reality. I have a perception of water, for example. How is it to be proved, Nāgārjuna is asking, that this perception actually apprehends water which exists in a mind-independent way?

The Purpose of Nāgārjuna's Attack

Nāgārjuna proceeds to examine and refute in turn the various ways in which *pramāṇa*-s themselves might be established (*siddha*) if they were to apprehend *prameya*-s with *svabhāva*. Nāgārjuna's intention, it appears, is to refute all of the possible ways in which *pramāṇa*-s which apprehend entities with *svabhāva* might be proved, thus undermining his opponent's pretensions to knowledge of *prameya*-s with *svabhāva*. The opponent says that he has knowledge of entities with *svabhāva*, but, Nāgārjuna contends, there can be no proof of this knowledge.

But note here – and this is very important – that there is a distinction between a knowledge-episode, i.e. a correct cognition, and the proof/validation of this knowledge-episode. A *pramāṇa* is a knowledge-episode in the sense of a correct cognition of an entity. Thus, a *pramāṇa* does not include the demonstration or justification that one's cognition is correct. (Contrast this notion of knowledge with the notion of knowledge as 'justified true belief', which I have employed in Chapter 2). A correct cognition is correct whether or not its correctness has been demonstrated. Which is to say that a *pramāṇa* is a *pramāṇa* whether or not it has been proved to be so.[2]

For example, I have a correct cognition of water in the distance. But, unless I take correct cognitions to be self-evident (a view which runs into difficulty, I think, because sometimes we think that our cognitions are correct when in fact they are not), I do not as of yet *know* that this cognition is correct. To gain this further knowledge, I would have to prove/validate in some way that the cognition is correct. For example, I could look again, I could ask other people what they see, I could throw pebbles at the object – do they make splashing noises? I could approach the object and taste or feel it. Such actions might constitute a proof/validation of my original correct cognition. (At precisely what point/under what conditions my cognition is proved to be correct is of course controversial). Note that the cognition was correct prior to the proof of its correctness.

In some cases one has knowledge-episodes, i.e. correct cognitions, and yet they are *never* proved/validated. I may have a correct cognition of water in the distance. As of yet I do not know that this cognition is correct. If I then walk away and never consider my cognition of the water in the distance again, I will never know whether or not it was correct. Yet, despite the fact that my cognition of the water in the distance was never proved/validated, this cognition was correct. One may know without knowing, on the basis of some proof, that the knowledge-episode in question was in fact a case of knowledge. So, one must be careful to distinguish (i) the *existence* of the knowledge-episode from (ii) the *proof* that it is a knowledge-episode. (i) can occur without (ii).

There is another important distinction to be made here..Even if it can be demonstrated that – not only can there be no *proof* that knowledge-episodes apprehend mind-independent entities but also – there *are* no knowledge-episodes of mind-independent entities, this does not mean that there *are* no mind-independent entities. It just means that, if there are mind-independent entities, they are entirely unknown. Thus, there are three distinct propositions:

(i) It cannot be proved that there are knowledge-episodes of mind-independent entities.
(ii) There are no knowledge-episodes of mind-independent entities.
(iii) There are no mind-independent entities.

It does not follow that if (i) therefore (ii) and (iii). It would appear, however, that Nāgārjuna's strategy is to establish only (i). Does Nāgārjuna himself think that, by establishing (i), he establishes (ii) and (iii)? It is impossible to be sure, of course. However, I suspect that Nāgārjuna (wrongly) thinks that the demonstration of (i) does entail (ii) and, most importantly, (iii). That is, perhaps Nāgārjuna erroneously thinks that the demonstration that there is no proof that knowledge-episodes apprehend mind-independent entities entails both that there is no knowledge of mind-independent entities, and, most importantly, that there are no mind-independent entities. This would certainly be in accord with the main contention of Nāgārjuna's thought – which is not that one cannot prove that knowledge-episodes apprehend mind-independent objects, nor that one does not know whether or not there are mind- independent entities but rather – that one does not have knowledge of mind-independent entities because there are no mind-independent entities (i.e. entities with *svabhāva*) to be known.

Perhaps at best Nāgārjuna might legitimately claim that the successful demonstration that there is no proof that knowledge-episodes apprehend *svabhāva*-endowed entities is an indication, or provides some evidence for the claim, that there are no entities with *svabhāva*. If it could be proved that knowledge-episodes apprehend *svabhāva*-endowed entities, then Nāgārjuna's claim that there are no entities with *svabhāva* would be proved false. If it cannot be proved that there are knowledge-episodes of *svabhāva*-endowed *prameya*-s, although this does not itself establish Nāgārjuna's claim that there are no *prameya*-s with *svabhāva*, it certainly may be used as supportive evidence for his claim. It would make his thesis more plausible.

Unfortunately for Nāgārjuna, however, as I will show, his demonstration that it cannot be proved that there are knowledge-episodes of *svabhāva*-endowed entities is in many ways flawed. Thus his demonstration does not succeed even as supportive evidence for his further claim that there are not any *prameya*-s with *svabhāva*.

The Theories of Validation Refuted by Nāgārjuna

The positions presented and criticized in Nāgārjuna's critique may conveniently be divided into two groups: (A) those positions which advocate the intrinsic validation of the *pramāṇa*-s, and (B) those positions which advocate the extrinsic validation of the *pramāṇa*-s. Intrinsic validation means validation of the *pramāṇa*-s by means of *pramāṇa*-s, without dependence on the *prameya*-s. Extrinsic validation means validation of the *pramāṇa*-s by means of dependence on the *prameya*-s. If *pramāṇa*-s were validated: (A) intrinsically, they might be (1) validated by other *pramāṇa*-s, or (2) self-evident, (B) extrinsically, they might be (1) validated by the *prameya*-s, or (2) mutually validated with the *prameya*-s.[3] In the *VV/VVC*, Nāgārjuna presents refutations of all of these positions. Furthermore, there is a very similar critique of intrinsic validation ((A) (1) and (2)) in the *Vaid/VaidC*. I shall examine and assess, in chapter 10, Nāgārjuna's attack on (A) and, in chapter 11, his attack on (B).

The Validation of Knowledge-episodes Versus the Reflexivity of Consciousness

However, before doing so, let me emphasize an important distinction. The issue of how one validates a knowledge-episode must not be confused with the issue of how consciousness is reflexive. The proof that a knowledge-episode is in fact a knowledge-episode is an entirely different phenomenon from the awareness that one is aware. For example, it is one thing to be aware that I am having a cognition of distant water; it is quite another thing to prove that my correct cognition of the distant water is a correct cognition. Indian philosophers in fact have plenty to say about the reflexivity of consciousness. However, Nāgārjuna's refutations are of various ways in which knowledge-episodes of *svabhāva*-endowed entities might be proved/validated. Which is to say that Nāgārjuna is not here, in my opinion, refuting various theories about the reflexivity of consciousness.

These issues are *especially* prone to be conflated in the present context for four reasons:

(i) The position that *pramāṇa*-s are validated by other *pramāṇa*-s is similar in form to the position, advocated by the Naiyāyikas, that reflexivity involves a second consciousness of the first consciousness. That is, consciousness$_2$ of consciousness$_1$ of an object. According to the Nyāya theory of reflexivity, there is usually an introspective cognition (*anuvyavasāya*), a mental perception, which immediately follows the cognition of an object, and which takes this cognition of the object as its object. One is consequently aware that one is aware.[4]

(ii) .Nāgārjuna argues, as we shall see, that the position that *pramāṇa*-s are validated by further *pramāṇa*-s entails an infinite regress. This is also a criticism which can be (and is, in Indian philosophy) made of the position that reflexivity involves a second consciousness of the initial consciousness of an object (is a third consciousness then required in order to be conscious of the second consciousness, etc?).[5]

(iii) The position that *pramāṇa*-s are self-validating, i.e. self-evident, is similar in form to the position, advocated especially by Buddhists influenced by Yogācāra thought, that consciousness is conscious of itself in the very act of being conscious of its object (thus a second consciousness is not required in order for reflexivity to occur). See, for example, Śāntarakṣita's theory of *svasaṃvedana*, according to which reflexivity does not involve a second and subsequent cognition; the very cognition of the object includes the simultaneous awareness of this cognition.[6] Cognition without this reflexivity, it is argued, would not be cognition, like a mirror which does not reflect would not be a mirror.

(iv) As we shall see, the opponent in the *VV/VVC* employs the analogy of the self-luminous light in support of the position that knowledge-episodes are self-validating, i.e. self-evident. *Pramāṇa*-s are 'self-luminous', so to speak. Consciousness is also said to be 'self-luminous' by some Indian philosophers in the sense that it is conscious of itself in the very act of being conscious of its object.[7] Thus, the same analogy is used in order to support two distinct philosophical positions.[8]

Now, I do not want to discuss in any detail theories of reflexivity in Indian philosophy. My point is that Nāgārjuna is engaged, in a critique – not of various theories about the reflexivity of consciousness but rather – of various theories about the validation of knowledge-episodes of *svabhāva*-endowed entities. Let us look in detail now, in chapter 10 and 11, at his critique.

Notes

1 See Monier-Williams (1899), pp. 1215–1216.

2 See Matilal (1986), pp. 135–140.

3 I borrow this categorization, with some modifications, from Siderits (1980), pp. 309–310. *VV* 51 is in fact a list of most of these positions, which are examined is detail in *VV/VVC* 31–50. The list adds the position that the *pramāṇa*-s might be established 'accidentally' or 'without a reason' (*akasmāt*). This position is not discussed anywhere else in the text, however. I assume that Nāgārjuna rejects it because it is obvious that the mere assertion that the *pramāṇa*-s are validated, without any explanation at all of how they are validated, is entirely vacuous. It is therefore not in need of any serious or sustained refutation.

4 See Siderits (1980), p. 324, Matilal (1986), pp. 143–147.

5 See, for example, *TS* 2025.

6 See, for example, *TS* 2011–2012. See also Williams (1998a).

7 See, for example, *TS* 2014, 3436–3437.

8 Bhattacharya (1978), p. 117, for example, seems to confuse the position in the *VV/VVC* that *pramāṇa*-s are 'self-luminous', i.e. self-validating/self-evident, with the position of the Vijñānavādins that consciousness is 'self-luminous', i.e. conscious of itself in the very act of being conscious of its object.

CHAPTER TEN

The Attack on Intrinsic Validation

Intrinsic Validation (1): Knowledge-episodes are Validated by Other Knowledge-episodes

At *VVC* 51, Nāgārjuna describes two different ways in which *pramāṇa*-s might be thought to be validated by other *pramāṇa*-s. (a) by other *pramāṇa*-s of the same type as themselves – such as a perception (*pratyakṣa*) by another perception, an inference (*anumāna*) by another inference, etc. For example, I might have a perception of a tree. This perception might be validated by a further perception of the tree. That is to say, I perceive a tree. I have another look and this second look confirms that the first perception of the tree was indeed correct, or (b) by *pramāṇa*-s of a different type from themselves, such as a perception by inference, comparison (*upamāṇa*), or verbal testimony (*śabda*), an inference by a perception, a comparison, or verbal testimony, etc. I might, for instance, be told by a reliable person (*āpta*) that there is a fire on the hill. This might be validated by the perception of a fire on the hill, or perhaps by the perception of smoke on the hill, followed by an inference that therefore there must be fire on the hill.

As Siderits notes,[1] Nāgārjuna's point here at *VVC* 51 can be taken in two ways: (i) it might be that *particular instances* of knowledge-episodes are validated by knowledge-episodes either of the same type or of other types (e.g. some verbal testimony might be validated by perception, some by inference, some by comparison, and some by other verbal testimony). Or (ii) it might be that it is a *generic trait* of particular types of knowledge-episode that they are validated by knowledge-episodes of the same type (e.g. all perceptions might be validated by perceptions) or a different type (e.g. all verbal testimony might be validated by perception).

Nāgārjuna's Refutation of Intrinsic Validation (1)

Nāgārjuna argues, both in the *VV/VVC* and the *Vaid/VaidC*, that the position that *pramāṇa*-s are validated by other *pramāṇa*-s entails an infinite regress (*anavasthā/thug pa med pa*), because the *pramāṇa*-s which validate the *pramāṇa*-s would themselves need to be validated by *pramāṇa*-s, etc.[2] For example, if my perception of a tree is validated by a further perception that the object is a tree, that further perception of the tree would need to be validated by another perception that the object is a tree, and so on. Consequently, no *pramāṇa* would ever be validated, because that on the basis of which it is validated would always itself be in need of validation. *X* cannot be validated on the basis of *y* if *y* has not been validated. *Z* might validate *y* but would itself be in need of validation, etc. The end result is that *x*, *y*, *z* etc are all unvalidated.

The point, then, (presumably) is that a knowledge-episode$_1$ which (supposedly) mirrors a mind-independent object of knowledge cannot be proved to do so through corroboration by another knowledge-episode$_2$ which (supposedly) mirrors the same mind-independent object of knowledge. For the knowledge-episode$_2$ must itself be proven to apprehend the mind-independent object of knowledge. If the knowledge-episode$_2$ is itself said to be proven to mirror the mind-independent object through corroboration by a knowledge-episode$_3$, the knowledge-episode$_3$ is itself in need of proof. And so on. If I have a perception of water, for example, the perception cannot be proven to be correct, i.e. to apprehend mind-independent water, by appeal to another perception of the water. For how is this second perception of the water itself proved to be accurate, i.e. proved to apprehend the water as it is independently of the knowing mind? A third perception of the water will suffer from the same problem. And so on. It will be a case of the unproven (supposedly) proving the unproven.

A Solution to the Infinite Regress Problem

I do not think, however, that Nāgārjuna's infinite regress argument is convincing as a refutation of the theory that knowledge-episodes are validated by other knowledge-episodes. If a knowledge-episode is corroborated by a (finite) number of other knowledge-episodes, it might be argued that this will be *sufficient proof* that the knowledge-episode is a correct cognition. If one has a perception of water, and this perception is corroborated by another perception of the water, etc, at some point one will be satisfied that one has proof that the perception of water is a correct cognition. One would only require endless corroboration by further knowledge-episodes, I think, if one's criterion for proof is *absolute certainty,* a criterion which is surely too strict. If my cognition is corroborated by a number of other cognitions, I may conclude that it is proved, i.e. *highly probable*, that my cognition is a correct cognition, i.e. actually apprehends a mind-independent entity. So the infinite regress can be stopped, I suggest, by relaxing the requirement that proof=certainty. Perhaps in rare cases, despite the proof of the correctness of my cognition by the corroboration of a finite number of cognitions, my initial cognition, and all of the corroborating cognitions, are in fact erroneous. In these cases, then, the proof that the cognition is correct fails. But these are exceptional cases which do not damage the general rule that it is proved, i.e. highly probable, that a cognition is a correct cognition if it is corroborated by other cognitions.

Perhaps Nāgārjuna would object, however, that this argument misses his point. According to Nāgārjuna, all entities are mind-dependent, i.e. they have conceptually constructed existence, although, for the unenlightened mind, these entities *appear* to be mind-independent (i.e. to have *svabhāva*). Thus, it may *seem* highly probable that a cognition which is corroborated by a finite number of other cognitions is a knowledge-episode in the Nyāya sense, i.e. a cognition which apprehends a mind independent state-of-affairs, but in no case is such a cognition *actually* a knowledge-episode. That is, in no case does the cognition really apprehend a mind-independent state-of-affairs. The initial cognition and all of the corroborating cognitions apprehend, by analogy with the illusion or the dream, an object which, though it appears to exist mind-independently, is actually a conceptual construction.

But it can be countered that Nāgārjuna has here made a very controversial – one might say, implausible – claim, namely, that cognitions never actually apprehend mind-independent entities (though they often seem to do so). Is not the onus therefore on Nāgārjuna to *prove* that cognitions do not apprehend a mind-independent state-of-affairs? Nāgārjuna has not here provided such a proof. And until this proof is forthcoming, is it not reasonable to continue to believe that cognitions which are corroborated by other cognitions do, in most cases at least, apprehend a mind-independent reality? It seems, then, that Nāgārjuna's refutation of the theory that knowledge-episodes are validated by other knowledge-episodes does not succeed.

Intrinsic Validation (2): The *pramāṇa*-s are Self-Evident

At any rate, Nāgārjuna thinks that the *pramāṇa*-s are not validated by other *pramāṇa*-s because an infinite regress would ensue. But, Nāgārjuna argues (in both the *VV/VVC* and the *Vaid/VaidC*), all objects other than *pramāṇa*-s can be validated by *pramāṇa*-s. The oak-tree is proven to exist, for example, if there is a correct perception of it, or a correct inference about it, etc. Why should the *pramāṇa*-s themselves be excepted from this rule? It would seem that such an exception is arbitrary, and undermines the entire *pramāṇa* theory. For the objects which are validated by the *pramāṇa*-s are validated by *pramāṇa*-s which, it would seem, are not themselves validated! In which case, the objects (supposedly) validated by the *pramāṇa*-s have not really been validated. The unvalidated cannot validate. The oak-tree, for example, cannot be proven to exist by a perception which has not been proven to be correct. The opponent must, then, give the special reason (*viśeṣahetu/khyad par gyi gtan tshigs*) or the difference (*mi 'dra ba nyid*) which excepts the *pramāṇa*-s from the general rule that, in order to be validated, entities must be proven by knowledge-episodes.[3]

The opponent's response, both in the *VV/VVC* and the *Vaid/VaidC*, is that the special reason why the *pramāṇa*-s are not validated by further *pramāṇa*-s (hence supposedly incurring an infinite regress) is that the *pramāṇa*-s are self-validating, i.e. self-evident. The opponent appears to mean that *pramāṇa*-s are made evident as *pramāṇa*-s whenever they apprehend their objects.[4] If there is a correctly cognized oak-tree, then there is no further proof of the correctness of the cognition necessary. The correctness of the cognition is evident in the very act of correctly apprehending the oak-tree. There is no need to produce another knowledge-episode to prove the existence of the knowledge-episode which apprehends the oak-tree. That a knowledge-episode is a knowledge-episode is obvious when it happens. Thus, the infinite regress of validation of *pramāṇa*-s by further *pramāṇa*-s does not occur. (The philosophical naivity of this position, if expressed without any qualifications, is striking. I shall have more to say about this later).

The Fire/Lamp Analogy

The opponent gives in the *VV/VVC* the example of fire (*agni/hutāśa/jvalana*) (in the *Vaid/VaidC* the word is *'mar me'*, which means 'lamp') which, he contends, illuminates (*prakāśayati/prasādhayati/dyotayati/gsal bar byed pa*) itself in the act of illuminating other things. Nāgārjuna has his opponent explain that just as (*yathā/ji ltar*) the fire/lamp is exceptional in illuminating itself simply in illuminating its object, similarly (*tathaiva/ de bzhin du*) the *pramāṇa*-s are exceptional in illuminating themselves simply in illuminating their objects.[5] The example of light (*pradīpa*) is also presented at *NS* II, 1, 19 in reply to the infinite regress argument and as what appears to be a defence, by the Naiyāyika, of the position that the *pramāṇa*-s are self-evident.[6]

It is of crucial importance here, I think, that the verbal forms *pra-√kāś*, *pra-√sad*, and *√dyut*, in their causative forms, in addition to meaning (i) 'to make bright, illuminate, irradiate', can also mean (ii) 'to make clear, evident, manifest'.[7] It seems obvious that the self-illumination of the fire/lamp must be understood in accordance with meaning (ii) rather than meaning (i). Surely the point is not that the fire/lamp literally illuminates itself in the act of illuminating others, as though there is somehow a light which is turned inwards upon the fire/lamp when it is lighting up its objects! Rather, the point must be that whenever an object is illuminated by a light, there is no need for any further proof that there is a light which is doing the illuminating. The very illuminating of the object makes it self-evident that there is indeed a light which is illuminating. If I can see the book on my desk, it must be the case that there is some light by means of which the book is illuminated. I do not need any further proof of the light. The proof of the existence of the light is its very illumination of the object. The 'self-luminosity of light' is simply a metaphor for this self-evident character which a light has in illuminating its object.

Similarly, it is being argued, the *pramāṇa*-s are self-evident when the objects of knowledge are apprehended. No demonstration that the knowledge-episode is indeed a knowledge-episode is required. (It is not that *pramāṇa*-s literally illuminate themselves, whatever that could possibly mean!)

In other words, expressed accurately, the argument from the fire/lamp example would read as follows: Just as (*yathā*) the fire/lamp is exceptional in being evident simply in illuminating its object, similarly (*tathaiva*) the *pramāṇa*-s are exceptional in being evident simply by apprehending their objects.

Nāgārjuna's Refutation of Intrinsic Validation (2)

Nāgārjuna's criticisms of the position that *pramāṇa*-s are self-evident are directed against the opponent's example of the fire/lamp. In fact, he devotes six whole verses in the *VV/VVC* and five verses in the *Vaid/VaidC*, to the refutation of the fire/lamp example. Clearly, he sees the fire/lamp example as central to the opponent's position that the *pramāṇa*-s are self-evident. This might seem rather strange, as the issue at stake is not really whether a fire/lamp is self-luminous, i.e. self-evident, but rather whether knowledge-episodes are self-luminous, i.e. self-evident. So why does Nāgārjuna see the example as having such vital importance?

Matilal argues that the example of the fire in the *VV/VVC* is the basis of an argument by analogy. Commonly accepted entity *x* has property *a*. Likewise, entity *y* has property *a*. The fire is self-evident when it illuminates its objects. Likewise *pramāṇa*-s are self-evident when they apprehend their objects. Obviously such an analogy cannot establish the self-evidence of the *pramāṇa*-s beyond doubt (for it could be that, whereas a light is self-evident, the *pramāṇa*-s are not. This is the weakness of arguments by analogy). But, Matilal says, the analogy makes the position that *pramāṇa*-s are self-evident plausible.[8] Presumably what Matilal means is that, if it is shown that there is one entity, i.e. the fire, which is self-evident, then this suggests that there might be others (e.g. the *pramāṇa*-s). But if there are no commonly acknowledged examples of self-evident entities, then it is highly unlikely that the *pramāṇa*-s are themselves self-evident.

Siderits says that it was widely accepted in ancient India that an entity cannot act on itself. Thus, for example, a knife cannot cut itself. Yet the theory of self-evidence entails that the *pramāṇa*-s act on themselves in the same way as they act on other things, i.e. they make both other things and themselves evident. Thus, the fire example is presented by the opponent as a counter-example to the prevailing Indian notion. And if there is one exception, the *pramāṇa*-s also might be excepted. But if the supposed exception is demonstrated actually not to act upon itself, then there will be no grounds at all for asserting the self-evidence of the *pramāṇa*-s. Nāgārjuna's strategy, then, is to refute the example in order to render implausible the theory that the *pramaṇa*-s are self-evident.[9]

There is another consideration, however. It is clear that Indian thinkers saw light and cognition/consciousness/the mind as strikingly parallel phenomena. Cognition is often described in terms of light imagery. Here, then, are some examples, from various Indian philosophical traditions.

In the *NS* an opponent objects to the Naiyāyika position that cognitions are transitory (*anavasthāyin*), claiming that, if this were the case, there could be only an indistinct apprehension (*avyakta-grahaṇa*) of an object, like a flash of lightning (*vidyutsampāta*) cannot give a distinct apprehension of the form (*rūpa*) which it lights up.[10] The Naiyāyika reply also uses light imagery: The transitory cognitions each give a distinct apprehension (*abhivyak-tagrahaṇa*) of the object, like a series of flashes of a lamp (*pradīpārci*).[11]

The opponent also objects to the Naiyāyika position that cognitions (*jñāna*) are not simultaneous (*ayaugapadya*), because, the opponent says, there can be the apprehension (*upalabdhi*) of many activities (*anekakriyā*) at the same time (*yugapad*),[12] as when one has simultaneously, for example, a visual cognition of a fire, an auditory cognition of running water, and a memory of talking with a friend.

The Naiyāyika response is that such cognitions have the appearance (*upalabdhi*) of simultaneity but in fact they occur in rapid succession (*āśusaṃcāra*), like the circle of the firebrand (*alātacakra*) appears because the firebrand is moved very quickly.[13]

Also, the *NS* describes visual cognition to be a result of an invisible ray (*raśmi*) emitted by the eye which contacts the object (*artha*).[14]

Further, in Sāṃkhya philosophy, 'illuminating' (*prakāśa*) is one of the three functions of the complex cognitive structure called the 'thirteenfold instrument' (*trayodaśakaraṇa*) (including *manas*, *buddhi*, *ahaṃkāra*, the sense capacities (*buddhindriya*), and motor capacities (*karmendriya*)) by which objects are apprehended.[15]

The *Sāṃkhyavṛtti* likens the process of cognition, whereby all objects in the three worlds are illuminated, to the illumination by a lamp within a house of the inside of the house.[16]

There are, in addition, many references to the luminosity of consciousness (*citta*) in Buddhist texts. Cittamātra-influenced thinkers, for example, employ the light imagery in their exposition of the reflexive nature of consciousness (*svasaṃvedana*).[17] Further, the **Bhadrapālaśreṣṭhiparipṛcchāsūtra*, from the *Ratnakūṭa* collection, describes consciousness (*vijñāna*) as able to occupy a large or a small body, like a light which, placed in the centre of a room, illuminates the room whether it is small or large.[18] This same *sūtra* compares the transmigration of consciousness to the light shed by the sun, the shining of the pearl, or the fire produced by wood (no explanation is given of the precise nature of the similarity).[19] There is a long tradition, present even in the *Aṅguttaranikāya* and other non-Mahāyāna texts, of describing consciousness as luminous (*cittaṃ prabhāsvaram*), in the sense that it is intrinsically pure though concealed by adventitious defilements (*kleśa*).[20] And so on.

My point is that, given the wide-spread acceptance of the similarity between light and cognition/consciousness/the mind in various ways, an analogy between light and a form of cognition, i.e. knowledge-episodes, would have been quite compelling. An ancient Indian thinker would have been strongly inclined to accept that what is true of light must also be true of cognition. Thus, if light is self-evident, then for the ancient Indian thinker it is more than likely that *pramāṇa*-s, as forms of cognition, would also be self-evident. I make no comment about the soundness of the analogy (other than to say that it seems pretty dubious). My point is simply that it would have appeared convincing to an ancient Indian thinker. This goes some way, I think, to explaining Nāgārjuna's sustained refutation of the self-luminosity of the fire/lamp. For if he is able to prove that light is not self-illuminating, i.e. self-evident, then, for the ancient Indian mind at least, this would be a strong argument against the self-evidence of the *pramāṇa*-s.

So, Nāgārjuna's response to the opponent's argument by analogy is that the opponent's example is inappropriate (*viṣama*).[21] The fire/lamp is not self-luminous, i.e. self-evident. Thus the argument by analogy breaks down. The *pramāṇa*-s might be self-luminous. i.e. self-evident, if the fire/lamp were self-luminous, i.e.

self-evident, but actually, Nāgārjuna argues, the fire/lamp is not self-luminous. Without the supportive analogy of the the fire/lamp, the opponent's position that the *pramāṇa*-s are self-evident is highly implausible.

I must admit, however, that, despite these explanations, I find Nāgārjuna's strategy philosophically disappointing to say the least. I think that a more direct attack on the notion of self-evident knowledge-episodes (rather than an attack on the notion of the self-luminous fire/lamp) would be more to the point. For clearly there are serious questions to be raised about a position which claims that knowledge-episodes are self-evident. How, for example, is the undeniable phenomenon of error to be explained? I shall have more to say about this matter a little later. For now, let us trace and evaluate Nāgārjuna's own attack on the theory of self-evident *pramāṇa*-s.

In the *VV/VVC* and the *Vaid/VaidC* there is a total of five distinct arguments which Nāgārjuna employs in his refutation of the fire/lamp example.The arguments given in the *Vaid/VaidC* to refute the example of the lamp appear in a different order from those found in the *VV/VVC*. Furthermore, one argument (argument (B)) is found only in the *VV/VVC*, whereas another argument (argument (E)) occurs only in the *Vaid/VaidC*. (See here table 3).

It is quite obvious that all five of these arguments are sophisms. It is, however, fairly difficult sometimes to identify the fallacy precisely. However, they are all unsound either because they are invalid, or because they rely on questionable premisses, as I shall demonstrate.

		VV/VVC	*Vaid/VaidC*
Order	(1)	Argument (A)	Argument (D)
in	(2)	Argument (B)	Argument (E)
text	(3)	Argument (C)	Argument (A)
	(4)	Argument (D)	Argument (C)

Table 3 Nāgārjuna's Refutations of the Self-Illuminating Fire/lamp

Critical Analysis of Nāgārjuna's Five Arguments

ARGUMENT (A). Illumination means making perceived, or lighting up, what was previously unperceived, or in the dark. It only makes sense to speak of 'illumination' as the removal of darkness. Something which is illumined must therefore be in the dark prior to its illumination. A pot can be illuminated because it can be in the dark. However, a fire/lamp-light cannot first be dark and then illuminated because there is no such thing as a dark fire/lamp-light. As the *Vaid/VaidC* says, darkness and light are contradictories (*'gal ba*). Thus, darkness cannot exist (*mun pa med pa*) in light in order to be subsequently illuminated.The self-illumination of the fire/lamp is therefore untenable.[22]

Nāgārjuna's argument employs causative forms of *pra-√kāś* and *pra-√sad* (in the *Vaid/VaidC 'gsal bar byed pa'* is used), both of which, as I have already explained, can mean both (i) 'to make bright, illuminate, irradiate.' (ii) 'to make clear, evident, manifest'. However, as I have already explained, it seems obvious that the fire/lamp example must be read in accordance with meaning (ii) rather than meaning (i). The fire/lamp makes itself evident simply in manifesting its object. Its illumination of the object is the proof of the existence of the light. No further proof is required in order to demonstrate that the light exists.

But in argument (A) Nāgārjuna takes the meaning of the verbs in sense (i) rather than sense (ii). He argues that a light cannot *illluminate itself* because it contains no darkness to be *illuminated.* His argument entirely misses the point that the opponent uses the fire/lamp example, not to prove that the fire/lamp illuminates itself, but rather to prove that fire/the lamp manifests itself – i.e. is evident, is proved – simply by its illumination of its object. In other words, Nāgārjuna's refutation depends upon a sense of the causatives of the verbs *pra-√kāś* and *pra-√sad* which the fire/lamp example (properly understood) does not itself depend upon. Argument (A) fails because Nāgārjuna incorrectly takes the fire/lamp example to be stating that the fire/lamp literally illuminates itself. In fact, the self-illumination of the fire/lamp this is simply a metaphor for the idea that the light is self-evident in its illumination of its object. So Nāgārjuna is here guilty of taking a metaphor literally.

ARGUMENT (B). If fire illuminates itself like (*iva*) it illuminates others, it will burn (*paridhakṣyati*) itself just as it burns others.

'Burn' here means, I take it, consumption or destruction by fire or heat, as when the fire burns its fuel, or the fire burns the forest. So 'burn' refers to the combustion of materials through contact with fire. The argument is, then, that fire consumes and destroys materials other than itself, but that it makes no sense to speak of fire consuming or destroying itself. Therefore, fire does not illuminate itself when it illuminates other things.[23]

Again, Nāgārjuna has taken the causatives of the verbs *pra-√kāś* and *pra-√sad* to mean 'illuminate' when they are, in the case of self-illumination, meant in the sense of 'self-evident' or 'self-manifest'. Nāgārjuna claims that the self-luminosity of fire would entail that fire illuminates itself in just the same manner (*evameva*) as it illuminates other things. But, given that fire's self-luminosity is a metaphor for the notion that the existence of the fire is proved by its illumination of its objects, Nāgārjuna is wrong to argue that the 'self-luminous' (so to speak) fire would illuminate itself in the same way in which it illuminates other objects. Strictly speaking, self-luminosity, i.e. self-evidence, is not a form of luminosity at all. The book is illuminated, thus it is self-evident that there must be a light which illuminates it. Thus, since fire does not literally illuminate itself just as it illuminates other things, it does not follow that fire must burn itself just as it burns other things.

Furthermore, even if a fire were self-luminous in the same way that it illuminates other things, it still would not follow that a fire must therefore burn itself just as it burns other things. It is not entailed that because one quality of fire, viz. its luminosity, is self-referring, therefore its other qualities, e.g. its ability to burn, must also be self-referring. One cannot argue validly, as Nāgārjuna attempts in argument (B), from the non-self-referential nature of one quality of an entity to the non-self-referential nature of another quality of the same entity.

ARGUMENT (C). If the fire/lamp is an entity with the capacity of illuminating (*prakāśayati/gsal bar byed pa*) itself then darkness (*tamas/mun pa*), as its opposite (*pratipakṣa/phyin ci log pa*), should have the opposite capacity, viz. the ability to conceal (*pracchādayiṣyati/chādayet/sgrib par byed pa*) itself.

One must appreciate again here that *prakāśayati* (used in the *VV/VVC*), the causative of the verb *pra-√kāś*, means – in addition to 'bringing to light' (i.e. illumining) – 'making manifest or evident.' (As does the Tibetan word, *gsal bar byed pa*, used in the

VaidC). *Pracchādayiṣyati* (used in the *VV*) is the simple future tense of the verb *pra-✓cchad*, whereas *chādayet* (used in the *VVC*) is the optative mode of the verb *✓chad*, both of which mean 'to cover, hide, conceal, keep secret'[24] (as does the Tibetan word, *sgrib pa byed pa*, used in the *Vaid/VaidC*). Thus, the point is that the opposite of illuminating or making manifest/evident, is concealing, making secret, hiding.

However, Nāgārjuna says, the concealing by darkness of itself is not seen or experienced (*dṛṣṭa*). I take this to mean that there is in fact plenty of observable evidence that darkness does not conceal itself. For there are many occasions on which darkness is perceived (for example, the darkness of the night-sky). As Nāgārjuna says, if darkness concealed itself the absurd consequence would follow that darkness would be imperceptible (*mi dmigs pa*). If darkness concealed itself, there would always and on every occasion simply be light (for darkness, as always hidden, would never be experienced!). Hence, it cannot make sense to say that light illuminates itself/makes itself manifest.[25] If x can do y then the opposite of x must do the opposite of y. If the opposite of x cannot do the opposite of y, then x cannot do y.

However, it seems to me that this argument relies on the assumption that darkness is in fact the opposite substance to light. But the Naiyāyikas maintain – sensibly, I think – that whereas light (*tejas*) is a substance (*dravya*), darkness (*tamas*) is an absence (*abhāva*).[26] Darkness is the absence of illumination or making manifest. The point is that *not illuminating or not manifesting is not equivalent to concealing or hiding*. 'Concealing' means not just the absence of manifestation, but the active prevention of manifestation. That darkness lacks the capacity to make manifest does not entail that it prevents manifestation. If, for example, I lack the ability to speak Mongolian, this does not mean that I actively prevent myself from learning Mongolian. I do not, for instance, burn any Mongolian-English dictionaries which come into my possession, or leave the room whenever my Mongolian friends speak in their native tongue.

Thus Nāgārjuna's argument fails: If light can illuminate itself, i.e. be self-evident, then the opposing substance to light might do the opposite of being self-evident, i.e. it might conceal itself. But darkness is not the opposing substance to light. Rather it is the mere absence of light. It is incorrect, therefore, to argue that because darkness cannot conceal itself, therefore light cannot be self-evident.

ARGUMENT (D). Illumination is by definition the removal or destruction of darkness (*andhakāravadha*). Nāgārjuna says that this removal of darkness would take place either through: (i) contact between the light and darkness or (ii) without contact between the light and darkness:

(i) If the removal of darkness by the fire/lamp requires contact (*prāpnoti/phrad*) between them, this cannot occur because contact requires co-existence whereas light and darkness are opposites. As Nāgārjuna expresses this point, there can be no darkness in the fire or in a place in which fire occurs. The idea is, I suppose, that *x* and the opposite of *x* cannot occupy an identical spatio-temporal location. Contact here entails that the two entities that have contact do occupy an identical spatio-temporal location, if only very briefly. But illumination and darkness are opposed to one another, i.e. they are contradictories, hence they cannot have contact. At no point in the process (*utpadyamāne*) of illumination, Nāgārjuna says in the *VV/VVC*, can the two opposite entities have contact, because they cannot, being contradictories, be at the same place at the same time.[27]

(ii) If the fire/lamp destroys darkness without contact (*aprāpta/ma phrad*), this would entail, according to the *VVC*, the absurd consequence that a particular fire would destroy all darkness in all parts of the world (*sarveṣu lokadhātuṣu*), because no contact would be required for the destruction to occur. As the *VaidC* says, a light in a single location would be able to illumine even the most remote of places, such as the darkness contained within the caves of all mountains (*ri thams cad kyi phug gi nang du gtogs pa'i mun pa*), because no contact would be required in order for the illumination to occur. There would be no reason why a particular darkness is destroyed by a particular light, for all darknesses are alike in being out of contact with light. (In the *VaidC* Nāgārjuna also gives the supportive analogy of the sword (*ral gri*). Just as a sword cannot cut without contact, likewise light cannot illuminate without contact with what it illuminates).[28]

So, Nāgārjuna concludes that illumination of darkness by light is impossible, given that it cannot occur either (i) by contact between light and darkness or (ii) without such contact.[29]

But Nāgārjuna's argument does not work as a refutation of self-illumination. As I have said, self-illumination, which is a metaphor for self-evidence, is not by definition 'the removal or destruction of darkness'. On the contrary, self-illumination (understood metaphorically) has nothing to do with darkness and its removal. Self-illumination means that a light is made evident, i.e. its existence is proved, simply by the fact that its object is illumined by it. The issue of whether in 'self-illumination' the light removes darkness with or without contact thus does not even arise. To take self-illumination literally, as Nāgārjuna does in his argument, is to miss the point of the metaphor.

Nevertheless, it might be argued that Nāgārjuna's argument works as a refutation, not of self-illumination, but of the illumination of objects in the normal, non-metaphorical sense, i.e, the illumination of other objects by light. Here, at least, it might be argued, light cannot illuminate either by contact or without contact the darkness which conceals such objects.

But this raises the question, why would Nāgārjuna want to refute this normal form of illumination? For the purpose of his critique is surely to refute the example of (so-called) 'self-illumination', as it is this phenomenon of self-illumination which is said by the opponent to support the argument that *pramāṇa*-s are self-evident. A critique of illumination in its normal sense would seem to be irrelevant (such a critique would bear no relation to the issue of self-evident *pramāṇa*-s) and, in fact, rather bizarre. Is Nāgārjuna seriously arguing that light does not illuminate objects? This would seem to be a very peculiar position to assert. (Perhaps he is refuting illumination with *svabhāva* of darkness with *svabhāva*, but he gives no indication that this is the case).

But even if he is (for some reason) refuting the illumination of objects by light, his argument is unsuccessful. The problem with this argument is that it depends on the assumption that light and darkness are two discrete things, which are diametrically opposed to one another. But, as I have explained, the Naiyāyikas (sensibly) considered darkness to be an absence of light, rather than a contradictory substance.

Thus, light and darkness are, one might say, actually two poles of a single phenomenon, which one might call 'the level of illumination'. In this case, there can be degrees of illumination or degrees of darkness. Darkness thus understood is simply the relative lack of light, rather than being an opposing substance which contradicts the nature of light. If there is no light whatsoever, then this is simply the complete absence of light, i.e. the very lowest possible level of illumination, rather than being a case of the removal of light by an opposing substance, darkness.

The point is, then, that light and darkness need not be seen as a battle between two contradictory, discrete entities. The problem of contact only arises if they are viewed in this way.

ARGUMENT (E). Nāgārjuna now admits that it is accepted both by ordinary men (*'jig rten pa*) and by investigators (*dpyod pa po*), i.e. philosophers, respected by the Nyāya tradition (of which he gives a long list) that darkness is the mere absence of light (*'od med pa tsam*). Darkness is an example (*dpe*) of a mere absence.

Nāgārjuna is here referring explicitly to the *NS*, which states that,

> *laukikaparīkṣakāṇāṃ yasminnarthe buddhisāmyaṃ sa dṛṣṭāntaḥ//*
>
> The *dṛṣṭānta* is the matter with regards which ordinary men (*laukika*) and investigators (*parīkṣaka*) have the same opinion. (*NS* I, 1, 25).

As Vātsyāyana explains in his commentary, the distinction between the ordinary man (*laukika*) and the investigator (*pārikṣaka*) is a distinction of intelligence, either innate or through training. Thus, the investigator has examined and understood the nature of the object in question more thoroughly and meticulously than the average man. An object is usable as a *dṛṣṭānta* when the careful examination has revealed the ordinary understanding of the entity in question to be correct.[30]

So, Nāgārjuna is now claiming that darkness is a *dṛṣṭānta* – i.e. a commonly and correctly understood instance – of an absence. In which case, Nāgārjuna argues, darkness is not accepted as an entity (*dngos po*) of any kind. Therefore, darkness is not anything which can be removed (*sel bar byed pa*) by light. So there can be no illumination, i.e. removal, of darkness by light.[31]

But Nāgārjuna has certainly gone astray here. He has, I think, confused two distinct meanings/uses of the term 'remove'.

First, 'remove' can mean 'relocate/eliminate'. One removes, i.e. relocates, the cup and one removes, i.e. eliminates, the spelling mistakes from the essay. In order to remove in this sense, there must be *an entity* which is relocated/eliminated. It would be wrong to say that in placing the cup on the table, I have relocated an entity called 'the absence of a cup', from the table (where do I put it, I wonder?) or that in inserting spelling-mistakes into my essay (surely a perverse activity), I have eliminated an entity called 'the absence of spelling mistakes' from my essay! It is true, as Nāgārjuna says, that an absence is not an entity which can be relocated/eliminated.

But, second, 'remove' can be used in a different sense, in relation to absences. To remove an absence means, I suggest, that an entity *x* exists where it did not exist/it was absent before (rather than that there is an entity called 'absence of entity *x*' which must be relocated or eliminated in order for entity *x* to exist). If I were to say that I remove the absence of a cup (admittedly, a rather unusual way of speaking), I would mean – not that there is an entity called 'absence of cup' which I relocate/eliminate in order for the cup to exist but rather – that the cup exists where previously it did not exist/it was absent. Similarly, the removal of darkness, an absence of light, by light means – not that there is an entity called 'darkness' which is relocated/eliminated by light but rather – that light exists where previously it did not exist/it was absent. So, when 'removal' is understood in this second sense, illumination, i.e. the removal of darkness by light, is unproblematic. Nāgārjuna's argument is therefore unsuccessful.

At any rate, argument (E) is irrelevant because, as I have argued already, the language of self-illumination is metaphorical. It is not that light 'lights itself up', as it were. Rather, the real point of the metaphor of self-illumination is that light is self-evident. It is proved that there is light simply by the fact that an object has been illuminated. No further proof is necessary. In the case of self-illumination, the issue of whether or in what sense illumination can remove darkness is spurious, for the phenomenon which is being referred to, i.e. self-evidence, is not really a case of illumination at all.

Some Further Reflections on Self-Evident Knowledge-episodes

All the arguments, therefore, which Nāgārjuna presents in refutation of the example of the fire appear to me to fail. This is not to say, however, that it is true that therefore *pramāṇa*-s are self-evident. It simply means that the attempt which Nāgārjuna makes to refute this position, by attacking the example which supports the position of self-evidence, is unsuccessful.

How, then, might one mount a more successful attack on the position that the *pramāṇa*-s are self-evident? Surely a problem with the self-evidence theory of validation is that it fails to explain the phenomenon of error. If knowledge-episodes are self-evident, how is it, then, that one sometimes thinks that one's cognition is correct, i.e. in accord with a mind-independent reality, and yet one is mistaken? And also, it might be argued, if it is sometimes the case that our supposedly self-evident knowledge-episodes are not in fact knowledge-episodes, then might it not be the case that none of our seemingly self-evident knowledge-episodes is in fact correct? That is, they might seem to mirror a mind-independent reality, but in fact they do not. Clearly, if a self-evidence theory of the validation of knowledge-episodes is to be refuted, this is the fracture-point.

Obviously, any successful reply to this objection will have to modify the naive theory that knowledge-episodes are simply self-evident. For if knowledge-episodes were simply self-evident, there would be no errors at all, which seems an impossible position to defend.

Perhaps one might attempt to defend the theory of self-evidence through recourse to some sort of internal characteristic, which distinguishes knowledge-episodes from non-knowledge-episodes. I have in mind here a theory like that of the Stoic criterion.[32] The knowledge episode has, it might be claimed, some essential characteristic or characteristics, such as clarity and distinctness, which mark it off from erroneous cognitions. A correct perception, for example, of a red chair, is (it might be argued) more vivid and well-defined than the red chair cognized in a dream. The appeal, then, would be to an experientially detectable criterion which indicates that the cognition in question is correct. Error occurs because one does not pay sufficient attention to the nature of the cognition in question. As such, one thinks that the criterion is there when in fact it isn't or *vice versa*. I may perceive, for example, a tree-stump where in fact there is a man. But, the proponent of the criterion theory might argue, if I examine carefully my perception, it will be evident that in fact the cognition lacks some characteristics (such as clarity and distinctness) which knowledge-episodes have.

However, it seems that, if the proponent of the theory of self-evidence appeals to criteria which indicate the correctness of his cognitions, then he has actually abandoned the theory of self-evidence. If a knowledge-episode has a detectable distinguishing characteristic, and yet one is not immediately aware of its presence, then the knowledge-episode is not self-evident. Self-evidence means 'not requiring any proof', but an appeal to criteria to distinguish a knowledge-episode from a non-knowledge-episode would appear to be a form of proof. That is, *because* this cognition has the criterion, it must be a knowledge-episode.

At any rate, the criterion theory is highly vulnerable to sceptical attacks, for the onus must be on its proponent to show that there is indeed some characteristic of knowledge-episodes which cannot be re-duplicated by erroneous cognitions. And it is difficult to argue convincingly for the existence of such a characteristic, for erroneous cognitions can be, it would seem, remarkably similar in all respects (including clarity and distinctness) to knowledge-episodes. It as at least doubtful, then, that the search for such a criterion can be successful. (In fact, the ancient sceptics, such as Arcesilaus, criticized the Stoics' attempts to identify some essential, distinguishing characteristic of veridical cognitions. Arcesilaus argued that a non-veridical cognition can have all of the characteristics of a veridical cognition).[33]

Another tactic would be to say that it is self-evident that most of our cognitions, most of the time, are correct. Erroneous cognitions occur due to abnormal conditions, such as intoxication, diseased sense-organs, or unusual external circumstances such as poor lighting, etc. Erroneous cognitions are the exceptions which prove the rule. The theory of self-evidence would then be a species of epistemological optimism, rather than epistemological infallibility.

This qualification certainly makes the theory more palatable, but surely it can be objected that if some cognitions are erroneous, all of them might be. The proponent of self-evidence will of course object that this possibility is highly unlikely, and thus such doubts are unreasonable.

But a Mādhyamika will respond that such doubts are not unreasonable, because there is a real sense in which all of our supposedly correct cognitions are in fact erroneous; for they are taken to mirror a mind-independent reality when in fact they do not. It may seem self-evident that most of our cognitions are correct, i.e. they are undistorted apprehensions of objects as they exist apart from the mind, but this is in fact a mistake. (Still, it seems to me that here the onus must be on the Mādhyamika to prove what is after all an extremely counter-intuitive position).

Note that this modified theory of self-evidence entails that any particular knowledge-episode is not, in fact, self-evidently correct. For it is always possible that one is under the influence of an abnormal condition, which makes what is not a knowledge-episode appear as a knowledge-episode. Thus, if one were to demonstrate that a particular knowledge-episode is in fact a knowledge-episode, there would have to be some test to ensure that no abnormal conditions were at play.

In conclusion, it is obvious that a naive theory of self-evident knowledge-episodes is easily refutable. It seems that a qualified theory of self-evident knowledge-episodes might be philosophically defensible; whether it is correct is a moot point. What is certain, however, is that Nāgārjuna's critique of a theory of self-evident knowledge-episodes – relying as it does on a series of fallacious arguments against self-illumination – is a complete failure.

An Argument Against Both Intrinsic Validation (1) and (2)

At *VV/VVC* 40–41, Nāgārjuna gives a general refutation of intrinsic validation, applicable both to the position that *pramāṇa*-s are self-evident and the position that *pramāṇa*-s are validated by other *pramāṇa*-s. He says that if *pramāṇa*-s were intrinsically established, then they would be established independently (*anapekṣya*) of their *prameya*-s. This follows analytically, because the definition of intrinsic establishment is establishment without relying upon the *prameya*-s. But, Nāgārjuna argues, if the *pramāṇa*-s are established independently of the *prameya*-s, then they would be independent of the *prameya*-s, i.e. they would not exist in dependence upon the *prameya*-s. They would not be the *pramāṇa*-s of anything (*kasyacit*). However, given that the *pramāṇa*-s are the *pramāṇa*-s of something, viz. the *prameya*-s, the position that the *pramāṇa*-s are intrinsically established is untenable.

But Nāgārjuna has here committed the fallacy of equivocation. Nāgārjuna wants to argue as follows:

Premiss$_1$.	If there were intrinsically established *pramāṇa*-s, they would be established independently of the *prameya*-s.
Premiss$_2$.	*Pramāṇa*-s are not established independently of *prameya*-s.
Conclusion.	There are not intrinsically established *pramāṇa*-s.

Apparently, the conclusion follows directly from the law of non-contradiction. X [=the *pramāṇa*] cannot be (y and $\sim y$). X is $\sim y$

[where ~*y* = not established independently of the *prameya*] ∴ *x* is ~(*y*). This argument is superficially persuasive. But consider the following analysis of Nāgārjuna's argument:

Premiss$_1$. If there were intrinsically established$_1$ *pramāṇa*-s, they would be established$_1$ independently of the *prameya*-s.
Definition$_1$. Established$_1$ = validated/proved.
Premiss$_2$. *Pramāṇa*-s are not established$_2$ independently of *prameya*-s.
Definition$_2$. Established$_2$ = existent.
Conclusion. There are not intrinsically established$_1$ *pramāṇa*-s.

This analysis makes it clear that Nāgārjuna employs two distinct senses of the term 'establishment' (*siddhi*) or 'established' (*siddha*). Which is to say that (independently established$_1$) and ~(independently established$_2$) are not contradictories. Thus, it does not follow that a *pramāṇa* cannot be both (independently established$_1$) and ~(independently established$_2$). Nāgārjuna's conclusion, therefore, is not entailed.

It seems to be true that a *pramāṇa* is established, i.e. *exists* in dependence upon its *prameya*. This follows from the intentionality of consciousness. A knowledge-episode is always and necessarily a knowledge-episode of an object. Thus, a knowledge-episode cannot exist apart from the object of knowledge which it knows. The object which it knows is its *prameya*. My correct perceptual apprehension of the copper beech tree, for example, simply cannot occur without a copper beech tree to be correctly perceptually apprehended. Thus, the *pramāṇa* exists in dependence upon the object.

However, that a knowledge-episode is established, i.e. *exists*, always as a knowledge-episode of an object does not in itself entail that the object itself establishes, i.e. *validates*, that the knowledge-episode accurately apprehends the object. It is logically possible that the knowledge-episode, though dependent for its existence upon its object, is self-evident, is validated by other knowledge-episodes, has not been validated (one can have correct cognitions without any proof that they are correct) or even cannot be validated at all (which would mean that there are correct cognitions, but there is no way of proving that there are correct cognitions).

Take, for example, the perceptual knowledge-episode of a tree. One might plausibly hold that, though the perception cannot exist independently of the tree perceived, the perception is proved to be correct because (i) the perception is self-evidently correct, or (ii) the perception has been confirmed by other perceptions. Alternatively, one may hold that one has not, or even cannot, prove that this knowledge-episode of the tree is in fact correct. So one cannot deduce, as Nāgārjuna attempts, that because a *pramāṇa* is dependent upon its *prameya* for its *existence*, therefore it is not *validated* independently of the *prameya*.

* * *

At *Vaid/VaidC* 2 there is a similar confusion of the issues of validation and existence. Here Nāgārjuna says that, because the *pramāṇa* is established (*grub pa*), i.e. exists (*yod*), in dependence on the *prameya* (and not just *vice versa*), therefore the *prameya* is the *pramāṇa* (here best understood as the 'means of knowledge') of the *pramāṇa*, and the *pramāṇa* is the *prameya* (i.e. the object known by means) of the *pramāṇa*. Hence, their natures are mixed (*'dres*).

But this appears to me to be bizarre reasoning. The fact that a *pramāṇa exists* in dependence on the object of knowledge *does not* entail that the object of knowledge is the means of knowledge of the *pramāṇa*, and that the *pramāṇa* is the object known by means of the object of knowledge. The mutual establishment, i.e. mutually dependent existence, of *pramāṇa* and *prameya* entails only that the *prameya* is the *means of existence* of the *pramāṇa* (and, of course, *vice versa*). Nāgārjuna has once again conflated the issue of the existence of the *pramāṇa*-s and *prameya*-s with the issue of their validation. It *would* follow that, if the *pramāṇa* were *validated* in dependence upon the *prameya*, then the object of knowledge would be the *means* by which the *pramāṇa* is *known* to be a *pramāṇa*. In this sense, then, the *prameya* would become the *pramāṇa* (here meaning the 'means of knowledge') of the *pramāṇa*, and the *pramāṇa* would become the *prameya* (i.e. the object known by means) of the *prameya*. But this 'mixing' of the natures of the *pramāṇa* and the *prameya*, I must stress, would not follow from their mutually dependent existence, as Nāgārjuna claims, but would occur if the *pramāṇa* and *prameya* were found to be dependent upon one another for their validation.

Notes

1 Siderits (1980), p. 310.
2 *VV/VVC* 32, *Vaid/VaidC* 5.
3 *VV/VVC* 33, *VaidC* 5.
4 *VVC* 33.
5 *VVC* 33, *Vaid/VaidC* 6.
6 But see Siderits (1980), pp. 332–325, Matilal (1986), pp. 59–61, and *NSBh* II, 1, 19 for Vātsyāyana's very different understanding of *NS* II, 1, 19.
7 See Monier-Williams (1899), p. 500, 653, 696. Note that, like the the causatives of the Sanskrit verbal forms *pra-√kāś*, *pra-√sad*, and *√dyut*, the Tibetan term used in the *Vaid/VaidC*, viz. *gsal bar byed pa*, in addition to meaning (i) 'to make bright, illuminate, irradiate', can also mean (ii) 'to make clear, evident, manifest'. See Chandra Das (1970), p. 1305.
8 Matilal (1986), pp. 57–58.
9 Siderits (1980), p. 313 and Siderits (1988), p. 313.
10 *NS* III, 2, 43.
11 *NS* III, 2, 45.
12 *NS* III, 2, 60–61.
13 *NS* III, 2, 62.
14 See *NS* III, 1, 32–50.
15 See Larson and Bhattacharya (ed.) (1987), pp. 52–53.
16 See Larson and Bhattacharya (ed.) (1987), p. 189.
17 See Williams (1998a).
18 See Chang (trans.) (1983), p. 235.
19 See Chang (trans.) (1983), p. 227. However, note that elsewhere in the **Bhadrapālaśreṣṭhiparipṛcchāsūtra* consciousness is said to be without light and to be like darkness (!) insofar as consciousness, like darkness, cannot be seen or grasped. See Chang (trans.) (1983), pp. 224–225.
20 See Lamotte (1962), pp. 52–56. See also again, for example, the **Bhadrapālaśreṣṭhiparipṛcchāsūtra* (Chang (trans.) (1983), p. 226), 'Sunlight impartially illuminates evil-doers and such filthy things as stinking corpses without being tainted by their foulness. Similarly, consciousness may reside in a pig, a dog, or a being of another miserable plane who eats dirty food, but is stained by none of them.' This tradition is continued and developed in various ways in Tibetan Buddhism, according to which the mind is commonly described as luminous by nature (*rang bzhin gyi 'od gsal ba=prakṛtiprabhāsvara*). See van der Kuijp (1983), p. 43, Williams (1998b), pp. 2–3.
21 *VV/VVC* 34.
22 *VV/VVC* 34, *Vaid /VaidC* 10.
23 *VV/VVC* 35.
24 See Monier-Williams (1899), p. 404, 657.
25 *VV/VVC* 36, *Vaid /VaidC* 11.
26 See, for example *VS*, V, 2, 21–22, summarized by Hattori in Potter (1977), p. 217. See also Potter (1977), pp. 110–111.
27 At *Vaid/VaidC* 8 the opponent presents a strange argument by analogy in support of the position that light contacts darkness. The opponent gives the analogy of the planets' (*gza'*) harmful influence (*gnod pa*) on people, such as

(the much-maligned) Devadatta. The point is, presumably, that light contacts darkness just as the planets contact the people upon whom they exert a harmful influence. It is (allegedly) established that the planets do exert a harmful influence upon people. (Perhaps the assumption here is that the planets emit a subtle matter which travels to certain unfortunate people and, through contact with them, causes them harm). Similarly, light illuminates darkness.

I suppose that in the ancient Indian context, light must have appeared as a very mysterious and even magical phenomenon. It may have thus seemed natural to compare light with other mysterious phenomena – such as the (supposed) evil influence of planets upon people.

But Nāgārjuna retorts that the analogy breaks down. Contrary to the opponent's opinion, light does not contact darkness, like the planets exert through contact their harmful influence on people. This is, according to Nāgārjuna, for two reasons:

(a) The harmful influence of the planets on people is possible because people are corporeal (*lus dang ldan pa*). The harmful influence of the planets only occurs when the entity influenced has a body which can be harmed, just as, for example, fire, a snake, illness, etc can only have a harmful influence upon the corporeal. Perhaps the notion is that the subtle matter emitted by the planets can only contact an entity which, similarly, is material. By contrast, darkness is a mere absence of light (*'od med pa tsam*). A mere absence cannot have a body, because, if it did have a body, insofar as it has the positive quality of corporeality, it would not be a mere absence.

(b) The planets are able to exert their influence on peoples' bodies at a great distance (*thag ring po na*), unlike a lamplight, which cannot illuminate very distant objects. The point appears to be, then, that, if the lamplight's alleged illumination of darkness through contact were like the planets' influence on people through contact, then lamplight would be able to contact darkness at a great distance. But it is clear that lamplight does not have this ability.

Note that both the opponent and Nāgārjuna maintain, it would appear, that the planets do indeed harmfully influence people. Their disagreement is about whether or not this harmful influence is similar or dissimilar to the alleged illumination of darkness through contact with light. The difficulty is, however, that neither party provides any proof for the harmful influence of the planets upon people. Perhaps it was a cultural assumption that such harmful influence occurs, and thus the point was taken as axiomatic. But this is a mistake, for the harmful influence of the planets upon people is not a self-evident truth.

However, Nāgārjuna might perhaps retort that he does *not accept* the position that planets harmfully influence people. He is engaging here in a *reductio ad absurdum* (*prasaṅga*). Nāgārjuna adopts *the opponent's assumption* that the planets have a harmful influence on people only for the sake of demonstrating the absurd consequences which follow *for the opponent*, who claims that the illumination of light is similar to this assumed harmful influence of the planets upon people. Nāgārjuna is claiming, in this case, that *even assuming for the sake of argument* that there is (as the opponent claims) an evil influence of planets upon people, the alleged illumination of darkness by light through contact cannot be similar to this evil influence of planets on people. Thus the opponent's argument by analogy does not work.

28 The analogy of the sword is also used in Mādhyamika texts in the refutation of *svasaṃvedana*. That is, just as a sword cuts others but cannot cut itself, so too cognition is not self-aware in the act of being aware of its object. See, for example, Śāntideva's *BC* IX, 18.

29 *VV/VVC* 37–39, *VaidC* 7–8.

30 *NSBh* 1, 1, 25, Jhā (trans.) (1984), pp. 340–341.

31 *VaidC* 9. As noted by Tola and Dragonetti (1995a), p. 185, *Vaid* 9, the verse to which this commentary corresponds, appears to be a corruption of the Sanskrit. They offer a possible reconstruction of it. I have chosen to rely on the commentary, without reference to the verse.

32 See Frede (1983), pp. 65–93.

33 See Hankinson (1995), pp. 81–82.

CHAPTER ELEVEN

The Attack on Extrinsic Validation

Extrinsic Validation (1): The *pramāṇa*-s are Validated by the *prameya*-s

The theory that *pramāṇa*-s are validated by *prameya*-s became the most commonly accepted explanation of validation among the Naiyāyikas. The tendency in Nyāya philosophy (despite the apparent claim at *NS* II, 1, 19 that *pramāṇa*-s are self-validating/self-evident) is to argue that knowledge-episodes are validated if the object functions or acts in the way in which it is cognized. Thus, a perceptual knowledge-episode of water is proved to be a correct perceptual cognition if, for example, the perceived water is found to be wet. But if the perceived water is not wet, it is a mirage rather than real water, and the perception of it as water is a case of error rather than of knowledge. In other words, the correctness of a knowledge-episode is attested by a further cognition of the efficacy (*phalajñāna*) or confirmatory behaviour (*pravṛttisāmarthya*) of the objects which are cognized. If the cognized object actually acts in accordance with its nature, then this proves that the initial cognition did apprehend an object which exists in the mind-independent world. The knowledge-episodes are, therefore, extrinsically validated, i.e. validated by the objects of which they are the knowledge-episodes.[1]

Nāgārjuna says that if the *pramāṇa*-s were validated by *prameya*-s, this might occur through: (i) objects of the same type or 'sphere of activity' (*viṣaya*)- e.g. a perceptual *pramāṇa* might be validated by a perceptual *prameya*, etc, (ii) a *prameya* of a different type, e.g. a perceptual *pramāṇa* might be validated by a *prameya* of an inference, an inferential *pramāṇa* might be validated by a perceptual *prameya*, etc.

Nāgārjuna also states that it might be that the *prameya*-s either individually (*vyasta*) or in an aggregate (*samasta*) could validate the *pramāṇa*-s.[2] For example, in the case of perceptual *pramāṇa*-s, it might be that: (i) one perceptual *prameya* validates a perceptual *pramāṇa*, (ii) an aggregate of perceptual *prameya*-s validates a perceptual *pramāṇa*, (iii) a perceptual *pramāṇa* is validated by an aggregate of *prameya*-s some of which are of the same type as itself, some of which are not of the same type as itself (e.g. some perceptual *prameya*-s, and some inferential *prameya*-s), or all of which are of a single different type from itself (e.g. a group of inferential *prameya*-s), or all of which are from a number of different types than it (e.g. a group of *prameya*-s consisting of inferential *prameya*-s, *prameya*-s of verbal testimony, and *prameya*-s of comparison, used to validate a perceptual knowledge-episode). And *mutatis mutandis* for the other *pramāṇa*-s.

The purpose of this list seems to be to cover all the conceivable possibilities. In fact, the later Naiyāyikas at least appear to have thought that the final, most reliable validation of all *pramāṇa*-s is by way of perceptual *prameya*-s. In this sense perceptual cognition is the basic type of knowledge-episode.[3] Perceptions of confirmatory behaviour provide the most reliable evidence upon which a proof of a knowledge-episode may proceed. Thus, the mechanics of the validation of a knowledge-episode are as follows: One has a knowledge-episode of an object. There is subsequently a perception of the confirmatory behaviour of the object. On this basis, there is an inference: *because* there is a perception of the confirmatory behaviour, therefore the original knowledge-episode of the object is proved to be a knowledge-episode.[4] If I rely on the verbal testimony, for example, of a trustworthy person (*āpta*), that the platypus lives in Australia, the consequent knowledge-episode that the platypus lives in Australia is most securely proved to be a knowledge-episode on the basis of the perception in Australia of the confirmatory behaviour of the curious duck-billed, egg-laying, amphibious creature in question. The trustworthy person has said that the platypus lives in Australia, and the receiver of this information subsequently perceives in Australia an animal behaving in accord with the description of the platypus provided by the trustworthy person. One infers that, because the confirmatory behaviour of the platypus is perceived in Australia, the cognition produced by the verbal testimony of the trustworthy person was a knowledge-episode.

Nāgārjuna's Refutation of Extrinsic Validation (1)

Nāgārjuna's argument is here particularly obscure. But I shall suggest an interpretation. His criticism is essentially that the theory that the *pramāṇa*-s are validated by the *prameya*-s commits the fallacy (*doṣa*) of the validation of the [already] validated (*siddhasya sādhana*).[5] What does this mean?

As I have emphasized, the theory of extrinsic validation (1) of *pramāṇa*-s means that the correctness of a cognition is proved by the confirmatory behaviour of the object cognized. When the object cognized behaves in accord with the initial cognition of it, then the initial cognition is confirmed to be correct. I have a cognition of fire. The fire actually behaves like fire, i.e. it burns, smokes, etc. My initial cognition of the fire is thereby proved to be correct.

There is, however, an obvious problem with this theory, which perhaps Nāgārjuna is pointing out here. The confirmatory behaviour of the object, which supposedly proves that my initial cognition of the object is correct, *must itself be apprehended by a cognition*. But how, then, does one prove that this cognition which apprehends the confirmatory behaviour is itself correct? I cognize that the fire behaves like fire, i.e. it burns, smokes, etc. How do I prove that the cognition of the fire's confirmatory behaviour is correct, i.e. actually mirrors a mind-independent state of affairs? If the cognition of the confirmatory behaviour is proved by further cognitions of confirmatory behaviour, then an infinite regress is entailed. One ends up, in other words, in the same position as the proponent of the theory that *pramāṇa*-s are validated by other *pramāṇa*-s. *Pramāṇa*$_1$ of *prameya*$_1$ is validated by *pramāṇa*$_2$ of the confirmatory behaviour of *prameya*$_1$. *Pramāṇa*$_2$ of the confirmatory behaviour of *prameya*$_1$ is validated by *pramāṇa*$_3$ of the confirmatory behaviour of *prameya*$_1$. And so on.

If one attempts to prove that a cognition is in fact a knowledge-episode, i.e. that it does mirror the mind-independent state of affairs, then it is futile to turn to the confirmatory behaviour of the object cognized as the means of proving the correctness of the initial cognition. For such a proof always relies on the confirmatory behaviour of the object as mediated by a further cognition. There is always the problem of whether this further cognition is itself accurate. In which case, the confirmatory behaviour of the *prameya* (given that the accuracy of the cognition of this confirmatory behaviour has not itself been proved) cannot be used to prove that the initial cognition of the *prameya* was correct.

Hence, perhaps, Nāgārjuna's claim that the theory that the *prameya*-s validate the *pramāṇa*-s entails the fault of validation of the [already] validated. If the confirmatory behaviour of the *prameya* is to validate the *pramāṇa*, i.e. prove that the *pramāṇa* apprehends its object as it is mind-independently, then this confirmatory behaviour of the *prameya* must itself *already* have been proven to be an object which has been correctly cognized, i.e. cognized as it is mind-independently. This means that there must be a cognition which has been proven *already* to cognize correctly the confirmatory behaviour of the *prameya*. To suggest otherwise would involve an absurd inversion (*vyatyaya*) of the theory of *pramāṇa*-s, which would render *pramāṇa*-s superfluous (for the confirmatory behaviour of the *prameya*-s would be said to be correctly cognized without a knowledge-episode!).[6] But how is it proved that the cognition of the confirmatory behaviour of the *prameya* has in fact cognized this confirmatory behaviour as it is mind-independently? Thus, the theory that a *pramāṇa* is validated by the confirmatory behaviour of the *prameya* presupposes (without proof) that there is a cognition which is correct (a *pramāṇa*), i.e. which mirrors the *prameya*'s behaviour as it exists mind-independently.

The later Naiyāyikas (much later than the *NS* and Nāgārjuna's critiques) were certainly aware of this difficulty. Their responses are complex and varied. In general, however, the Naiyāyikas counter that one does not generally doubt the correctness of the cognitions which apprehend confirmatory behaviour. If the water quenches my thirst, I do not usually doubt the perceptual knowledge-episode of the water quenching my thirst. If the fire burns my hand, then I do not doubt that the knowledge-episode of the fire burning my hand is in fact correct. If on some unusual occasion one were to doubt such a knowledge-episode of confirmatory behaviour, the cognition would be validated by appeal to further confirmatory behaviour (e.g. not only did the water quench my thirst, it quenched other people's thirst, it felt like water, etc). This does not lead to an infinite regress, however, because the psychological need for validation stops as soon as the doubt which impedes action is dispelled. Sooner or later, the evidence that the water which I perceive is in fact water will be sufficient for me to believe that it is water. I am then able to act successfully on the basis of this conviction. I will be happy, for example, to take a bath in the water now that my doubts have been vanquished.[7]

It could of course be argued that this pragmatic answer to the problem of validation of knowledge-episodes of confirmatory behaviour is actually an evasion of the issue, for it is still possible that, despite one's psychological convictions, the cognitions of confirmatory behaviour are in fact false, in the sense that they do not correspond to a mind-independent reality (for example, by analogy with a dream in which one believes that one is tasting water, one believes that other people are tasting the water too, etc and yet there is not in fact any water which is being tasted).

But the Naiyāyika can, I think, reasonably object that it is *highly unlikely* that one's psychological convictions, on the basis of cognitions of confirmatory behaviour, are wrong. Granted, it is *theoretically* possible, by analogy with the dream, that all of one's cognitions of the confirmatory behaviour are actually false. That is, it is theoretically possible that not just my initial perception of the water, but my subsequent cognitions of the water as wet, thirst-quenching, cool, etc are delusions. It *might* be, then, that there is no mind-independent water. But a theoretical possibility (especially such an implausible one) is not the same as an actuality. If it is claimed that nevertheless one cannot be *certain* that the cognitions of the confirmatory behaviour are themselves correct, then the Naiyāyika could respond that the requirement of certainty is too strict. The Naiyāyika can say, quite reasonably, that it is *highly probable* that the cognitions of confirmatory behaviour are correct, and this is sufficient grounds for proof. The Naiyāyika might insist, I think, that the onus is on the opponent to prove his (the opponent's) *highly improbable* thesis that the cognitions of the confirmatory behaviour *are not* correct, i.e. do not apprehend a mind-independent state-of-affairs, and thus cannot be used as proof of the correctness of the initial knowledge-episode.

Extrinsic Validation (2): *Pramāṇa*-s and *prameya*-s are Mutually Validating

Nāgārjuna's Refutation of Extrinsic Validation (2)

The final theory which Nāgārjuna considers is that the *pramāṇa*-s and the *prameya*-s are validated in mutual dependence. Nāgārjuna says, if the *pramāṇa*-s validate the *prameya*-s and the *prameya*-s validate the *pramāṇa*-s, then in effect neither *pramāṇa*-s nor *prameya*-s are validated, because they both rely on something unvalidated for their own validation. There is a vicious circle of unvalidated entities depending upon one another for their validation.[8]

Such mutual validation would be like saying, Nāgārjuna argues by analogy, that a father (*pitṛ*) is to be produced (*utpādya*) by a son (*putra*) and that the son himself also is to be produced by the father. In this case both the son and the father would have both the characteristic (*lakṣaṇa*) of the father, i.e. producing, and the son, i.e. being produced. Such a situation, Nāgārjuna says, would raise a doubt (*saṃdeha*) about, i.e. leave the question unanswered as to, which of the two is the father and which the son. For something which is produced cannot really also be the producer of what produces it. Similarly, if both the *pramāṇa* and the *prameya* have the characteristic of validating the other and being validated by the other, then the question of validation remains unanswered. For something which is validated cannot really also be the validator of that which validates it.[9]

I understand Nāgārjuna to mean here that the position that the *pramāṇa* validates the *prameya* and that the *prameya* validates the *pramāṇa* is obviously circular. If $pramāṇa_1$ validates $prameya_1$ and $\mathrm{prameya}_1$ validates $pramāṇa_1$ then neither $pramāṇa_1$ nor $prameya_1$ has in fact been validated. For example, take my perception of the copper beech tree. If I am asked to prove that this perception is correct, I might say that it is correct because there is a copper beech tree. If I am asked to prove that there is a copper beech tree, and I reply that there is a copper beech tree because I have a perception of it, then I have very obviously begged the question.

A Reply to Nāgārjuna's Refutation

One might, however, imagine a more sophisticated version of the theory of mutual validation. Such a theory might state that *pramāṇa*-s and *prameya*-s gain their trustworthiness through their interaction over time and with experience. The cognitions are attested by the repeated confirmatory behaviour of the objects cognized, and the objects cognized are attested by the fact that they are repeatedly objects of (increasingly) reliable forms of cognitions.

This is, in fact, a position which appeals to common-sense, and which seems to describe how cognition actually evolves in experience. One gradually builds up a sense that certain cognitions and types of cognition are correct, because they have been proved so by their object's confirmatory behaviour in the past. And one gradually builds up a sense that certain objects exist as they are cognized, because similar cognitions of them have been correct in the past. Take, for example, the following scenario.

I perceive from a distance a pool of water. I may confirm that it is a pool of water when it quenches my thirst. Here the initial perception of the pool of water is validated by the confirmatory behaviour of the pool of water. If at a later date I again perceive at some distance a pool of water I will perhaps trust my perception. The perception is now a means of validating the object itself. I again may confirm that it is a pool of water when it quenches my thirst. The confirmatory behaviour again reinforces the validity of the perception, and the perception can be trusted even more to be a means of validating a similar perceived object in the future. If I perceive at a distance a pool of water I shall be justified in believing that it is in fact a pool of water because I have perceived it thus. I may judge that the perceived pool of water is in fact a pool of water, simply on the basis that I know my perception to be reliable in this matter. The object is validated by the cognition and the cognition has itself been validated on the basis of the previous confirmatory behaviour of the object. *Pramāṇa* and *prameya* are mutually validating.

I want to suggest that experience in general develops in this manner. One gradually becomes accustomed to trusting one's cognitions on the basis of their repeated success at apprehending objects. Their success has been measured by the fact that the object cognized has behaved as one would expect such an object to behave.

But it can be objected that this explanation remains hopelessly circular. That one gradually becomes accustomed to trusting one's cognitions in this way does not prove that the objects apprehended exist independently of the mind. For it might be that, although one comes to *trust* that one's cognitions are reliable in apprehending mind-independent objects, *in fact* the objects which are apprehended do not exist independently of one's mind. The perception of the pool of water might be attested by the fact that it can quench one's thirst, etc, and one will subsequently trust one's perceptions of pools of water as reliable, but perhaps the pool of water, and its thirst-quenching capacity are fabrications of the cognition which apprehends them.

Once again, however, I must repeat my objection to this sort of criticism. It is admittedly theoretically possible that all the objects of cognitions are in fact conceptual constructs. In this sense, the circularity of the above explanation cannot be denied. That is, the explanation does not *disprove* the theoretical possibility that the whole process of mutual validation of knowledge-episodes and objects of knowlege depends on objects which are in reality simply products of the mind. But this theoretical possibility seems so unlikely, I contend, that it is the (Mādhyamika) opponent who must *prove* that this theoretical possibility is an actuality. Until such a proof is forthcoming, the thesis that, generally speaking, the objects of cognitions have a mind-independent nature can be safely assumed to be correct.

Notes

1 My account of the Nyāya theory of extrinsic validation depends on Chatterjee (1978), pp. 81–89, Matilal (1986), pp. 160–179. They rely primarily on the *Nyāyamañjarī* of Jayanta Bhaṭṭa, the *Nyāyavārttikatātparyaṭīkā* of Vācaspati Miśra, and Udayana's *Pariśuddhi*.

2 *VVC* 51.

3 See Van Bijlert (1989), p. 33. See also Matilal (1986), p. 5, who writes that, for the Naiyāyikas, perceiving is 'the most direct, basic, and indubitable knowing.'

4 See Matilal (1986), p. 164.

5 *VV/VVC* 42.

6 See *VV/VVC* 43–45.

7 See Matilal (1986), pp. 172–179, Chatterjee (1978), pp. 81–89.

8 *VV/VVC* 46–48.

9 *VV/VVC* 49–50.

CHAPTER TWELVE

The Attack on Validation: Conclusion

Nāgārjuna's attack on the validation – intrinsic and extrinsic – of *pramāṇa*-s is, I conclude, a philosophical failure. This is for two reasons.

First, in many ways (which I have outlined above in chapters 10 and 11) the arguments which Nāgārjuna presents in order to refute the various ways in which the *pramāṇa*-s might be validated are simply untenable. Nāgārjuna's arguments do not establish even that there is no *proof* that knowledge-episodes apprehend mind-independent objects, let alone that *prameya*-s do not *exist* in a mind-independent manner.

Second, the position which underlies Nāgārjuna's arguments – namely, that objects of knowledge (*prameya*) exist without *svabhāva* = are one and all entirely conceptual constructs – would seem (regardless of the fact that his arguments are so often fallacious) to be a highly implausible account of the way things really are. It seems much more likely that – as the Naiyāyikas maintain – the objects which one apprehends by means of *pramāṇa*-s actually exist independently of the apprehension of them (in many cases at least). Nāgārjuna's critique of the validation of knowledge-episodes has certainly given us no good reasons to think otherwise.

CHAPTER THIRTEEN

The Argument from the Three Times

Analysis of the Argument

At *Vaid/VaidC* 12, Nāgārjuna presents an argument which is meant to prove that the *pramāṇa*-s and *prameya*-s are not established, i.e. do not exist (with *svabhāva*? See my discussion below), in the three times (*dus gsum du tshad ma dang gzhal bya dag ma grub pa*). This is an argument which is presented, in a somewhat different form, by a (possibly Mādhyamika) opponent at *NS* II, 1, 8–11. It also appears, in a very similar form to the argument in the *Vaid/VaidC*, in the **Dvādaśanikāyaśāstra*, attributed to Nāgārjuna.[1]

The argument, as it occurs in the *Vaid/VaidC*, is as follows. If there are *pramāṇa*-s and the *prameya*-s, they must be mutually dependent. Mutual dependence is a form of causation. Causation occurs in time. Which is to say that the *pramāṇa* must occur: (i) prior to (*snga rol*) the *prameya*, (ii) subsequent to (*phyis*) the *prameya*, or (iii) at the same time as (*cig car du*) the *prameya*. But (i), (ii), and (iii) are all impossible. (Impossible if the *pramāṇa*-s and *prameya*-s have *svabhāva*?). Therefore, the *pramāṇa*-s and *prameya*-s do not exist (with *svabhāva*?).

How does Nāgārjuna argue that (i), (ii) and (iii) are impossible?

(i) If the *pramāṇa* occurs prior to its *prameya* it would not in fact be a *pramāṇa*. Nāgārjuna perhaps means that knowledge-episodes are intentional, i.e. they must have objects of which they are the knowledge-episodes. But for a *pramāṇa* which existed before its *prameya* there would be no object of which the *pramāṇa* would be the *pramāṇa*. As the opponent at *NS* II, 1, 9 expresses this point, if the *pramāṇa* existed before the *prameya*, then perception (*pratyakṣa*), for example, would not be produced by connection (*sannikarṣa*) of the sense-organ (*indriya*) with the object (*artha*). That is, the *pramāṇa* would exist without its object. There would be knowledge without something which is known, which is absurd.

(ii) If the *pramāṇa* occurs after the *prameya*, then the *pramāṇa* would be unarisen at the time that the *prameya* is arisen. But a *pramāṇa* which has not yet arisen cannot be the *pramāṇa* of an arisen *prameya*. What is unarisen simply cannot abide together with (*lhan cig mi gnas pa*), i.e. be in relation to, what is arisen. Only things which have arisen already can be in relation to one another. Nāgārjuna says that if an unarisen *pramāṇa* were asserted to be the *pramāṇa* of an arisen *prameya*, then a horn of a rabbit could be a *pramāṇa*! This analogy seems to be making the (rather obvious) point that an unarisen *pramāṇa* is actually non-existent, and it is absurd that a non-existent could be the *pramāṇa* of a *prameya*.

Thus, the consequence of the position that the *pramāṇa* occurs after the *prameya* is that the *prameya* exists without a *pramāṇa*. But this is impossible, because, the intended object relies on the intentional cognition just as much as the intentional cognition relies on the intended object. There is no such thing as an object of knowledge without a knowledge-episode which cognizes it.

I stress here the ambiguity of this last assertion. Does Nāgārjuna mean (i) that the object in its quality of 'being known' is dependent upon the knowledge-episode or (ii) that the knowledge-episode itself is constitutive of the object known? Surely Nāgārjuna's argument only establishes (i), which is a trivial finding. One suspects that Nāgārjuna actually means that (ii) is the case. But his argument does not in fact prove this point. Nāgārjuna is either stating something so obvious as to be uninteresting (namely, that the 'being known' of an object requires and cannot exist prior to the knowing of this object) or something neither obvious nor at all substantiated by Nāgārjuna's argument (namely, that an object which is known cannot exist prior to the knowing of this object).

At any rate, positions (i) and (ii) are (according to Nāgārjuna) impossible because, on account of their mutual dependence, the *pramāṇa* cannot exist prior to, i.e. without, the *prameya*, and the *prameya* cannot exist prior to, i.e. without, the *pramāṇa*. This would seem to imply, therefore, that they are simultaneous. But Nāgārjuna explains that this cannot be the case either:

(iii) If the *pramāṇa* and the *prameya* were to exist at the same time, then they would not be mutually dependent, because mutual dependence is a relation of causation, and simultaneous entities cannot cause one another. Nāgārjuna gives the analogy of the two horns of the ox, which arise together but do not cause one another. In order for one entity to cause another entity, it must exist prior to the caused entity. (This certainly rules out certain notions of causation, such as, for example, Aristotle's final cause). *X* is the cause of *y* when *y* is a result of *x*. But results necessarily follow, i.e. exist at a later time than, that of which they are the results. But, as we have seen, a *pramāṇa* cannot exist at a later time than a *prameya*, and neither can a *prameya* exist at a later time than a *pramāṇa*.

The most obvious weakness in this argument against the simultaneity of *pramāṇa* and *prameya* is that it employs a very restrictive notion of causation, viz. as involving a temporal series. A cause must be, according to Nāgārjuna, prior to the effect which it produces. Thus a cause must not be simultaneous with its effect. But this argument is unconvincing, because it may well be that causation can in fact occur in some cases without temporal succession. Some entities may be effects, i.e. depend upon their causes, without those causes preceding them. That this is the case is certainly recognized by the Abhidharma. The *AKBh*, for example, says that simultaneous mutual causation (*sahabhūhetu*) is one ot the six types of causes (*hetu*). The Pāli Abhidhamma also accepts the *sahajāta paccaya* (the simultaneous condition) and says that it has a reciprocal (*aññamañña*) form. According to both the Vaibhāṣika and Theravāda traditions, such simultaneous mutual causation is typified by the four great elements (*mahābhūta*), which cannot exist apart from one another. Though the Sautrāntikas did not accept reciprocal causation, they did admit that non-reciprocal, simultaneous causation occurs (as between, for example, the sense organ and its corresponding consciousness).[2] Nāgārjuna is, then, out on a limb (in terms of Buddhist philosophy) when he says that simultaneous causation is impossible. But he provides no justification (other than the implausible analogy of an ox's horns) for his unusual and far from self-evident assertion.

In fact, it appears to me to be entirely plausible that the *pramāṇa* and *prameya* do exist, in one sense at least, in mutual dependence and simultaneously. For the knowledge-episode must have an object of knowledge in order to be known, and an object, in order to be an object of knowledge, must be the object of a knowledge-episode. (Which does not, I stress, prove that there is no object which exists independently of its being an object of knowledge. I would argue that the *prameya*, understood as the object which is known (as opposed to its 'being known') can (in many cases) exist before, simultaneously with, and after the knowledge-episode. A tree, for example, can exist before, simultaneously with, and after the knowledge of it). It seems, then, that the notion of simultaneous causation in this respect is quite unproblematic. It certainly is not refuted by simply pointing out that an ox's horns exist simultaneously and are not causes of one another!

The Naiyāyika Objection

Nāgārjuna's argument from the three times thus seems very dubious indeed. But what precisely does Nāgārjuna intend to demonstrate by means of this argument? It would seem that his position here is that the *pramāṇa*-s and the *prameya*-s do not exist at all. For he appears to have denied even the possibility of simultaneous, mutually dependent *pramāṇa*-s and *prameya*-s. He seems to claim that *pramāṇa*-s and *prameya*-s cannot exist, even in mutual dependence. Nāgārjuna appears to argue that the occurrence of *pramāṇa*-s and *prameya*-s is impossible.

This is certainly how Nāgārjuna's argument is understood by the Naiyāyika opponent at *Vaid/VaidC* 13. The Naiyāyika opponent objects that, if for Nāgārjuna the *pramāṇa*-s and the *prameya*-s are non-existent, because any temporal relation between them is impossible, then surely Nāgārjuna must claim that he has a knowledge-episode that this is the case. But then, Nāgārjuna contradicts himself, because he has claimed both that knowledge-episodes and their objects do not exist, and that he has a knowledge-episode, arrived at by a correct inference, that there are no knowledge-episodes and objects of knowledge-episodes. As the Naiyāyika opponent says, Nāgārjuna's negation of the *pramāṇa*-s, which itself has the character of a *pramāṇa*, should itself be impossible in the three times.

I think that this objection is sound, if Nāgārjuna is indeed claiming that the *pramāṇa*-s and *prameya*-s do not exist. The assertion that there is a knowledge-episode that there are no knowledge-episodes is self-contradictory. If, as seems to be suggested in the *NS*,[3] the Mādhyamika might attempt to avoid the problem by excepting this one knowledge-episode from the general rule, then this is arbitrary. Why should the knowledge-episode that there are no knowledge-episodes be excepted by the Mādhyamika from the general rule that *pramāṇa*-s and *prameya*-s cannot exist in the three times? It is incumbent upon the Mādhyamika to explain how the existence of a *pramāṇa* and a *prameya* is possible in this special case, and this he cannot do, of course, without contradicting his own reasoning that the *pramāṇa*-s and *prameya*-s are not established in the three times.

Nāgārjuna's Response to the Naiyāyika Objection

The unconvincing response given to this problem by Nāgārjuna in the *Vaid/VaidC* is that the opponent's objection commits the fallacy (*skyon*) of previous acceptance (*sngar khas blangs pa*). In other words, according to Nāgārjuna, the opponent argues:

Premiss$_1$: The *pramāṇa*-s and *prameya*-s cannot be established in the three times.

Premiss$_2$: The cognition (the *pramāna*-s and the *prameya*-s cannot be established in the three times) is itself a *pramāṇa*.

Conclusion: Therefore, the cognition (the *pramāṇa*-s and the *prameya*-s cannot be established in the three times) cannot itself be established in the three times.

Nāgārjuna claims that the opponent first *accepts* premiss$_1$, i.e. that the *pramāṇa*-s and *prameya*-s cannot be established in the three times, before proceeding to refute it. And, Nāgārjuna says, in that the Naiyāyika first accepts premiss$_1$, the debate is finished (*rtsod pa rdzogs pa*)! Which is to say that Nāgārjuna's position, i.e. that the *pramāṇa*-s and the *prameya*-s cannot exist in the three times, is established.[4]

But this argument is pure sophistry. The Naiyāyika does not *accept* premiss$_1$, i.e. that the *pramāṇa*-s and *prameya*-s are not established in the three times. On the contrary, the Naiyāyika argument is intended to point out the undesirable consequences *for Nāgārjuna* of Nāgārjuna's own acceptance of this premiss. The Naiyāyika is engaging here in *tarka*, i.e. in a *reductio ad absurdum*. (See chapter 6 for a discussion of *tarka*). That is, *if* one were to accept, as does Nāgārjuna (and as certainly the Naiyāyika himself does not), that the *pramāṇa*-s and *prameya*-s are not established in the three times, then the knowledge-episode, i.e. *pramāṇa*, that the *pramāṇa*-s and the *prameya*-s are not established in the three times would be impossible. But Nāgārjuna claims that he knows, i.e. has a *pramāṇa*, that the *pramāṇa*-s and the *prameya*-s are not established in the three times. Nāgārjuna's position entails that *Nāgārjuna* is caught in a paradox, i.e. a contradiction.[5] The Naiyāyika is surely right here, if Nāgārjuna is in fact claiming that he knows that there are no *pramāṇa*-s and *prameya*-s.

Another Mādhyamika Response Considered

The Mādhyamika might, I suppose, alternatively try to answer the Naiyāyika objection by claiming that his argument from the three times is *not* in fact intended to negate the existence of the *pramāṇa*-s and *prameya*-s. Rather, the argument is meant to negate a particular notion of how it is that *pramāṇa*-s and *prameya*-s exist. The Mādhyamika might say, then, that he negates only the notion that *pramāṇa*-s and *prameya*-s exist with *svabhāva*. Thus, the knowledge-episode that knowledge-episodes and their objects do not exist in the three times is possible because it is in fact a knowledge-episode without *svabhāva* (but a knowledge-episode nonetheless) that knowledge-episodes with *svabhāva* and their objects with *svabhāva* do not exist in the three times. His refutation that *pramāṇa*-s and *prameya*-s can exist in the three times is not a refutation of *pramāṇa*-s and *prameya*-s *per se*, but is rather a refutation of the compatibility of their mutual dependence with the possession of *svabhāva*. This is, of course, an attractive solution; it appears to get the Mādhyamika out of his paradox.

However, this interpretation of the argument from the three times is far from unproblematic. In the *Vaid*/*VaidC* Nāgārjuna does not make explicit that the argument that the *pramāṇa*-s and *prameya*-s are not established in the three times is intended to refute the existence with *svabhāva* of *pramāṇa*-s and *prameya*-s. Instead he resorts to the previously mentioned and completely sophistical accusation that the Naiyāyika objection commits the fallacy of previous acceptance. If Nāgārjuna thinks that he refutes only the existence with *svabhāva* of *pramāṇa*-s and *prameya*-s by means of the argument from the three times, then why does he not say so?

Nevertheless, earlier in the *Vaid*/*VaidC*, as I have explained (see Chapter 8), Nāgārjuna advocates that the *pramāṇa*-s and *prameya*-s are mutually dependent, and that this mutual dependence entails that they exist but without *svabhāva*. Perhaps, then, the argument that the *pramāṇa*-s and *prameya*-s are not established in the three times is simply meant to support this position.

Furthermore, at *Vaid/VaidC* 16, Nāgārjuna gives the analogy of a man who becomes afraid (*'jigs par 'gyur ba*) because he wrongly thinks that a river (*chu*) is deep (*gting ring*). This concept (*blo*) that the river is deep may be negated when he is informed that the river is in fact not deep. The negation removes a misunderstanding, a misconception. Nāgārjuna says that his negation of the *pramāṇa*-s and *prameya*-s (by means of the argument from the three times) similarly simply removes a misconception.

See here the similar analogy given at *VVC* 64, in which Nāgārjuna compares his negation, 'the *svabhāva* of entities does not exist' (*nāsti svabhāvo bhāvānām*), to the negation, stated to someone who thinks that 'Devadatta is in the house', that 'Devadatta is not in the house.' The negation 'Devadatta is not in the house' makes known (*jñāpayati*) that Devadatta is not in the house. Similarly, the negation 'the *svabhāva* of entities does not exist' makes known that entities do not in fact have *svabhāva*. There is no *svabhāva* whatsoever of any entities, yet the negation is necessary in order to remove the misunderstanding in people's minds that entities do have *svabhāva*. At *VVC* 64, at least, Nāgārjuna clearly wishes to remove the misconception that entities have *svabhāva*, and his intention is not to negate the existence *per se* of entities.

It is arguable, then, that the misconception which Nāgārjuna's negation of the *pramāṇa*-s and *prameya*-s (by means of the argument from the three times at *Vaid/VaidC* 12) is meant to remove is that these *pramāṇa*-s and *prameya*-s have *svabhāva*. Nāgārjuna negates the misconception that *pramāṇa*-s and *prameya*-s have *svabhāva* rather than the *pramāṇa*-s and *prameya*-s as such.

* * *

But there is a problem with this Mādhyamika response to the Naiyāyika objection. *Why* would the *pramāṇa*-s and *prameya*-s which exist without *svabhāva* escape Nāgārjuna's argument from the three times, whereas the *pramāṇa*-s and *prameya*-s which exist with *svabhāva* are (supposedly) refuted by this same argument? It would appear that, if Nāgārjuna's argument from the three times were successful, it would apply equally to *pramāṇa*-s and *prameya*-s which have *svabhāva*, and to *pramāṇa*-s and *prameya*-s which do not have *svabhāva*. That is to say, even a *pramāṇa* without *svabhāva* would not – according to Nāgārjuna's argument – be able to exist prior to, after, or at the same time as a *prameya* without *svabhāva*. Thus, even *pramāṇa*-s and *prameya*-s which exist without *svabhāva* would not be established in the three times. Must not Nāgārjuna's arguments apply equally well (or badly) to *pramāṇa*-s and *prameya*-s which exist with *svabhāva* and *pramāṇa*-s and *prameya*-s which exist without *svabhāva*? In which case, either his argument from the three times is unsuccessful and refutes neither *pramāṇa*-s and *prameya*-s which exist with *svabhāva* nor *pramāṇa*-s and *prameya*-s which exist without *svabhāva*, or else his argument from the three times is successful and refutes both *pramāṇa*-s and *prameya*-s which exist with *svabhāva* and *pramāṇa*-s and *prameya*-s which exist without *svabhāva*. The exception of *pramāṇa*-s and *prameya*-s without *svabhāva* from the refutation would be arbitrary.

Furthermore, I have argued (see chapter 4) that Nāgārjuna's assertion of universal absence of *svabhāva* reduces to nihilism (despite Nāgārjuna's intention to tread the Middle Path between nihilism and eternalism). Given Nāgārjuna's contention that everything lacks *svabhāva*, there is not actually a real distinction between existence without *svabhāva* and complete non-existence. In which case, the existence without *svabhāva* of *pramāṇa*-s and *prameya*-s is after all equivalent to their complete non-existence. It just will not work for Nāgārjuna to say that his argument from the three times refutes – not the existence of *pramāṇa*-s and *prameya*-s but rather – the misconception that *pramāṇa*-s and *prameya*-s have *svabhāva*. If everything lacks *svabhāva* (as Nāgārjuna claims), then the knowledge-episode without *svabhāva* that there are no knowledge-episodes and objects of knowledge with *svabhāva* entails the nihilistic paradox that there is a knowledge-episode that knowledge-episodes and objects of knowledge do not exist at all. The Naiyāyika objection to Nāgārjuna's argument from the three times still stands.

Notes

1 See Cheng (1982) (trans.), pp. 101–103. Lindtner (1982), p. 11 argues that the **Dvādaśanikāyaśāstra*, which survives only in Chinese, is 'decidedly spurious'.

2 See *AKBh* II, 49–50. Karunadasa (1967), pp. 131–132.

3 See *NS* II, 1, 14. See also *NSBh* II,1, 14 and *NSV* II, 1, 14, Jhā (trans.) (1984), pp. 627–628.

4 *Vaid* /*VaidC* 14–15.

5 See *NSV* II, 1, 12, Jhā (trans.) (1984), pp. 620–621. Uddyotakara's opponent states that, 'by urging that "denial is not possible, as it cannot be connected with any of the three points of time," you admit (the force of our argument and contention) that "as they cannot be connected with any of the three points of time, perception and the rest cannot be regarded as *pramāṇa*."' This is essentially the fallacy of previous acceptance, of which Nāgārjuna, in the *Vaid* and *VaidC*, accuses the Naiyāyika. Uddyotakara responds that, 'This does not affect our position, we reply; as all that we mean by urging this argument is to show that your view involves a self-contradiction on your part; what we are urging is that you are open to the charge that the reasoning that you have put forward goes directly against your own view; and we do not admit the validity of that reasoning ... '. I am strongly inclined to agree with Uddyotakara here.

CHAPTER FOURTEEN

Further Arguments in the *Vaidalyaprakaraṇa*

At *Vaid/VaidC* 18–20 Nāgārjuna presents three further arguments intended to refute the Nyāya *pramāṇa* theory. I shall, in the present chapter, examine these arguments, and attempt to evaluate them. (A task which, I might add, is not aided by the laconic and obscure nature of Nāgārjuna's presentation of his points).

The Analysis of the Perception of a Pot

At *Vaid/VaidC* 17, the Naiyāyika opponent argues that the *pramāṇa* apprehends the *prameya*, and this is attested by the confirmatory behaviour of the *prameya*. This is, then, a statement of the Nyāya *pramāṇa* theory, according to which the *pramāṇa* ascertains the *prameya* as it exists independently of the mind. That the *pramāṇa* is a *pramāṇa*, i.e. that the *pramāṇa* does actually apprehend its object as it exists independently of the mind, is demonstrated when the object is found to behave in accordance with the nature of the object as cognized by the *pramāṇa*.

Nāgārjuna responds, at *Vaid/VaidC* 18, that although (*kyang*) the *pramāṇa*-s might exist, the object of knowledge (*prameya*) cannot be admitted (*'thad pa ma yin*). He then says that if the *pramāṇa*-s existed (*tshad ma rnams ni grub na*), there would have to be an object of knowledge! Nāgārjuna's point appears to be that, given that the object of knowledge cannot be admitted, therefore there are no knowledge-episodes. That is, even if one were to admit the existence of *pramāṇa*-s, their corresponding *prameya*-s could not occur. Thus, in fact, there are no *pramāṇa*-s. I think that what

Nāgārjuna means is that there is no mind-independent object of knowledge, i.e. no object of knowledge with *svabhāva*, and thus it is wrong to claim, as do the Naiyāyikas, that there are knowledge-episodes which mirror a mind-independent state of affairs. But how does Nāgārjuna justify his position?

Nāgārjuna gives the example of the perception (*mngon sum*) of the pot (*bum pa*). Nāgārjuna does not deny that there is a perception of a pot. However, the perception of the pot is not, according to Nāgārjuna, a perception of a mind-independent entity. What are initially perceived, he claims, are the various sense-objects (*don*). They are apprehended by means of their corresponding sense-organs (*dbang po*). Thus, for example, the sight sense-organ (*mig gi dbang po*) perceives the colour sense-object. Furthermore, this perception of the colour sense-object itself depends on conditions (*rkyen la ltos pa*), such as light (*snang ba*). Redness, for example, is only perceived if there is light by means of which the sense-organ can apprehend it. (Nāgārjuna's point here seems to be that the perception of a sense-object requires further conditions in addition to the sense-organ and the sense-object).

Nāgārjuna seems to be making a distinction between two types or stages of perception. First, there is the perception of various sense-objects, such as colour, by means of the respective sense-organs (along with certain other conditions (such as light, in the case of vison)). Second, there is the perception of the pot. This second stage is a construction by the mind on the basis of the perception of the sense-objects. The entity 'pot' is a name/concept which is attributed by the mind on the basis of the perception of various sense-objects, such as colour. Thus, the knowledge-episode of the pot does not mirror a mind-independent state of affairs. The same is true, Nāgārjuna says, about inferences, comparisons and verbal testimony about the pot. They will, like the perception of the pot, be inferences, comparisons, and verbal testimonies about a pot which is conceptually constructed on the basis of sense-objects.

Nāgārjuna appears here to be re-stating the basic Abhidharma position. What is initially apprehended are various aggregations of *rūpadharma*-s. For example, aggregations of colour *dharma*-s, aggregations of tactile *dharma*-s, etc. These *rūpadharma*-s are apprehended by their respective sense-organs, which produce the corresponding sense-consciousness. An aggregation of colour *dharma*-s, for example, is apprehended by a visual sense-organ, which produces a visual sense-consciousness. An aggregation of sound *dharma*-s is apprehended by a hearing organ, which produces an instance of auditory consciousness. And so on.

The sense-organs and their respective objects are called the twelve *āyatana*-s (visual organ and colour (and, according to some, shape),[1] hearing organ and sound, nasal organ and smell, taste organ and taste, touch organ and touch, and mental organ and mental objects), whereas these twelve *āyatana*-s together with their six corresponding consciousnesses (visual consciousness, auditory consciousness, olfactory consciousness, gustatory consciousness, tactile consciousness, and mental consciousness) are named the eighteen *dhātu*-s.[2]

The Abhidharma position states that perceptions of the mind-independent world are perceptions of aggregations of atomic particles. Thus, there is a mind-independent world, but it is not the world of pots, mountains, and trees which one ordinarily experiences. Rather, it is the world of imperceptible atomic particles which, in aggregation, may be perceived as colours, sounds, smells, etc. The perceived world of tables, mountains, and trees, etc is constructed by the mind on the basis of the apprehended aggregations of *dharma*-s.[3]

Thus, the pot is not an object of knowledge in the sense in which the Naiyāyikas use the term 'object of knowledge'. That is, it is not an entity which exists mind-independently. Consequently, there can not be a knowledge-episode of it, if one means by a knowledge-episode, as do the Naiyāyikas, a mirroring of a mind-independent state of affairs.

(The Naiyāyika will of course object to this explanation. For him the mind-independent world is a much richer place than that envisaged by the Ābhidharmika. The mind-independent world includes, not only atomic particles which cluster together (which, the Naiyāyika does, however, accept) but also the whole entities (*avayavin*), which are not just concepts/names attributed by the mind to the aggregates of parts (*deśa*). Pots, mountains and trees *do* exist mind-independently. They are said to exist in their parts through the relation of inherence (*samavāya*). Consequently, a perception of a pot, for example, is a perception of a mind-independent entity. And because the pot inheres in its parts, one may have a perception of the whole entity 'pot' simply by perceiving a part of the pot.[4])

One would expect here, I think, that Nāgārjuna would make the further point that even the Abhidharma *dharma*-s, which form in aggregation the sense-objects, are themselves conceptually constructed. In this case – not only would knowledge-episodes of ordinary entities, such as pots, not mirror a mind-independent reality but also – there would be no mind-independent reality at all upon which such knowledge-episodes are based. One cannot have knowledge-episodes which apprehend a mind-independent reality even in the case of the sense-objects out of which pots, etc are conceptually constructed. The sense-objects themselves are *prajñaptisat*. This is a point which is made explicitly at *ŚS* 52–54, where Nāgārjuna argues that the *āyatana*-s (the sense-organs and their objects) are themselves empty (*stong pa*). That is, they are empty of *svabhāva*, which is to say that they are *prajñaptisat*. It seems surprising to me that Nāgārjuna, here in the *Vaid/VaidC*, does not make a similar point. As his argument stands, it appears to be an explication of Abhidharma position, and it does not (clearly, at any rate) take the further distinctively Mādhyamika step of denying even the *svabhāva* of the sense-objects themselves. (Nāgārjuna's argument is very obscure, however. One cannot be sure of what point he intends to make).

Refutation of the *pramāṇa* as a Cognition which Corresponds to the Object as *prameya*

At *VaidC* 19, the Naiyāyika opponent asserts once again his realist thesis. The *prameya* is the object, such as a pot, to which corresponds a cognition (*blo= buddhi*), e.g. the perception of the pot, which is the *pramāṇa*. The point is, it would appear, that a knowledge-episode is a mental mirroring of the mind-independent state of affairs. The pot exists and is there to be contacted, as it were, by the cognition. Nāgārjuna presents two arguments in refutation of this position. He argues that: (1) the object cognized is just a condition of the knowledge-episode, and (2) the cognition is a *prameya*, according to the Naiyāyikas themselves.

The Object Cognized is Just a Condition of the Knowledge-episode

Nāgārjuna writes,

> *de rkyen du gyur pa nyid yin pa'i phyir shes pa yang ma yin zhing shes bya yang ma yin no//*

> Because the [pot] only occurs as a condition, it is neither the knowledge nor the object of knowledge. (*Vaid* 19)
>
> *gang gi phyir dbang po dang don phrad pa las blo skye bar 'dod pa de'i phyir bum pa ni rkyen du gyur pa nyid yin pa de'i phyir blo ni tshad ma ma yin la bum pa yang gzhal bya ma yin no/*
>
> Because it is accepted that the cognition [of the pot] arises as a result of the contact of the sense-organ and the object, therefore the pot only occurs as a condition [of the knowledge-episode]. Therefore, the cognition [of the pot] is not the knowledge-episode and the pot is not the object of knowledge. (*VaidC* 19).

What does Nāgārjuna mean when he states that the pot is a only a condition (*rkyen*) of the knowledge-episode? It would seem that he means that the pot is the object of the sense-organ. The sense-organ and the pot are both required in order for a knowledge-episode to occur. They are both conditions required for the production of a knowledge-episode. Thus, the pot is only a necessary but not a sufficient condition for the occurrence of a knowledge-episode. But why should it follow from this that the pot is not the object of knowledge, and the cognition of the pot is not the knowledge-episode? I do not understand Nāgārjuna's reasoning. (One is tempted, perhaps, to find a 'Kantian' sort of argument here. Because the sense-organ, as well as the pot, is a condition for the possibility of knowledge, what is actually known is not the pot as it is in itself, but rather the pot as mediated by the sense-organ (and, indeed, the sense-consciousness). The pot as it is in itself is just a cause of the cognition, and lies behind the 'veil of ideas'. But this interpretation seems rather far-fetched).

At any rate, it seems that Nāgārjuna is being very inconsistent. As I have explained, at *Vaid/VaidC* 18 Nāgārjuna says that the sense-organs apprehend the sense-objects, such as colour, smell, etc, on the basis of which the object, such as a pot, is conceptually constructed. Now, at *Vaid/VaidC* 19, Nāgārjuna appears to say that the object which is contacted by the sense-organ is the pot. Therefore the pot is only one of the conditions (along with the sense-organ) which produces the knowledge-episode. But, surely, Nāgārjuna should say, rather, that the contact of the sense-organ with the sense-object (such as colour) is the condition in dependence upon which the mind constructs the cognition of the pot. The pot is not a condition for the production of the knowledge-episode; it is, rather, the object of knowledge which occurs dependent upon conditions such as the contact of the sense-organ and the sense-object, and the constructive activity of the mind. I suspect that Nāgārjuna is guilty here of (very) confused thinking. (It is hard to know, however, exactly what Nāgārjuna has in mind. His argument is so undeveloped that it is difficult confidently to make much philosophical sense of it).

The Cognition is a *prameya*, According to the Naiyāyikas Themselves

Nāgārjuna's final argument, at *Vaid/VaidC* 20, is that the Naiyāyikas claim, at *NS* I, 1, 9, that cognitions (*buddhi*) are in fact a class of *prameya*-s. But the Naiyāyikas also want to claim, Nāgārjuna notes, that the *pramāṇa* is a cognition. How then can the cognition be both a *prameya* and a *pramāṇa*? Nāgārjuna clearly means that the Naiyāyikas are inconsistent in claiming that one thing, viz. a cognition (*blo*), can be both a knowledge-episode and the object of knowledge. However, Nāgārjuna's argument is obviously fallacious, and this is for two reasons:

(i) It does not follow that, because *pramāṇa*-s are cognitions, all cognitions are *pramāṇa*-s. In fact, this is obviously not the case (according to the Naiyāyikas themselves there are plenty of erroneous cognitions, cognitions characterized by doubt, etc. See chapter 6). Thus, cognitions which are not knowledge-episodes might become the object (*prameya*) of a knowledge-episode. For example, one may have the introspective knowledge-episode which apprehends, i.e. takes as its object of knowledge, an erroneous cognition. I might have the correct cognition of my erroneous cognition. I know that my cognition of the twelve-headed ogre in my back garden (for instance) is incorrect. There is no contradiction, then, in the claim that *pramāṇa*-s are cognitions, and that other non-*pramāṇa* cognitions might become the *prameya*-s of these *pramāṇa*-s.

(ii) It is true that it is contradictory to assert that a cognition which is a *pramāṇa* might simultaneously be a *prameya*. However, there is no contradiction in the position (advanced by the Naiyāyikas[5]) which asserts that a cognition which is a *pramāṇa* might become subsequently the *prameya* of another *pramāṇa*. This might occur when the *pramāṇa* is itself validated. For then the correct cognition itself becomes the object attested. There is a knowledge-episode of a knowledge-episode.

Take, for example, my correct cognition of the pot. A subsequent correct cognition might take the correct cognition of the pot as its object (*prameya*). For example, as a result of validation, I might have the knowledge-episode that my earlier cognition of the pot was a knowledge-episode. I have a knowledge-episode of a knowledge-episode (which is thus, in this context, a *prameya*).

So, Nāgārjuna's claim that it is inconsistent to assert that *pramāṇa*-s and (some) *prameya*-s are both cognitions fails both because cognitions which are not *pramāṇa*-s can be *prameya*-s, and because cognitions which are *pramāṇa*-s can be *prameya*-s of subsequent *pramāṇa*-s. There is thus no contradiction in the Naiyāyika assertion that *pramāṇa*-s are cognitions, and that one class of *prameya*-s is cognitions.

Nāgārjuna's argument is, then, fallacious. As we have seen, the employment of fallacious reasoning is, in fact, a pervasive characteristic of Nāgārjuna's critique of the *pramāṇa* theory in the *Vaid/VaidC*. One often gets the impression that the critique in the *Vaid/VaidC* is designed, not to establish the truth, but to defeat opponents by whatever means, fair or foul (i.e., in Nyāya terms, Nāgārjuna is engaging in *jalpa*[6]). Either that or its author was a very poor logician! Many of the arguments which Nāgārjuna uses for the pulverization (*vaidalya*) of the Nyāya categories of *pramāṇa* and *prameya* are themselves easily obliterated. Nāgārjuna engages in what appears to be shameless sophistry, but I think that in identifying the fallacies which he commits some light is thrown on the philosophical issues at stake.

Notes

1 The Vaibhāṣika Abhidharma claims that the visual organ apprehends both colour and shape. The Sautrāntikas and Theravādins, by contrast, say that the visual organ apprehends only colour. Shape or figure (*saṃsthāna*) has, according to the Sautrāntikas, a conceptually constructed existence (*prajñapti-sat*). This is because, otherwise, shape would be apprehended by both the visual and the tactile organ, which would violate the principle that each sense-organ has an exclusive objective domain. (For example, the visual organ cannot apprehend a sound, the nasal organ cannot apprehend a colour, etc). See *AKBh* IV, 3a-3c, Karunadasa (1967), pp. 49–52, Matilal (1986), pp. 250–254.

2 For the *dhātu*-s and *āyatana*-s see *AKBh* I. See also Karunadasa (1967), p. 34–55, Matilal (1986), p. 241.

3 See Williams (1981), p. 238. Cox (1995), pp. 138–139.
4 See *NS* II, 1, 32. See also *NSBh* and *NSV* II, 1, 32, Jhā (trans.) (1984), pp. 697–706, and Matilal (1986), pp. 255–291.
5 See *NSBh* II, 1, 16, Jhā (trans.) (1984), pp. 632–633.
6 On *jalpa*, see See *NS* I, 2, 2. See also Potter (1977), p. 208.

CHAPTER FIFTEEN

Conclusion

I have answered the questions which I raised at the beginning of the introduction to this study of Nāgārjuna's philosophy.

Is Nāgārjuna a sceptic? Despite some striking formal parallels between Nāgārjuna's arguments and the arguments of the classical sceptics, Nāgārjuna is not a sceptic. Whereas the sceptic claims not to have knowledge, Nāgārjuna emphatically says that he has knowledge of emptiness (*śūnyatā*), i.e. the absence of *svabhāva* of entities. In what sense is knowledge of the ultimate truth (*paramārthasatya*) or reality (*tattva*) non-conceptual for Nāgārjuna? I have investigated and assessed in detail two interpretations. Non-conceptual knowledge might be, for Nāgārjuna, (1) a trans-rational gnosis of an unconceptualizable reality or (2) a focussed, not explictly conceptual, meditative knowledge by acquaintance (as opposed to a merely theoretical knowledge) of a conceptualizable reality (the emptiness, i.e. the absence of *svabhāva*, of entities). I have favoured the latter interpretation as perhaps closer to Nāgārjuna's intentions, though I found that both interpretations entail serious philosophical problems. Does Nāgārjuna's understanding of the ultimate truth/reality as emptiness (*śūnyatā*) condemn him to nihilism? Understood in the Abhidharma context in which Nāgārjuna was functioning, Nāgārjuna's philosophy of emptiness, i.e. universal absence of *svabhāva*, probably does entail nihilism, despite Nāgārjuna's claim to tread the Middle Path. These were the principal issues which I discussed at length in the first part of this study.

In the second part of this study, I considered Nāgārjuna's critiques, in the *VV/VVC* and the *Vaid/VaidC*, of the Nyāya theory of knowledge (*pramāṇa*). What is the Nyāya *pramāṇa* theory which Nāgārjuna attacks? I have explained in some detail the main features of this *pramāṇa* theory. The Nyāya *pramāṇa* theory is, most fundamentally, a form of philosophical realism, according to which knowledge is the correct apprehension of mind-independent objects. What is the precise purpose of Nāgārjuna's critiques? Nāgārjuna's critiques are intended to refute this Nyāya realism. According to Nāgārjuna, there can be no knowledge (*pramāṇa*) of mind-independent entities, because there *are* no mind-independent entities. Are Nāgārjuna's criticisms successful, from a philosophical perspective? I think that I must answer with a definite 'no'. Nāgārjuna's arguments certainly fail to establish that there are no mind-independent entities and that there can be no knowledge of mind-independent entities.

★ ★ ★

It is not uncommon for Buddhists, particularly perhaps those Buddhists influenced by Madhyamaka, to quote the scriptural passage to the effect that Buddhist teaching must be tested by reason, i.e. it must be analyzed, like gold is tested by melting, cutting, and polishing. Buddhist teaching should not be accepted out of devotion or respect.[1]

The present study of Nāgārjuna's has been an attempt to conduct such a test with regard to Nāgārjuna's thought, at least. I have attempted an appraisal of Nāgārjuna's philosophy of emptiness. The results of this test have not been entirely complimentary to Nāgārjuna. Nāgārjuna's reasoning is very often flawed, and the basic philosophical position which underlies his thinking – namely, that all entities lack *svabhāva*=have conceptually constructed existence (*prajñaptisat*) – seems to me to be untenable.

This is certainly not to say, I must stress, that Buddhism *as a whole* is flawed. Nāgārjuna's philosophy represents only one among many Buddhist expressions of how things really are. Perhaps, then, there are more satisfactory explanations given by other Buddhist thinkers. I must also add that I do not think that anything which I have said in this critical study disproves what I consider to be basic Buddhist teachings, such as dependent origination, the four noble truths, the eightfold path, the teaching of the importance of compassion, etc. What I have perhaps proved, however, is that Nāgārjuna's philosophy of emptiness, despite his claims to the contrary, is incompatible with these basic Buddhist teachings. If everything is empty the Buddhist path would be destroyed (regardless of Nāgārjuna's protestations). But the problem lies, not with the basic Buddhist teachings, but with Nāgārjuna's philosophy of emptiness.

Nevertheless, as I hope that this book has made clear, study of Nāgārjuna's thought raises important philosophical questions – about the way things really are, and the nature of knowledge-claims about the way things really are. His thinking has certainly provided the present author with an opportunity to reflect on, and grapple with, these issues. In my opinion, Nāgārjuna does not provide a convincing answer to the question 'how are things actually?' but critical engagement with his thought does seem to lead one to a deeper questioning. From a philosopher's perspective, at any rate, this is salutary. In the final analysis, Nāgārjuna's philosophy may not pass the test of reason, but it is certainly not fool's gold.

Notes

1 For a translation of this passage see Lopez (1988), p. 5. Lopez (1988), p. 10 says that this passage is cited by Tsong kha pa in his *Drang nges legs bshad snying po*, and that R. Thurman has found it quoted also in Śāntarakṣita's *Tattvasaṃgraha* The quote appears to be from the *Jñānasārasamuccaya*. See Nagao (1991), p. 237. Williams (1991), p. 511 says that the present Dalai Lama is fond of quoting this passage.

APPENDIX

Some Further Reflections on *Svabhāva* in Indian Madhyamaka

I have explained in chapter 4 that for Nāgārjuna *svabhāva* is uncreated (*akṛtrima*) and independent of another (*nirapekṣaḥ paratra*). I have also said that Nāgārjuna claims that all entities lack, i.e. are empty of, *svabhāva*. I have argued that, seen in the context of Abhidharma philosophy, this denial of *svabhāva* must mean, not just that all entities dependently originate but also, that all entities are *prajñaptisat*. That is to say, no entity exists independent of/uncreated by conceptual construction.

Candrakīrti's Claim that the Actual *svabhāva* of Entities is Their Lack of *svabhāva*

The Mādhyamika reflections on the notion of *svabhāva* are actually more complex, however. According to Candrakīrti, for example, although in the sense which I have just explained all entities lack *svabhāva*, there is another special sense in which entities actually have *svabhāva*.

At *PP* 264–265 Candrakīrti comments on Nāgārjuna's statement, at *MMK* XV 2c–d, that *svabhāva* is uncreated and independent of another. Candrakīrti takes this statement as an affirmation that there is such an uncreated and independent nature of entities. Candrakīrti describes this actual *svabhāva* of entities as having 'the state of not changing' (*avikāritva*) and as 'invariableness always' (*sadaiva sthāyitā*). This actual *svabhāva* of entities is, in other words, what invariably is truly the case about all entities. It is thus *uncreated or unfabricated* in the specific sense that it is the *true/actual* nature of entities, and it is *independent* in the specific sense that it is the true nature of all entities, *irrespective of circumstances.* Candrakīrti equates this *svabhāva* with the *dharmatā*, *svarūpa*, *prakṛti*, and *tathatā*. But what is this uncreated, independent true nature of all entities? It is, Candrakīrti says, *śūnyatā*, which is the state of absence of *svabhāva* (*naiḥsvabhāvya*). Emptiness – i.e. the absence of existence independent of conceptual construction – without exception/independent of circumstances characterizes entities as their ultimate truth. In this special sense this emptiness may be called the *svabhāva* of entities.

Candrakīrti makes this same point in a particularly succinct fashion in *YṢV* 25, where he declares that 'the *svabhāva* of entities it the absence of *svabhāva*' (*dngos po'i rang bzhin ni ngo bo nyid med pa yin*). As Williams[1] points out, the Tibetan translators have here attempted to make a distinction between *svabhāva* as: (i) 'inherent existence' or 'own being' (i.e. more-than-conceptually constructed existence) – translated as *ngo bo nyid* – which entities do not have, and (ii) 'true/actual nature' – translated as *rang bzhin*, – which entities do have. Thus the *rang bzhin* of entities is their lack of *ngo bo nyid.*

Adumbrations of Candrakīrti's View in Nāgārjuna's Writings

Candrakīrti does not present his interpretation of *svabhāva* here as an innovation. He seems to think that Nāgārjuna himself accepts that entities' absence of *svabhāva* is the actual *svabhāva* of entities. This is, Candrakīrti appears to think, the intended meaning of the statement describing *svabhāva* at *MMK* XV, 2c–d.

However, Nāgārjuna does not say here (at *MMK* XV, 2c–d) that he accepts that anything exists which satisfies his description of *svabhāva*. And, in fact, there are many passages in texts reliably attributed to him in which he simply denies that there is any *svabhāva* of entities. In other words, Nāgārjuna usually seems to claim that there is nothing which satisfies his definition of *svabhāva*.[2] The category 'entities with *svabhāva*' would appear to be simply an empty set for Nāgārjuna. He at no point clearly takes the position that the absence of *svabhāva* is the actual *svabhāva* of entities. It appears, then, that Candrakīrti is not simply a faithful commentator in this regard. There is perhaps an element of innovation in his explanation of Nāgārjuna's text. (Unless, of course, Candrakīrti was party to no longer extant Mādhyamika texts or an oral tradition about this matter).[3]

I have, however, located four passages in texts attributed to Nāgārjuna which might imply that the actual *svabhāva* of entities is their lack of *svabhāva*. I shall consider them in turn.

(1) Nāgārjuna says, at *MMK* XVIII, 7c–d that the *dharmatā* (like *nirvāṇa*) is without origination (*anutpannā*) and without cessation (*aniruddhā*). In his commentary on this verse, Candrakīrti says that this *dharmatā* is the *svabhāva* of *dharma*-s.[4] As I have explained, for Candrakīrti the actual *svabhāva* of *dharma*-s, and hence of entities in general, is their absence of *svabhāva*. It does seem reasonable to infer, as Candrakīrti has done, that the *dharmatā* is *śūnyatā*, i.e. the absence of *svabhāva* in entities. The absence of *svabhāva* does not originate or cease, i.e. it is what is always truly the case about entities. Nevertheless, Nāgārjuna does not actually state either that the *dharmatā* is *śūnyatā*, i.e. the absence of *svabhāva* of entities, or that the *dharmatā* is the *svabhāva* of entities. Candrakīrti's extrapolation from *MMK* XVIII 7c–d seems quite sensible, but this does not necessarily mean that it is an extrapolation made by Nāgārjuna himself.

(2) In the *YṢ*, Nāgārjuna states that:

> *bālā rajyanti rūpeṣu vairāgyaṃ yānti madhyamāḥ/*
> *svabhāvajñā vimucyante rūpasyottamabuddhayaḥ//*
>
> Fools are attracted to forms, the middling reach freedom from all worldly desires. Those with the best intellects, knowing the *svabhāva* of form, are liberated. (*YṢ* 55).

The idea here might be, then, that those with the best intellects, i.e. the *āryan*-s, know that the *svabhāva*, i.e. the invariable true nature, of form (*rūpa*) is its lack of *svabhāva*, i.e. its conceptually constructed existence. It is this knowledge which liberates them from *saṃsāra*. Candrakīrti certainly thinks so, for his commentary on this verse states that:

> *gang dag gzugs kyang ngo bo nyid kyis med de/ gzugs brnyan bzhin du khong du chud pa de dag ni gzugs la sogs pa'i rnam par rtog pa rnams las gdon mi za bar/ gzugs kyi rang bzhin shes pa yi/ blo mchog rnams ni rnam par grol//*
>
> Also, whoever comprehends that form is without *svabhāva*, like a reflection, they, the best intellects who know the

svabhāva of form, are liberated undoubtedly as a result of the understanding of form, etc. (*YṢV* 55).

Note the addition of the 'etcetera' (*la sogs pa*). Candrakīrti clearly thinks that Nāgārjuna intends that form (*rūpa*) here is merely illustrative. In fact, it is by knowing the *svabhāva* (which is the absence of *svabhāva*) of all entities, and not just form, that those with the best intellects are liberated.

It is evident, I think, that Candrakīrti has explored the implications of Nāgārjuna's statement here quite convincingly. Nevertheless, this does not mean that Nāgārjuna himself was necessarily aware of these implications. Nāgārjuna simply says, after all, that liberation is by means of knowing the *svabhāva* of form. One might protest that the implications which Candrakīrti states are obvious. However, one should not assume that what seems obvious was in fact obvious to Nāgārjuna. There is, after all, no evidence here to suggest that Nāgārjuna had thought the matter through. Candrakīrti is, then, cleverly developing the implications of Nāgārjuna's statement, implications of which Nāgārjuna himself might or might not have been aware.

(3) In the *MMK*, Nāgārjuna writes that,

tathāgato yatsvabhāvastatsvabhāvamidaṃ jagat/
tathāgato niḥsvabhāvo niḥsvabhāvamidaṃ jagat//

That which is the *svabhāva* of the *tathāgata* is the *svabhāva* of this world.
The *svabhāva* of the *tathāgata* does not exist. The *svabhāva* of this world does not exist. (*MMK* XXII, 16.)

Nāgārjuna does not actually say here that:

(a) the *svabhāva* of the *tathāgata* is his absence of *svabhāva*.

(b) because the *svabhāva* of the *tathāgata* is the *svabhāva* of the world, therefore the *svabhāva* of the world is its absence of *svabhāva*.

However, one is certainly tempted to make this interpretation of the text.

(4) In the *AS*, Nāgārjuna states:

hetupratyayasaṃbhūtā paratantrā ca saṃvṛtiḥ/
paratantra iti proktaḥ paramārthastvakṛtrimaḥ//
svabhāvaḥ prakṛtistattvaṃ dravyaṃ vastu sadityapi/

Convention arises from causes and conditions and is dependent.
The dependent is thus proclaimed [by the Buddha].
But the ultimate is uncreated.
Also it is called, *svabhāva*, nature, reality, substance, essence, [and] true being. (*AS* 44–45b)

Clearly convention (*saṃvṛti*), which is dependently originating, is here contrasted with the ultimate (*paramārtha*), which is uncreated. It seems that a list of synonyms, including '*svabhāva*', is given for *paramārtha*. It is difficult to know, however, quite what Nāgārjuna has in mind. Does he mean that the ultimate – i.e. the *svabhāva*, *prakṛti*, etc – is the absence of *svabhāva* of entities? Is the ultimate 'uncreated' in the sense that it is the true (i.e. unfabricated) nature of all the dependently originating conventions, i.e. the entire conceptually constructed world? This is certainly a plausible inference to make, especially given that many other passages of the *AS* assert the absence of *svabhāva* of entities.

This interpretation is strongly supported by the following passage:

yaḥ pratītyasamutpādah śūnyatā saiva te matā/
tathāvidhaśca saddharmastatsamaśca tathāgataḥ//
tattattvaṃ paramārtho 'pi tathatā dravyamiṣyate/
bhūtaṃ tadavisaṃvādi tadbodhādbuddha ucyate//

Dependent origination is just what you [i.e. the Buddha] understand to be emptiness, and so too is the true doctrine, and identical to that is the *tathāgata*.
That is regarded [by you to be] the truth, and the ultimate, suchness [i.e. the true nature of things], the substance [of things].
That is the incontrovertible truth.
On account of [one's] knowing that, a Buddha is proclaimed. (*AS* 40–41).

Here, Nāgārjuna says that dependent origination is what is meant by emptiness. This statement arguably implies that emptiness is the absence of a nature which is independent (of conceptual construction). That is, because entities originate in dependence upon the mind, therefore they are empty of *svabhāva*. Nāgārjuna describes this emptiness as, among other things, the *paramārtha* and the *dravya* of entities. Thus, one might argue:

(a) the *paramārtha* and the *dravya* are emptiness.
(b) emptiness, the lack of *svabhāva* of entities, is the entities' absence of a nature independent of conceptual construction.
(c) *svabhāva* is given in *AS* 44–45b as a synonym of *paramārtha* and *dravya*, therefore,
(d) the actual *svabhāva* of entities is emptiness, i.e. the absence of *svabhāva* of entities.

Again, a reasonable inference, but one which Nāgārjuna himself does not make in the text.

A *gzhan stong* Interpretation of *AS* 44–45b

There is an alternative reading of *AS* 44–45b. It is sometimes said in the Tibetan Jo nang pa school, which advocates a *gzhan stong* ('other empty') interpretation of emptiness, that Nāgārjuna's highest teaching, the so-called 'Great Madhyamaka', can be found in the collection of his verses of praise (*bstod tshogs*), which includes the *AS*.[5] These verses of praise are said to communicate that there is an Ultimate Reality which is immutable. This Ultimate Reality is not itself empty of, i.e. it does not lack, *svabhāva*. The Ultimate Reality is empty only in the quite different sense that it is devoid of what is other (*gzhan*) than it, viz. the dependently originating, conceptually constructed world.[6] According to this interpretation, then, the quoted passage from the *AS* does not mean that the *svabhāva*, i.e. the invariable true nature, of entities is their lack of *svabhāva*. Rather, it communicates that there is an ultimate (*paramārtha*), an Ultimate Reality, which, by contrast with the conditioned (*saṃskṛta*) world, has a more-than-conceptually constructed existence (*dravyasat*) and is permanent. This would then be a very different Mādhyamika attitude to *svabhāva* than I have so far considered.

However, I suspect that such a *gzhan stong* interpretation of the term '*svabhāva*', if applied to *AS* 44–45b, does not pay sufficient attention to the text as a whole in which the passage in question is embedded. The *AS* is replete with declarations that entities lack *svabhāva*. It seems, in fact, to be the main message of the text. Thus, in the opening verse (*AS* 1), Nāgārjuna makes obeisance to the Buddha who, he says, spoke of the absence of *svabhāva* of dependently originating entities.[7] He does not say that he makes obeisance to the Buddha for speaking of an Ultimate Reality which exists permanently and with *svabhāva*!

Of course, the *gzhan stong* interpreter might still object that it is not contradictory for Nāgārjuna to teach in most verses of the *AS* that dependently originating entities lack *svabhāva*, and also, at *AS* 44–45b, that there is an Ultimate Reality which is empty of such dependently originating entities. However, one wonders how this *gzhan stong* interpretation of *AS* 44–45b might be reconciled with, for example, the following verse:

etattat paramaṃ tattvaṃ niḥsvabhāvārthadeśanā/
bhāvagrahagṛhītānāṃ cikitseyamanuttarā//

This is the ultimate truth[8]: The teaching that objects are without *svabhāva*.
This is the best medicine for those trapped through grasping at entities. (*AS* 52).

Here Nāgārjuna does not say only that dependently originating entities are without *svabhāva*. He says that the teaching (*deśanā*) of this absence of *svabhāva* is the ultimate truth (*paramaṃ tattvam*). He does not say that the ultimate truth is that there is an Ultimate Reality which, by contrast with dependently originating entities, has *svabhāva*. And surely, if the ultimate truth were for Nāgārjuna that there is an Ultimate Reality, existing with *svabhāva* – i.e. an Ultimate Reality which is *dravyasat* and permanent – then Nāgārjuna would not declare that the ultimate truth is simply that entities lack *svabhāva*. Surely Nāgārjuna would be clearer than this about such an important point. Surely he would at least say that the ultimate truth is that entities (other than the Ultimate Reality) lack *svabhāva*, *and* that there is an Ultimate Reality, existing with *svabhāva*. It seems, then, that a *gzhan stong* interpretation of Nāgārjuna's assertion of *svabhāva* at *AS* 44–45b is rather implausible.

Notes

1 Williams (1992a), p. 34.

2 *MMK* XXIV is replete with references to the absence of *svabhāva* of entities. See also *MMK* XIII, 3, *YṢ* 19, *ŚS* 3, 12, 16, 35.

3 Note, however, that Bhāvaviveka also says that his position (*phyogs*) is that the *svabhāva* (*ngo bo nyid*) of *dharma*-s (*chos rnams*) is their emptiness of *svabhāva* (*ngo bo nyid stong pa nyid*). See *TJv* (96, 28, 1–1) (Iida (1980), p. 88). It might be that the origin of the idea is to be found in the *Prajñāpāramitā sūtra*-s. In the *Aṣṭasāhasrikā Prajñāpāramitā*, probably an early *sūtra* of this genre (see

Williams (1989a), pp. 41–42), it is declared that the *prakṛti* (which might be a synonym for *svabhāva*) of *dharma*-s is their lack of *prakṛti*, and their lack of *prakṛti* is their *prakṛti*. (*yā ca prakṛtiḥ sāprakṛtiḥ, yā cāprakṛtiḥ sarvadharmāṇam* ...). Quoted in Bhattacharya (1978), pp. 113–114.

4 See *PP* 364.

5 See Williams (1989a) pp. 107–108 and Hookham (1991), pp. 82, 154–155. It should be noted, however, that the *gzhan stong* interpretation of Nāgārjuna relies primarily, not on the *AS*, but on the *Dharmadhātustava*, which is extant in Tibetan and Chinese. Lindtner (1982), p. 17 says, however, that this work is probably not actually by Nāgārjuna. Lindtner argues that it would be a 'glaring inconsistency' for Nāgārjuna to assert, as the ultimate truth, the 'positive ontology' which is found in the *DS*. Nevertheless, Lindtner contends, one cannot rule out the possiblity that this work is written by Nāgārjuna from a conventional or non-definitive (*neyārtha*) perspective. In other words, Nāgārjuna might have written the *DS* for those without the spiritual maturity to hear the highest truth, i.e. the universal emptiness (absence of *svabhāva*) of entities. However, a *gzhan stong* interpretation would argue the exact opposite. The works written from a conventional or non-definitive perspective are the *MMK*, etc, which teach universal absence of *svabhāva*, whereas the 'positive ontology' of the *DS* is the highest truth, i.e. the definitive (*nītārtha*) teaching. One thing is certain here. One cannot argue simply that the *DS* is not by Nāgārjuna because it contains apparent *gzhan stong*-type teachings. This would be, of course, to beg the question.

6 Versions of this *gzhan stong* position appear to be advocated by, for example, Dol po pa Shes rab rgyal mtshan (1292–1361) and also Mi bskyod rdo rje (1507–1554). More recent proponents have included members of the *ris med* movement. See Hookham (1991), p. 4, 53 and Cabezón (1992), p. 6, 424, 508. One should note, however, that this reading of Nāgārjuna's verses of praise is influenced by the *tathāgatagarbha* doctrine of the *Ratnagotravibhāga*, etc. *Tathāgatagarbha* influenced *sūtra*-s undeniably sometimes refer to a permanent Ultimate Reality, e.g. the *dharmakāya*, which is concealed by the adventitious defilements of the unenlightened person. (Of course, the interpretative issue becomes whether or not to take these references literally. See Ruegg (1989), pp. 26–28). Even the earliest of the *tathāgatagarbha sūtra*-s probably post-dates Nāgārjuna. See Williams (1989a), p. 96–109.

7 *AS* 1, 'I make obeisance to him whose knowledge is unequalled, who is inconceivable, incomparable, who spoke of the absence of *svabhāva* of dependently-born entities.' (*pratītyajānāṃ bhāvānaṃ naiḥsvābhāvyaṃ jagāda yaḥ/ taṃ namāmyasamajñānamacintyamanidarśanam//*).

8 '*Tattva*' is often best translated by 'reality'. However, in this context the appropriate translation seems to be 'truth', given that it is a teaching (*deśanā*) (rather than the reality to which the teaching refers) which is described as (*paramaṃ*) *tattvam*.

BIBLIOGRAPHY

Ames, W.L. 1982. 'The Notion of *Svabhāva* in the Thought of Candrakīrti'. *JIP* 10, pp. 161–177.

Ames, W.L. 1993. 'Bhāvaviveka's *Prajñāpradipa* [A Translation of Chapter One: "Examination of Causal Conditions" (*Pratyaya*)].' *JIP* 21, pp. 209–260.

Annas, J and Barnes, J. 1994. Sextus Empiricus. *Outlines of Scepticism*. Cambridge: Cambridge University Press.

Aung, S.Z. and Rhys Davids, C.A F. 1969. *Points of Controversy (Kathā-Vatthu)*. London: Luzac and Company.

Bagger, M. 1991. 'Ecumenicalism and Perennialism Revisited. (Critical Notice Concerning The Problem of Pure Consciousness edited by Robert K.C. Forman).' *RS*, 27, pp. 399–411.

Barnes, J. 1983. 'Ancient Skepticism and Causation'. In Burnyeat (1983), pp. 149–203.

Barnes, J. 1988. 'Scepticism and Relativity'. *PhS* 32, pp. 1–31.

Barnes, J. 1990. 'Some Ways Of Scepticism'. In Everson (1990), pp. 204–224.

Beyer, S. 1974. *The Buddhist Experience: Sources and Interpretations*. Dickenson: Encino and Belmont.

Bhattacharya, K. 1990 (3rd ed.). *The Dialectical Method of Nāgārjuna*. Delhi: Motilal Banarsidass.

Bocking, B. 1995. *Nāgārjuna in China. A Translation of the Middle Treatise*. Lewiston: The Edwin Mellen Press.

Buescher, J.B. 1982. *The Buddhist Doctrine of Two Truths in the Vaibhāṣika and Theravāda Schools*. PhD thesis. University of Virginia.

Burnyeat, M.(ed.) 1983a. *The Skeptical Tradition*. Berkeley: University of California Press.

Burnyeat, M. 1983b. 'Can the Sceptic Live His Scepticism?'. In Burnyeat (1983), pp. 117–148.

Burnyeat, M. 1984. 'The Sceptic in His Place and Time'. In Rorty (et al.) (1984), pp. 225–254.

Cabezón, J.I. 1992 *A Dose of Emptiness*. Albany: State University of New York Press.

Chandra Das, S. 1970. *A Tibetan-English Dictionary*. Delhi: Motilal Banarsidass.

Chang, G.C.C. (ed.) 1983. *A Treasury of Mahāyāna Sūtras. Selections from the Mahāratnakūṭa Sūtra*. University Park: The Pennsylvania State University Press.

Chatterjee, S. 1978. *The Nyāya Theory of Knowledge*. Calcutta: University of Calcutta.

Cheng, H. 1982. *Nāgārjuna's Twelve Gate Treatise*. Dordrecht: D. Reidel.

Conze, E. 1973a. *The Short Prajñāpāramitā Texts*. London: Luzac.

Conze, E. 1973b. *The Perfection of Wisdom in Eight Thousand Lines and Its Verse Summary*. San Francisco: Four Seasons.

Coulson, M. 1992 (2nd ed.). *Sanskrit. An Introduction to the Classical Language*. London: Hodder and Stoughton.

Cox, C. 1995. *Disputed Dharmas. Early Buddhist Theories of Existence*. Tokyo: The International Institute For Buddhist Studies.

Crosby, K. and Skilton A. (trans.) 1996. *The Bodhicaryāvatāra*. Oxford: Oxford University Press.

Dancy J. and Sosa E. (ed.) 1992. *A Companion to Epistemology*. Oxford: Blackwell.

Dayal, H. 1932. *The Bodhisattva Doctrine In Buddhist Sanskrit Literature*. Delhi: Motilal Banarsidass.

De Jong, J. W. 1949. *Cinq Chaiptres de la Prasannapadā*. Paris: Guethner.

De La Vallée Poussin, L. 1971/1980. *L'Abhidharmakośa de Vasubandhu*. (6 vols.). Bruxelles: Institut Belge Des Hautes Études Chinoises.

De La Vallée Poussin, L. 1988. *Abhidharmakośakārikā and Abhidharmakośabhāṣya*. (translated from French into English by L.M. Pruden). Berkeley: Asian Humanities Press.

Dreyfus, G. 1997. *Recognizing Reality. Dharmakīrti's Philosophy And Its Tibetan Interpretations*. Albany: State University of New York Press.

Dreyfus, G. and Lindtner C. 1989. 'The Yogācāra Philosophy of Dignāga and Dharmakīrti', *SC* 2, pp. 27–52.

Eckel, M.D. 1980. *Bhāvaviveka's Response to the Fundamental Problems of Mādhyamika Philosophy*. Unpublished Doctoral Thesis. Harvard University.

Eckel, M.D. 1987. *Jñānagarbha's Commentary on the Distinction Between the Two Truths*. Albany: State University of New York Press.

Evans, G. 1982. *The Varieties of Reference*. Oxford: Clarendon Press.

Everson, S (ed.). 1990. *Epistemology. Companions to Ancient Thought, 1*. Cambridge: Cambridge University Press.

Fenner, P. 1990. *The Ontology of the Middle Way*. Dordrecht: Kluwer Academic Publishers.

Forgie, J. W. 1985. 'Hyper-Kantianism in Recent Discussions of Mystical Experiences.' *RS* 21, pp. 205–218.

Forman, R. K.C. 1991. 'Reply: Bagger and the Ghosts of GAA.' *RS* 27, pp. 413–420.

Franco, E. 1983. 'Studies in the *Tattvopaplavasiṃha*.' *JIP* 11, pp. 147–166.

Frede, M. 1983. 'Stoics and Skeptics on Clear and Distinct Impressions.' In Burnyeat (1983), pp. 65–93.

Frede, M. 1984. 'The Sceptic's Two Kinds of Assent and the Question of the Possibility of Knowledge.' In Rorty (et al.) (1984), pp. 255–278.

French, P.A. et al. (ed.). 1989. *Midwest Studies in Philosophy, Vol XIV. Contemporary Perspectives in the Philosophy of Language II*. Notre Dame: University of Notre Dame.

Garfield, J.L. 1995. *The Fundamental Wisdom of the Middle Way*. Oxford: Oxford University Press.

Gethin, R.M.L. 1992. *The Buddhist Path to Awakening. A Study of the Bodhi-Pakkhiyā Dhammā.* Leiden: E.J. Brill.

Griffiths, P.J. 1986. *On Being Mindless: Buddhist Meditation and the Mind-Body Problem.* La Salle: Open Court.

Griffiths, P.J. 1994. *On Being Buddha. The Classical Doctrine of Buddhahood.* Albany: State University of New York Press.

Hahn, M. 1982. *Nāgārjuna's Ratnāvalī. Vol 1. The Basic Texts.* Bonn: Indica et Tibetica Verlag.

lHa mKhar yongs dzin bsTan pa rGyal mTshan. 1972 (ed.). *sTong thun chen mo.* New Delhi.

Hankinson, R.J. 1995. *The Sceptics.* London: Routledge.

Hattori, M. 1968. *Dignāga, On Perception, Being the Pratyakṣapariccheda of Dignāga's Pramāṇasamuccaya from the Sanskrit and Tibetan Versions.* Cambridge: Harvard University Press.

Hayes, R. 1988. *Dignāga on the Interpretation of Signs.* Dordrecht: Kluwer Academic Publishers.

Hayes, R. 1994. 'Nāgārjuna's Appeal.' *JIP* 22, pp. 299–378.

Hegel, G.W.F. 1977. (trans. J.N. Findlay). *The Phenomenology of Spirit.* Oxford: Oxford University Press.

Heidegger, M. 1962. (trans. J. Macquarrie and E. Robinson). *Being and Time.* London: SCM Press.

Hookham, S.K. 1991. *The Buddha Within. Tathagatagarbha Doctrine According to the Shentong Interpretation of the Ratnagotravibhaga.* Albany: State University of New York Press.

Hopkins, J. 1975. *The Precious Garland and The Song of the Four Mindfulnesses.* London: George Allen and Unwin.

Hopkins, J. 1989. 'A Tibetan Delineation of Different Views of Emptiness in the Indian Middle Way School.' *TJ* 14, pp. 10–43.

Hopkins, J. 1996. (revised ed.). *Meditation on Emptiness.* Boston: Wisdom.

Huntington, C.W. 1989. *The Emptiness of Emptiness: An Introduction to Early Indian Mādhyamika.* Honolulu: University of Hawaii Press.

Iida, S. 1980. *Reason and Emptiness. A Study in Logic and Mysticism.* Tokyo: The Hokuseido Press.

Inada, K.K. 1970. *Nāgārjuna.* Tokyo: Hokuseido.

Jackson, D.P. 1987. *The Entrance Gate for the Wise (Section III). Sa-sKya Paṇḍita on Indian and Tibetan Traditions of Pramāṇa and Philosophical Debate.* Vol II. Wien: Arbeitskreis für Tibetische und Buddhistische Studien Universität Wien.

Jackson, R. 1985. 'For Whom Emptiness Prevails: An Analysis of the Religious Implications of Nāgārjuna's *Vigrahavyāvartanī* 70.' *RS* 21, pp. 407–414.

Jackson, R. 1993. *Is Enlightenment Possible? Dharmakīrti and rGyal tshab rje on Knowledge, Rebirth, No-Self and Liberation.* Ithaca: Snow Lion.

Jhā, G. 1984. *The Nyāya-Sūtras of Gautama with the Bhāṣya of Vātsyāyana and the Varṭika of Uddyotakara.* 4 vols. Delhi: Motilal Banarsidass.

Jha, G. 1986. *The Tattvasaṅgraha of Shāntarakṣita.* Delhi: Motilal Banarsidass.

Kajiyama, Y. 1973. 'Three Kinds of Affirmation and Two Kinds of Negation in Buddhist Philosophy.' *Wiener Zeitschrift für die Kunde Südasiens*, 17, pp. 161–175.

Kajiyama, Y. 1991. 'On The Authorship Of The *Upāyahṛdaya*', in Steinkellner (ed.). (1991), pp. 107–117.

Kalupahana, D.J. 1986. *Nāgārjuna. The Philosophy of the Middle Way.* Albany: State University of New York Press.

Karunadasa, Y. 1967. *Buddhist Analysis of Matter.* Columbo: Department of Cultural Affairs.

Katz, S.T. (ed.). 1978. *Mysticism and Philosophical Analysis.* London: Sheldon Press.

Katz, S.T. 1978. 'Language, Epistemology and Mysticism.' In Katz (1978), pp. 22–74.

Katz, S.T. (ed.). 1992. *Mysticism and Language.* Oxford: Oxford University Press.

Katz, S.T. 1992. 'Mystical Speech and Mystical Meaning.' In Katz (1992).

Klein, A. 1986. *Knowledge and Liberation. Tibetan Buddhist Epistemology in Support of Transformative Religious Experience.* Ithaca: Snow Lion.

Klein, P.D. 1992. 'Scepticism.' In Dancy and Sosa (1992), pp. 457–458.

Kunjunni Raja, K. 1963. *Indian Theories of Meaning.* Madras: The Adyar Library.

Kvaerne, P. 1994. (ed.). *Tibetan Studies. Proceedings of the 6th Seminar of the International Association for Tibetan Studies.* Vol 2. Oslo: The Institute for Comparative Research in Human Culture.

Lamotte, E. 1962. (trans.). *L'Enseignment de Vimalakīrti.* Louvain: Université de Louvain Institut Orientaliste.

Lang, K. 1983. *Āryadeva on the Bodhisattva's Cultivation of Merit and Knowledge.* PhD dissertation. University of Washington.

Larson, G. J. and Bhattacharya, R.S. 1987 (ed.). *Encyclopedia of Indian Philosophies. Sāṃkhya. A Dualist Tradition in Indian Philosophy.* Princeton: Princeton University Press.

Lindtner, C. 1982. *Nagarjuniana. Studies in the Writings and Philosophy of Nāgārjuna.* Delhi: Motilal Banarsidass.

Lopez, D. 1987. *A Study of Svātantrika.* Ithaca: Snow Lion Publications.

Lopez, D. (ed.) 1988. *Buddhist Hermeneutics.* Honolulu: University of Hawaii Press.

Matilal, B.K. 1968. *The Navya-Nyāya Doctrine of Negation. The Semantics and Ontology of Negative Statements in Navya-Nyāya Philosophy.* Cambridge: Harvard University Press.

Matilal, B.K. 1977. *A History of Indian Literature. Nyāya-Vaiśeṣika.* Wiesbaden: Otto Harrassowitz.

Matilal, B.K. 1986. *Perception: An Essay on Classical Indian Theories of Knowledge.* Oxford: Clarendon Press.

May, J. 1959. *Candrakīrti Prasannapadā Madhyamakavṛtti (Commentaire limpide au Traité du Milieu).* Paris: Maisonneuve.

McGhee M. 1992. (ed.). *Philosophy, Religion, and the Spiritual Life. Cambridge Philosophy Supplement 32.* Cambridge: Camdridge University Press.

Monier-Williams. 1899. *A Sanskrit-English Dictionary.* Delhi: Motilal Banarsidass.

Murti, T.R.V. 1960 (2nd ed.). *The Central Philosophy of Buddhism.* London: George Allen and Unwin.

Nagao, G. 1991. *Mādhyamika and Yogācāra.* Albany: State University of New York Press.

Nagel, T. 1974. 'What Is It Like To Be A Bat?' *Philosophical Review* 83, pp. 435–450.

Nagel, T. 1997. *The Last Word.* Oxford: Oxford University Press.

Napper, E. 1989. *Dependent-Arising and Emptiness.* London: Wisdom.

Newland, G. 1992. *The Two Truths in the Mādhyamika Philosophy of the Ge-luk-ba Order of Tibetan Buddhism*. Ithaca: Snow Lion.

Nyanaponika Thera. 1976. *Abhidhamma Studies: Researches In Buddhist Psychology*. Kandy: Buddhist Publication Society.

Pagel, U. 1995. *The Bodhisattvapiṭaka. Its Doctrines, Practices and their Position in Mahāyāna Literature*. Tring: The Institute of Buddhist Studies.

Peacocke, C. 1989. 'What are Concepts?' In French, P.A. et al. (1989), pp. 1–28.

Pendlebury M. 1992. 'Experience, Theories of'. In Dancy and Sosa (ed.). (1992), pp. 125–129.

Pivčevic, E. 1986. *The Concept of Reality*. London: Duckworth.

Popkin, R. 1992. 'Scepticism, Modern'. In Dancy and Sosa (ed.). (1992), pp. 462–464.

Potter, K. (ed.). 1977. *The Encyclopedia of Indian Philosophies, Vol. 2, Nyāya-Vaiśeṣika. Indian Metaphysics and Epistemology: The Tradition of Nyāya-Vaiśeṣika up to Gangeśa*. Delhi: Motilal Banarsidass.

Ray, R. 1994. *Buddhist Saints In India*. Oxford: Oxford University Press.

Robinson, R. 1953 (2nd ed.). *Plato's Earlier Dialectic*. Oxford: Clarendon Press.

Rorty, R. et al. (ed.). 1984. *Philosophy in History. Essays on the Historiography of Philosophy*. Cambridge: Cambridge University Press.

Runes, D.D. (ed.). 1984. *Dictionary of Philosophy*. Totowa: Rowman and Allanheld.

Ruegg, D.S. 1977. 'The Uses of the Four Positions of the *Catuṣkoṭi* and the Problem of the Description of Reality in Mahāyāna Buddhism.' *JIP* 5, pp. 1–56.

Ruegg, D.S. 1981. *The Literature of the Madhyamaka School of Philosophy in India*. Wiesbaden: Otto Harrassowitz.

Ruegg, D.S. 1989. *Buddha-nature, Mind, and the Problem of Gradualism in a Comparative Perspective. On the Transmission and Reception of Buddhism in India and Tibet*. London: School of Oriental and African Studies, University of London.

Ruegg, D.S. 1991. 'On *Pramāṇa* Theory in Tsong kha pa's Madhyamaka Philosophy.' In Steinkellner (1991), pp. 281–310.

Sastri, N.A. '*Madhyamārthasaṅgraha* of Bhāvaviveka.' *Journal of Oriental Research*, (date unknown), pp. 41–49.

Schayer, St. 1931. *Ausgewählte Kapitel aus der Prasannapadā*. Krakow.

Scherrer-Schaub, C. A. 1991. *Yuktiṣaṣṭikāvṛtti. Commentaire à la soixantaine sur le raisonnement ou Du vrai enseignement de la causalité par le Maître indien Candrakīrti*. Bruxelles: Institut Belge Des Hautes Études Chinoises.

Schopen, G. 1987. 'The Inscription on the Kuṣān Image of Amitābha and the Character of the Early Mahāyāna in India.' *The Journal of the International Association of Buddhist Studies*, 10, pp. 99–137.

Searle, J.R. 1995. *The Construction of Social Reality*. London: Allen Lane. Penguin.

Sharma, P. 1990. *Śāntideva's Bodhicharyāvatāra*. New Delhi: Aditya Prakashan.

Shastri, D.N.D. 1964. *The Philosophy of Nyāya-Vaiśeṣika and its Conflict with the Buddhist Dignāga School (Critique of Indian Realism)*. Delhi: Bharatiya Vidya Prakashan.

Siderits, M. 1980. 'The Madhyamaka Critique of Epistemology, I'. *JIP*, 8, pp. 307–335.

Siderits, M. 1988. 'Nāgārjuna as Anti-Realist.' *JIP*, 16, pp. 311–326.

Sprung, M. 1979. *Lucid Exposition of the Middle Way. The Essential Chapters from the Prasannapadā of Candrakīrti*. Boulder: Prajñā Press.

Steinkellner, E. and Tauscher, H. (ed.). 1983. *Contributions on Tibetan and Buddhist Religion and Philosophy*. Wien: Universität Wien.

Steinkellner, E. (ed.). 1991. *Studies in the Buddhist Epistemological Tradition. Proceedings of the Second International Dharmakīrti Conference, Vienna, June 11–16, 1989*. Wien: Verlag Der Österreichischen Akademie Der Wissenschaften.

Striker, G. 1983. 'The Ten Tropes of Aenesidemus'. In Burnyeat (1983), pp. 95–115.

Striker, G. 1990. 'The Problem of the Criterion'. In Everson (1990), pp. 143–160.

Swanson P.L. 1989. *Foundations of T'ien T'ai Philosophy. The Flowering of the Two Truths Theory in Chinese Buddhism*. Berkeley: Asian Humanities Press.

Tauscher, H. (ed. and trans.) 1981. *Madhyakakāvatāraḥ und Madhyamakāvatārabhāṣyam (Kapitel VI, Vers 166–226)*. Wien: Arbeitskreis für Tibetische und Buddhistische Studien Universität Wien.

Tillemans, T. 1983. 'The "Neither One Not Many" Argument For *Śūnyatā* And Its Tibetan Interpretations.' In Steinkellner and Tauscher (ed.) (1983), pp. 305–320.

Tola, F. and Dragonetti, C. 1995a. *Nāgārjuna's Refutation of Logic (Nyāya)*. Delhi: Motilal Banarsidass.

Tola, F. and Dragonetti, C. 1995b. *On Voidness. A Study On Buddhist Nihilism*. Delhi: Motilal Banarsidass.

Tuck, A.P. 1990. *Comparative Philosophy and the Philosophy of Scholarship. On the Western Interpretation of Nāgārjuna*. Oxford: Oxford University Press.

Vaidya, P.L. 1960. *Madhyamakaśāstra of Nāgārjuna with the Commentary: Prasannapadā by Candrakīrti*. Darbhanga: The Mithila Institute.

Van Bijlert, V.A. 1989. *Epistemology and Scriptural Authority. The Development of Epistemology in the Old Nyāya and the Buddhist School of Epistemology With an Annotated Translation of Dharmakīrti's Pramāṇavārttika II (Pramāṇasiddhi), vv 1–7*. Wien: Arbeitskreis für Tibetische und Buddhistische Studien Universität Wien.

Van der Kuijp, L.W.J. 1983. *Contributions to the Development of Tibetan Buddhist Epistemology From the Eleventh to the Thirteenth Century*. Wiesdaden: Franz Steiner Verlag GmbH.

Vidyābhuṣana, S, C. 1975. (2nd ed.). *The Nyāya Sūtras of Gotama*. Delhi: Oriental Books Reprint Corporation.

Walshe, M. 1987. *Thus Have I Heard*. London: Wisdom.

Warder, A.K. 1970a. 'The Concept of a Concept'. *JIP* 1, pp. 181–196.

Warder, A.K. 1970b. 'Dharmas and Data'. *JIP* 1, pp. 272–295.

Williams, P. 1978. 'Book Review of Karl Potter (ed.) *Indian Metaphysics and Epistemology: The Tradition of Nyāya-Vaiśeṣika up to Gangeśa*.' *JIP* 6, pp. 277–297.

Williams, P. 1980. 'Some Aspects of Language and Construction in the Madhyamaka. *JIP*, 8. pp. 1–41.

Williams, P. 1981. 'On The Abhidharma Ontology.' *JIP* 9, pp. 227–257.

Williams, P. 1983. 'A Note on Some Aspects of Mi Bskyod Rdo Rje's Critique of Dge Lugs Pa Madhyamaka.' *JIP* 11, pp. 125–145.

Williams, P. 1984. 'Review Article of *Nagarjuniana: Studies in the Writings and Philosophy of Nāgārjuna*.' *JIP* 12, pp. 73–104.

Williams, P. 1989a. *Mahāyāna Buddhism*. London: Routledge.

Williams, P. 1989b. 'Introduction – Some Random Reflections on the Study of Tibetan Madhyamaka.' *TJ* 14, pp. 1–9.

Williams, P. 1991. 'Some Dimensions of the Recent Work of Raimundo Panikkar: A Buddhist Perspective.' *RS* 27, pp. 511–521.

Williams, P. 1991b. 'On the Interpretation of Madhyamaka Thought: Review Article of Huntington's *The Emptiness of Emptiness*.' *JIP* 19, pp. 191–218.

Williams, P. 1992a. 'Review of C.A. Scherrer-Schaub, *Yuktiṣaṣṭikāvṛtti. Commentaire à la soixantaine sur le raisonnement ou Du vrai enseignement de la causalité par le Maître indien Candrakīrti*.' *Journal of the Royal Asiatic Society*.

Williams, P. 1992b 'Non-Conceptuality, Critical Reasoning and Religious Experience. Some Tibetan Buddhist Discussions.' In Michael McGhee (ed.). (1992).

Williams, P. 1994. 'An Argument for Cittamātra – Reflections on *Bodhicaryāvatāra* 9: 28 (Tib 27) cd.' In Kvaerne (ed.) (1994), pp. 965–974.

Williams, P. 1998a. *The Reflexive Nature of Awareness (Rang Rig): A Tibetan Madhyamaka Defence*. Richmond: Curzon Press.

Williams, P. 1998b. *Altruism and Reality: Studies in the Philosophy of the Bodhicaryāvatāra*. Richmond: Curzon Press.

Williams, P. (manuscript 1) *Indian Philosophy*. Forthcoming (1998) in A. Grayling (ed). *Philosophy 2: Further Through the Subject*. Oxford: Oxford University Press.

Williams, P. (manuscript 2) 'Mahāyāna Buddhism In India: A Doctrinal Overview'.

Wood, T.E. 1994. *Nāgārjunian Disputations. A Philosophical Journey Through An Indian Looking Glass*. Honolulu: University of Hawaii Press.

INDEX

Abhidhammāvatāra 120
Abhidharma/Abhidhamma x–xi, 3–4, 8, 83–4, 88–96, 99, 101–3, 110–21, 125, 129, 143, 147, 193, 202–3, 209, 213
Abhidharmakośabhāṣya (*AKBh*) 84, 117–8, 121, 193, 198, 207 *see also* Sautrāntika *and* Vaibhāṣika
Ābhidharmika *see* Abhidharma
absence (*abhāva*) 168, 170–2
Absolute/Ultimate Reality 11, 31, 38, 52–3, 218–20
Academic and Pyrrhonian sceptic(ism) 27–31, 37, 41
Acintyastava (*AS*) 13, 42, 46–7, 51, 83, 96, 98–100, 117, 119, 144, 150, 216–20
activity (*kāritra*) 111
actual *svabhāva* 7, 213–8
afflictions/defilements (*kleśa*) 32, 38–9, 164, 220
āgama x–xi, 129, 141
analyzable (entities/existence) 91, 94, 114–6 *see also* unanalyzable (entities/existence)
Anesidemus 25–6, 41–2
Aṅguttaranikāya 164
Anuruddha II of Kāñcī 120
anuvyavasāya 155
aparapratyaya 74
Arcesilaus 27, 174
argument from the three times 191–9
Aristocles 33
Aristotle 193
Āryadeva 119
asaṃskṛta dharma-s 91, 93, 117 *see also* dharma-s *and* saṃskṛta dharma-s
Aṣṭasāhasrikā 219–20.
ātman 89, 101, 130, 139
attachment 76–7, 116
āyatana 150, 203–4, 207

Bagger, M. 64–5
balance (*tulā*) analogy 137–8
Being and Time see Heidegger, M.
**Bhadrapālaśreṣṭhiparipṛcchāsūtra* 164, 178
Bhattacharya, K. 3, 129, 156
Bhāvanākrama (*BK*) 85
Bhāvaviveka 5–7, 50–1, 68–9, 81, 219
Bodhicaryāvatāra (*BC*) 119–20, 180
Bodhicittavivaraṇa (*BV*) 13, 120–1
bodhisattva ideal 109, 120
Bodhisattvapiṭaka 85
Brentano, F. 131
Buddha x–xi, 37, 42, 46, 57, 97–8, 104, 119, 217–8 *see also* tathāgata
Buddhadatta 120
buddhavacana xi

calm (*śānta*) 45–6, 79

Candrakīrti 5–7, 35–6, 39, 42, 59–60, 68, 74, 85, 98, 101, 103–4, 108, 113–4, 117, 120–1, 146, 213–6
Cartesian sceptic(ism) 25 *see also* Descartes, R. *and* modern sceptic(ism)
Cārvāka 139–40
Catuḥśataka (*CŚ*) 119
Catuḥstava (*CS*) 13–14, 119 *see also* Acintyastava (*AS*) *and* Lokātītastava (*LS*)
catuṣkoṭi 33, 46, 51, 53
causation 33, 42, 191, 193–4
cavil (*vitaṇḍā*) 133, 139
The Central Philosophy of Buddhism see Murti, T.R.V.
Chatterjee, S. 139
Chih-tsang 51
Chung-lun 85
Cittamātra *see* Yogācāra
classical sceptic(ism) 23–34, 37, 40–1, 209 *see also* sceptic(ism)
classical sceptical method 24–7
cognition (*jñāna*/*buddhi*) 130–3, 146, 204, 206–7
comparison (*upamāna*) 134–5, 137, 140–1, 151, 157, 182, 202
concept(s) 48–9, 62, 84 *see also* saṃjñā
conceptual construction/conceptually constructed (existence) xi, 2, 4–5, 35–6, 38, 60–2, 68, 76, 82–3, 91–116, 118–21, 138, 147–50, 159, 188, 202–7, 210, 213–5, 217–8
conceptual diffusion (*prapañca*) 3, 45–6, 50–1, 79, 81, 85 *see also* niṣprapañca
conceptual discrimination (*vikalpa*) 97–8 *see also* nirvikalpa
confirmatory behaviour 181–5, 187–8, 201
content and character of experience 69–70, 84
convention/conventional (truth) (*saṃvṛti* (*satya*)) 57–62, 91–2, 96–7, 104–6, 110, 115, 118–20, 216–7, 220 *see also* vyavahāra
critique of *pramāṇa*-s 1, 10, 13–4, 128–30, 138, 141–210
cultural/linguistic conditioning 105–7
Dalai Lama 211
darkness 167–72, 178–9
darśana 75, 77, 85
dependent arising(s)/origination x–xi, 4, 31, 35–6, 38, 42, 52–3, 87–121, 143, 148, 150, 210, 213, 217–20
dependently arisen/originated *see* dependent arising(s)/origination
Derrida, J. 8
Descartes, R. 27, 40
dharma 46, 57, 96, 119
Dharmadhātustava (*DS*) 220
Dharmakīrti 6, 10, 121
dharma-s x–xi, 5, 46, 53, 68, 88, 90–4, 98, 103, 111–4, 116–7, 119–20, 202–3, 215
dharmatā 19, 45, 53, 68, 214–5
dhātu 101, 203, 207
dhyāna/*jhāna* 80–1, 84–5
Dīghanikāya (*DN*) 85
Dignāga 10, 140
dogmatism 21–2, 37, 40, 42
dogmatic/undogmatic global sceptic(ism) *see* global sceptic(ism)
Dol po pa Shes rab rgyal mtshan 220
doubt (*saṃśaya*) 132, 206
Drang nges legs bshad snying po 211
dravya(*sat*) 35–6, 38, 42, 90–2, 99, 104, 114, 119–20, 135, 216–8
dreams/illusions 99–100, 150, 159, 185
Dreyfus, G. 3, 136
dṛṣṭi see view/position/thesis
Dummett, M. 62
**Dvādaśanikanikāyaśāstra* 191, 198

emptiness of emptiness (*śūnyatāśūnyatā*) 68, 118
empty/emptiness (*śūnya*(*tā*)) ix–xi, 1–3, 19, 31, 35–9, 42–3, 47, 73, 75–9, 81–3, 85, 87–9, 95, 101, 103, 109, 111, 118–9, 141–3, 150, 204, 209–11, 213–5, 217–20
epistemological categories 128, 138
equipollence (*isosthenia*) 25–7, 39
error (*viparyaya*) 132, 134, 206
establishment ((*pra*)*siddhi*) 151, 175–7
ethics (*śīla*) 11, 76
eternalism 4, 37–8, 42, 46, 87, 125, 198

Evans, G. 48
example (*dṛṣṭānta*) 133, 137, 171
experience, nature of 69–73
extrinsic validation 154, 181–9
eye-disease *see* taimirika

fallacy of equivocation 175
fallacy of previous acceptance 195, 199
fallacy of validation of the [already] validated 183
fire/lamp analogy 161–72, 178–9
first/second-order conceptual construction 91–2
five modes of Agrippa 42
four great elements (*mahābhūta*) 193
further arguments in *Vaidalyaprakaraṇa* 201–8
further reflections on *svabhāva* 213–20

dGe lugs (pa) 4, 11, 73, 85, 118
general characteristics (*sāmānyalakṣaṇa*) 91, 117
global sceptic(ism) 22–4, 28, 31
Go rams pa bSod nams seng ge 3
Great Madhyamaka 51, 218
Griffiths, P. 53

Hankinson, R.J. 29
Hastavālanāmaprakaraṇa (HV) 119
Hayes, R. 3, 10
Hegel, G.W.F. *see* Phenomenology of Spirit
Heidegger, M. 77, 85
hindrance (*nīvaraṇa*) 80
Hume, D. 27, 40
Huntington, C. 9
Husserl, E. 131

illumination *see* lamp/fire analogy *and* luminous mind/consciousness
impressions (*phantasia*) 24, 30–1
Inada, K. 3
Indian epistemology 125–6 *see also* Nyāya pramāṇa theory
inference (*anumāna*) 12, 132–4, 137, 139, 141, 151, 157, 160, 182, 202
infinite regress 13, 33, 42, 110, 140, 155, 158–61, 183–4
inherence (*samavāya*) 136, 203
intentional(ity) 131, 146, 176, 191–2 *see also* viśayatā
intrinsic validation 154, 157–80

Jainas 139
jalpa 207–8
Jayanta Bhaṭṭa 188
Jayarāśi Bhaṭṭa *see* Cārvāka
Johnston, E. H. and Kunst, A. 129
Jo nang pa 218 *see also* gzhan stong
Jñānasārasamuccaya 211
justified true belief 20, 24, 29–30, 41–3, 152

kalpanā 97–8
Kamalaśīla 5–6 *see also* Bhāvanākrama (BK)
Kant, I. 205
karma(vipāka) 104–7, 109–10, 112, 120
Kathāvatthu 101, 120
Katz, S. 64
mKhas grub dGe legs dpal bzang/mKhas grub rje 4, 7, 119 *see also* dGe lugs (pa) *and* sTong thun chen mo
mKhas pa 'jug pa'i bzhag pa see Sa skya Paṇḍita
knowledge by acquaintance 2, 42–3, 73–7, 79, 81, 83, 209
knowledge-episode *see* pramāṇa/prameya

lack of explicit conceptualization 77–9, 81, 84
lamp analogy *see* fire/lamp analogy
Lang, K. 54
Lindtner, C. 13, 32, 80, 119, 129, 198, 220
local sceptic(ism) 21–2
Locke, J. 114
Lokātītastava (*LS*) 13, 42, 46, 66–7, 97, 102, 117, 146
Lopez, D. 211
luminous mind/consciousness 156, 163–4, 178 *see also* fire/lamp analogy

Madhyamakālaṃkāra 119
Madhyamakāvatāra (*MA*) 68, 84, 120–1

Madhyamakāvatārabhāṣya (*MABh*) 84, 120
Madhyamārthasaṅgraha (*MS*) 83
Mahāyāna ix, xi, 10–11, 46, 53, 109
Matilal, B.K. 3, 130, 133, 135, 139, 162
meditation 4, 11, 43, 66–7, 70, 72–85, 209
memory 111–2, 131, 139–40
Meno 130
Middle Path/Way 4, 5, 83, 87, 90, 101, 103, 125, 143, 144, 198, 209
Mi bskyod rdo rje 3, 15, 220
Mīmāṃsaka 127
Mi pham (rgya mtsho) 51–2, 81
modern sceptic(ism) 23–4, 26–7, 40–1 *see also* Cartesian sceptic(ism) *and* sceptic(ism)
modes of Anesidemus *see* Anesidemus
momentariness 91, 111–3
Monier-Williams, M. 32, 139
Mūlamadhyamakakārikā (*MMK*) 13–4, 19, 31, 37–8, 40, 42, 45–6, 51, 57, 66, 74, 76, 79, 85, 88, 96–7, 99, 101, 103, 117, 119–20, 129, 144, 213–6, 219
Murti, T.R.V. 5–9
mutually dependent existence 145–50, 177, 191–8
mutual validation 154, 186–8
mystic(ism) 2, 64–5

Nagel, T. 71
nāmamātra 97–8, 101
Napper, E. 73
neyārtha/nītārtha 119, 220
nihilism 2, 4–5, 10, 37–8, 42, 46, 83, 87–121, 125, 142, 198, 209
nirodhasamāpatti 82, 84–5
nirvāṇa 38, 45, 60, 97, 215
nirvikalpa 45–6, 61, 67, 72–3 *see also* conceptual discrimination (vikalpa)
niṣprapañca 50–1, 60–1, 67, 72, 78, 81, 85 *see also* conceptual diffusion (prapañca)
non-apprehension of entities 141–4
non-assertion (*aphasia*) 26–7, 31, 39, 40
non-conceptual knowledge 1–4, 45–85, 125, 209
non-memory (*anubhava*) 131–2, 134–5, 139
non-origination 98–9
Nyāyamañjarī 139, 188
**Nyāyānusāra* 117
Nyāya *pramāṇa* theory 1, 13–4, 41, 126–40
Nyāyasūtra (*NS*) 12, 126, 128, 130–1, 135–40, 161, 163, 171, 178, 181, 184, 191, 194, 199, 206, 208
Nyāyasūtrabhāṣya (*NSBh*) 139–40, 178, 180, 199, 208
Nyāyasūtravārṭika (*NSV*) 139, 199, 208
Nyāya taxonomy of cognition 131–5
Nyāya theory of validation 151–2, 161, 181–3
Nyāyavārttikatātparyaṭīkā 188

ontological categories 135–7, 140
Outlines of Pyrrhonism (*OP*) 28, 41–2 *see also* Sextus Empiricus

pakṣa see view/position/thesis
Pāli 80, 101, 127
paradox of nihilism 111
paradox of unconceptualizability/ineffability 55–7
paramārtha (meaning of) 68–9
Paramatthavinicchaya 120
paratantrarūpa/paratantrasvabhāva 120–1
parikalpa 97
Pariśuddhi 188
parts 90–1, 93–6, 101, 103, 114–6, 119
Pendlebury, M. 69
perception (*pratyakṣa*) 126, 134, 137, 139, 141, 151, 157–8, 160, 181–2, 186–8, 192, 202
permanent *dharma*-s (with *svabhāva* only) 111–4, 116
Phenomenology of Spirit 62
Pivcevic, E. 71–2
planet analogy 178–9
Plato 27, 130
post-meditative experience 75–7
Potter, K. 136, 138, 140
Prajñāpāramitā sūtra-s xi, 219
prajñaptimātra 94–111, 118, 120

prajñāptirupādāya 101–4
prajñapti(sat) see conceptual construction/conceptually constructed (existence)
pramā 41, 130–1, 133–5, 144
pramāṇa/prameya 1, 13–4, 33, 41, 125–10
prasaṅga 179
Prasannapadā(PP) 59–60, 74, 117, 120, 146–7, 213, 220
pratijñā see view/position/thesis
pratītyasamutpāda see dependent arising(s)/origination
Pratītyasamutpādavyākhyāna 119
pre-conceptual cognition 84
preta 105
private nature of experience 70–3
proponent of emptiness (*śūnyatāvādin*) 6, 128
public world 107–9

radical sceptic(ism) 23, 28, 37
rational analysis 11–2, 73–4, 85
Ratnāvalī (*RV*) 13–4, 38, 52, 95–6, 99–100, 104, 119
realism 136–8, 141, 144, 147, 204, 210
reflexivity 155–6
resting-place (*gnas*) 32, 38
Robinson, R. 54
Ruegg, D.S. 3

Sa skya pa 3
samādhi 79, 85
Samādhirājasūtra 85
śamatha 74, 85
Saṃdhinirmocanasūtra 85
saṃjñā 83–4
saṃjñāved(ay)itanirodha see nirodhasamāpatti
saṃskṛta dharma-s 90–4, 111–4, 116 *see also* dharma-s *and* asaṃskṛta dharma-s
Saṃyuttanikāya 84
Saṅghabhadra 91
Śāntarakṣita 5–6, 119, 155
Śāntideva *see* Bodhicaryāvatāra
Saptapadārthī 139
Sarvāstivāda *see* Vaibhāṣika
sasvabhāvamātra see permanent dharma-s (with svabhāva only)
Sautrāntika 42, 104, 113, 117, 193, 207
sceptic(ism) 2–4, 19–43, 45, 50, 125, 143, 209 *see also* classical sceptic(ism) *and* modern sceptic(ism)
Schelling, F.W.J. 62
Scherrer-Schaub, C.A. 32
Searle, J.R. 108
self-characteristic (*svalakṣaṇa*) 91, 117
self-evidence 152, 154–6, 160–81
Sextus Empiricus 24–6, 28, 33, 42 *see also* classical sceptic(ism) *and* Outlines of Pyrrhonism
Siderits, M. 126, 157, 162
simultaneous (mutual) causation 193
skeptikos 28
Socrates 23, 27
solipsist/solipsism 109, 111
Stoic(ism) 42, 173–4
suffering (*duḥkha*) 76–7, 82, 127–8
Śūnyatāsaptati (*ŚS*) 13–4, 35, 42, 83, 88, 117, 119, 129, 150, 204, 219
suspension of judgement (*epoche*) 24–7, 31–2, 39–40
sustained thought (*vicāra*) 80
svasaṃvedana 155, 164, 180
sword analogy 169, 180
syllogism 34, 132–3

taimirika 74
tarka 132–3, 195–6
Tarkabhāṣā 139
Tarkajvālā (*TJv*) 68, 83–4
Tarkasaṃgraha 139
tathāgata 35, 68, 216–7 *see also* Buddha
tathāgatagarbha 6, 11, 220 *see also* gzhan stong
tattva 1, 19, 45, 74, 79, 209, 219–20
Tattvadīpikā 139
tattvajñāna 50, 128
Tattvopaplavasiṃha see Cārvāka
theoretical knowledge 73–7, 81
Theravāda 193, 207
three levels of wisdom 74, 85
Tola F. and Dragonetti, C. 100, 126, 137–9, 180

sTong thun chen mo (*sTong*) 14, 119
tranquillity (*ataraxia*) 26–7, 31, 39
(trans-)mundane ultimate truth 50–1, 53, 58–61, 81
Tsong kha pa 6–7, 73, 211 *see also* dGe lugs (pa)
Tuck, A. 8
two truths 57–62, 96, 120

Udayana 188
Uddyotakara 133, 199
ultimate (truth) (*paramārtha*(*satya*)) 1, 5, 11–2. 19, 35, 45, 47, 50–1, 57–61, 68, 79, 81, 87–91, 94, 97, 110, 118–9, 209, 214, 217–20
unanalyzable (entities/existence) 92–4, 111, 113 *see also* analyzable (entities/existence)
unconceptualizable reality 49–66, 81–2, 121, 209

Vācaspati Miśra 188
Vaibhāṣika 42, 90, 104, 111–4, 116, 193, 207
Vaidalyaprakaraṇa and commentary (*Vaid/VaidC*) 1, 13–4, 34, 42, 102, 125–6, 128–9, 137–9, 145–50, 158–80, 191–209
Vaiśeṣika 42, 136, 139
Vaiśeṣikasūtra (*VS*) 135, 140
validation 151–89
Vasubandhu *see* Abhidharmakośabhāṣya
Vātsyāyana 135–6, 171
Vedānta 127
verbal testimony (*śabda*) 129, 134, 137, 140–1, 151, 157–8, 182, 202
view/position/thesis 2, 19, 31–2, 34, 36–8, 45, 50, 54, 76–7, 79, 81, 85, 219
Vigrahavyāvartanī and commentary (*VV/VVC*) 1, 13–4, 19, 42, 85, 111, 117, 120, 125–6, 128–9, 141–4, 151–89, 197, 209
Vijñānavāda *see* Yogācāra
viśayatā 139 *see also* intentional(ity)
vivikta 35, 80–1, 85
vyavahāra 53, 59, 96–7, 119 *see also* convention/conventional (truth) (saṃvṛti(satya))
**Vyavahārasiddhi* 119

Warder, A.K. 101–2
whole entities 203
Williams, P. 3, 11, 13, 51, 117–20, 211, 214
without diversity (*anānārtha*) 45–6, 79
Wittgenstein, L. 8
Wood, T. 90
words and concepts 48–9

yod min med min position 51
Yogācāra 11, 42, 104, 110, 113, 120, 155, 164
Yuktiṣaṣṭikā (*YṢ*) 13–4, 19, 32, 35–6, 38–9, 42, 76, 80, 85, 97, 104, 119, 215, 219
Yuktiṣaṣṭikāvṛtti (*YṢV*) 35–6, 39, 85, 98, 104, 113, 120, 214, 215

Zen 59
gzhan stong 6, 218–20 *see also* tathāgatagarbha